SWEET DREAMS

MUSIC IN AMERICAN LIFE

A list of books in the series appears at the end of this book.

SWEET DREAMS

The World of Patsy Cline

EDITED BY WARREN R. HOFSTRA

UNIVERSITY OF ILLINOIS PRESS

Urbana, Chicago, and Springfield

Library of Congress Cataloging-in-Publication Data
Sweet dreams : the world of Patsy Cline / edited by Warren R. Hofstra.
pages ; cm. — (Music in American life)
Includes bibliographical references and index.
ISBN 978-0-252-03771-9 (cloth : alk. paper)
ISBN 978-0-252-07930-6 (pbk. : alk. paper)
ISBN 978-0-252-09498-9 (ebook)
1. Cline, Patsy, 1932–1963. 2. Country music—History and criticism.
3. Country music—Social aspects.
I. Hofstra, Warren R., 1947- editor
ML420.C57S84   2013
782.421642092—dc23 [B]   2012050575

PUBLICATION OF THIS BOOK
IS SUPPORTED BY A GRANT FROM
Figure Foundation

Mike Foreman, 1941–2012
Friend, Colleague, Scholar

CONTENTS

ACKNOWLEDGMENTS

The world of Patsy Cline is immense. It is no surprise therefore that a project about her and her impact on American popular music and culture would obligate the efforts of many people. A major milestone on the road to completing this book was the 2008 conference "Sweet Dreams: The Life and Times of Patsy Cline" sponsored and organized by the Virginia Historical Society in Richmond, Virginia. Paul Levengood is now president and CEO of the society; at the time he contributed his organizing abilities and intellectual vision to the conference project as its cochair with me, he was associate editor of the society's journal, the *Virginia Magazine of History and Biography*. It was Paul's predecessor in the society's chief leadership position, the eminent Charles F. Bryan Jr., however, who saw the great promise in giving Patsy Cline top billing in the programs of the society, which contribute so abundantly to the culture and history of Virginia. He adopted the conference at a critical point in its development and guaranteed its ultimate success by giving freely of his energy and vision to it. Also at the Virginia Historical Society, Pam Seay, vice president for institutional advancement, worked hard with great skill and understanding to ensure that all the moving parts of a complex undertaking functioned smoothly and effectively together. Tim Timberlake—freelance voice talent, producer, stage manager, and emcee—put together the evening concert that graced the conference with such country music greats as Jimmy Dean and George Hamilton IV as well as a host of younger artists who creatively and sensitively reinterpreted the music that Patsy Cline made famous.

A number of individuals contributed mightily to the initial conceptualization and development of not only the conference but also the book that was always intended as its outcome. Perhaps the greatest debt of gratitude belongs to colleagues at the History and Tourism Center of Shenandoah

University, most notably William Austin, director; Pat Zontine, development coordinator; and Sandy Snyder, administrative assistant, all of whom worked closely with me and contributed their valuable time and great talents during the initial stages of the project. Sandy Snyder has stayed with it until its culmination, coordinating the work of the book's authors and providing invaluable assistance in collecting and preparing its numerous illustrations. Jane Radford, a passionate fan of Patsy Cline and principal in the consulting firm of Cultural Communications, provided wise counsel to staff at the History Center at some of the most sensitive stages in the process of conference development.

Numerous individuals and institutions in and around Patsy Cline's hometown community of Winchester, Virginia, have also supported the conference and the book. Rebecca A. Ebert, archivist at the Stewart Bell Jr. Archives of the Handley Regional Library, with other members of her excellent staff, especially Bettina Helms, pitched in time and time again with tips about archival sources and with services above and beyond any call of duty, especially in identifying and obtaining illustrations for the book and tracking down sometimes obscure references to many aspects of Cline's eventful life in the community. Tim Youmans, planning director of the City of Winchester, also provided invaluable assistance in identifying sources for illustrations. Readers will note the absence of photographs or other images of Patsy Cline in this volume. Most unfortunately, permission for these images could not be secured.

Farther afield, the interest and enthusiasm of Laurie Matheson, editor in chief of the University of Illinois Press, provided the impetus to get this project over the top at just the right moments in its evolution. To copy editor Nancy Albright we owe our gratitude for bringing the text as close to perfection as is humanly possible. Thanks are also due to Robert Grogg for the excellent index and to Andrew Flory for his assistance and advice throughout the early stages of the project. And personally, my greatest debt belongs to all the authors in this book, each of whom also gave conference presentations. Not a single one ever balked at any of the numerous and sometimes burdensome tasks a scholarly collaboration entails upon its victims; nor did anyone flag in supporting each other and me throughout the many twists and turns of working together for more than half a decade on the life and times of one of America's greatest, and perhaps most complex and enigmatic, musical artists.

One among us, however, will never be able to enjoy the satisfaction of seeing this book through to publication. But from its inception, Michael M. Foreman has been critical to its development and realization. Mike grew up in Winchester, went to school here, and returned from college to teach at the local high school as well as serve on the city council. He then gave twenty-eight years as clerk of the Winchester City Court and on retirement became my colleague as an adjunct on the faculty of Shenandoah University, where I teach. As the result of a lifetime of service, Mike knew more about this community than anyone I ever met, and no one cared more about it. He most generously shared his abundant knowledge—not the least with numerous people involved in this project. It was Mike's insights, information, and stories that immeasurably enlivened and deepened the manuscript we wrote together for it. His unfortunate passing in October 2012, while this book was in production, dealt a blow to everyone who depended upon him for guidance and wise counsel. In works such as this book, his memory and spirit will live on to enliven the imaginations of those who care about American communities like Winchester and who appreciate their capacity to give to the world those individuals with the remarkable talents of a woman such as Patsy Cline.

SWEET DREAMS

INTRODUCTION

Country Music and Cultural History in the World of Patsy Cline

Warren R. Hofstra

What interests us in Patsy Cline is her enduring popularity. If she had not entered the Country Music Hall of Fame as the first female soloist a full decade after her death in 1963, merited a commemorative first-class stamp issued in her honor in 1993, earned a Grammy Award for lifetime achievement two years later, secured a star on the Hollywood Walk of Fame in 1999, received the Recording Industry Association of America Diamond Award for ten million sales of her greatest hits album, all amid numerous other recognitions and honors, the essays in this collection would seem stillborn. Cline may be better known and more widely appreciated today than she was in her own time.

That her artistry and voice—an instrument of great range, beauty, and subtlety—renders Cline's work timeless and enduring is undeniable. But her expansive popularity and the burgeoning network of her fans can only be explained by the evolving meaning and appeal of her music with new and different audiences. The dynamic of this relationship between musical production and reception thus reflects many of the major themes of American cultural history in the late twentieth and early twenty-first centuries. In exploring the world of Patsy Cline, the articles in this volume trace the development and significance of these themes.

Not least in thematic importance is the growing nostalgia for the 1950s as the seeming stability and normalcy of the era have gained appeal by contrast to the upheavals of the 1960s. As the generation that produced turmoil over the Vietnam War, the counterculture, civil rights, and women's rights sought new forms of social and political security in the 1980s and 1990s, the earlier, midcentury decade took on an idyllic, sentimental, and dreamy aura. Interest in Cline soared as contemporary artists covered more and more of her hit songs, and any number of impersonators donned black curls, red lipstick, and cowgirl outfits in the attempt to bring Cline back to life.

Although nostalgia, like memory, serves present needs, yearning for Cline and her times calls out a consideration of the world into which she emerged in the 1950s as a country music star. Thus many of the articles in this volume focus on Cline's character and career amid the historical themes of her own age. If what interests us in the past is its countenance as a foreign country wherein one encounters strange people and exotic ways of life, then the strictures of race, class, gender, and identity as they functioned in Cline's world can alienate and offend us as much as they intrigue and beguile. Insofar as these qualities ordered life in her world, however, they also figure prominently as analytical devices in the articles that follow.

In its scope this volume, therefore, embodies a paradox. At the same time that Cline's music generates a contemporary audience on its own merits, the powerful force of nostalgia roots her in a particular past. This contrast of past and present, history and memory, reality and imagination are all embodied in the complexity and contradiction of the title of Cline's hit song "Sweet Dreams." Like so many songs of its era, this one is about love, loss, and a yearning for what might have been. It evokes Cline's own longing for success—her eager anticipation of each rise in an ever-widening arena of recognition—as well as a defining, determined ambition in which every achievement became only a stage for the next. But what made these dreams sweet for Cline was their fulfillment with each new hit and an expanding national reputation during the late 1950s and early 1960s. In a dark paradox, however, Cline recorded "Sweet Dreams" in early February 1963, only one month before her tragic death in a plane crash in rural Tennessee on March 5. Amid premonitions of her own passing, the poignant congruence of singer and song deepened one month later with its posthumous release on April 15. Sweet as her dreams may have been, she was fated never to enjoy their full realization.

The paradox of Cline's "Sweet Dreams" also serves as a metaphor for her times and in this sense as a method for this book. Although premised upon stardom in the field of country music, Cline's dreams paralleled the rise of a consumerist middle class amid the post–World War II prosperity of a consumer economy. Gross national product increased during the 1950s to almost two and one-quarter times what it had been in 1940. That median family income was 90 percent greater in 1959 than it had been fifteen years earlier mirrored a tripling of disposable income, or real purchasing power, and a dramatic expansion of consumer credit. Rates of home ownership from 1940 to 1960 increased from 44 to 62 percent of American households. Most remarkable in the unprecedented creation of new wealth was its distribution among the middle ranks of the national income hierarchy. In 1929 on the eve of the stock market crash, America's wealthiest 5 percent consumed one-third of the national income. By 1958 this elite received only 22 percent of income. At the same time that earnings in the middle brackets rose and the salaried middle class mushroomed, the number of factory workers dropped. By 1956 white-collar personnel outnumbered blue-collar workers for the first time in American history. By 1960 three-fifths of Americans enjoyed a middle-class standard of living defined now by home ownership, suburbanism, an automobile, and a fair share of the surfeit of consumer goods flooding American markets.[1] Patsy Cline and her contemporaries witnessed the rise of a capacious, enveloping middle class defined by consumption that engulfed the older social polarity of production pitting workers against the owners and managers of its means. By the end of the 1950s the vast majority of Americans would identify themselves as "middle class" in spite of income or employment.[2]

Thus the American dream was transformed from economic independence through owning land in a rural society to dependence in the labor-saving lifestyle of suburbia. More paradoxes abounded. Left out by race were African Americans for whom the disparity of privilege and wealth drove a freedom movement for economic parity and social justice in the 1950s. Although women benefitted immensely by the material comforts of middle-class living, a feminine mystique bound many of them to a numbing domesticity and the frustration of thwarted aspirations for personal advancement. And in one of the deepest ironies of the age, a large part of its affluence depended upon military spending in a Cold War conflict in which annihilation represented the ultimate peril of prosperity. All of these developments and their ironies would play out in the life of Patsy Cline—as they also play out in the articles that follow. They argue that Cline's own dreams for success and material comfort evolved side by side with the emergent American dream of middle-class society.

* * *

Patsy Cline was born Virginia Patterson Hensley in Winchester, Virginia, on September 8, 1932, less than one week after her mother and father were married in the same Shenandoah Valley town. Sam Hensley was a blacksmith, and Hilda Patterson took in sewing for extra income. A desultory search for work during the Great Depression and the war that followed kept the family on the move until "Ginny" was sixteen and two more children had joined the family. Music, however, was a constant in family life. Sam, by all accounts, bore the voice of an angel even if in life his demons of alcohol, violence, and domestic abuse tortured the souls of those around him. His eldest daughter learned to play the piano as a child, but so loved song that she became known for singing on the sidewalks of Shenandoah

Valley towns—sometimes for spare change—where her family sojourned. Radio, movies, and the pop sound of big bands that regularly visited dance venues in the Shenandoah Valley no doubt also shaped the musical tastes and styles of the young performer. American popular music, especially the artistry of female vocalists such as Dolly Dawn or Jo Stafford, provided the fare on which Cline developed and her style evolved, at least by the time she first sang publically. But this talented singer had also imbibed the ethos of country music and adopted the western styling of a cowgirl yodeler.[3]

In 1948 the family moved back to Winchester and took a house on South Kent Street in the working-class, east side of town. Because her father was now out of the family picture, Patsy left school and worked first in a chicken factory and then archetypically behind the soda fountain at a local drugstore. There she served vanilla cokes, lime rickeys, and chocolate uniques, but her true passion lay with singing and a life in music. Perhaps her earliest appearance came on Joltin' Jim McCoy's live Saturday morning country music show on local radio station WINC.[4] By all accounts, she appeared one Saturday and inveigled McCoy for a chance to sing with his band, the Melody Playboys. With her mother's help and lots of gumption, she did everything possible to gain attention. She recorded aluminum demonstration disks at a local music store studio to send off for the instant fame hucksters promised in magazine advertisements. More practically, her mother persuaded Ralph "Jumbo" Rinker to let her sing on Saturday evenings with his band at honky tonks such as the Melody Lane a few miles out of town. There were talent contests at the local Palace Theater, which she often won, and minstrel shows at the high school as well as a chance to sing pop songs while draped in a black cocktail dress with bandleader Jack Fretwell at a more upscale Winchester haunt, the York Inn, or at Front Royal's John Marshall Nightclub.

Although marked in youth as a prodigy, Cline fit the mold of most aspiring musicians in building ambition upon small, local beginnings. Her course to stardom was marked by achievement in ever widening circles until she hit it big on the stage of national notoriety. She first broke out of the narrow circuit of Winchester gigs when *Grand Ole Opry* star Wally Fowler and the Oak Ridge Quartet came to town for a gospel performance at the Palace. So aggressive was Cline in pressing Fowler for a chance to sing with him and so impressed was he by the sixteen-year-old's talent that he arranged an *Opry* audition. But the experience proved a forlorn hope for a girl too young to appear on the Nashville stage. Back home Cline next picked up with Bill Peer and sang with his Melody Boys in honky tonks, dance halls, and Moose Lodges in a classic example of a territory band playing all the options their range of recognition would allow. In 1953 Cline assumed what would become her stage name when she married Gerald Cline in a match promising little more than cold comfort. It lasted fewer than three years. Meanwhile her fame spread locally, and no one was surprised when she won a major country music contest with Peer at the Warrenton Fair in summer 1954. Her victory attracted the attention of Washington, D.C., country music impresario Connie B. Gay, who soon headlined her on his Town and Country Network of radio and television variety shows. Because so many rural southerners had moved to Washington to take government jobs during the New Deal and World War II, D.C. had become a hub of country music interest and activity. Cline did well and joined the company of Jimmy Dean, Roy Clark, and George Hamilton IV as country music celebrities. She still sang in and around Winchester with the Kountry Krackers and wrangled an exploitive recording contract with California promoter Bill McCall at 4 Star Records that robbed her of earnings and opportunity for years. Under agreement with Decca Records, however, she already had four recording sessions and sixteen releases with producer Owen Bradley before her big break came in January 1957 when she took first place on *Arthur Godfrey's Talent Scouts* singing "Walkin' After Midnight." This song soon rose to number two on the country chart and twelve on the pop chart establishing Cline as a crossover, pop-country singer, a move reinforced by her Godfrey appearance not as a cowgirl but in a sleek, sheath dress. Success led to further national exposure as she subsequently sang with Brenda Lee and appeared on Tex Ritter's *Ranch Party Show*, Alan Freed's *The Big Beat*, the *Ozark Jubilee*, and notably the *Grand Ole Opry*.

By 1960 Cline had remarried, moved to Nashville, and signed a Decca contract that allowed her to continue her work with Owen Bradley. In Bradley's famous Quonset Hut studio, Cline, with singing groups such as the Jordanaires or the Anita Kerr Singers and various instrumentalists, crafted a new sound—the Nashville Sound—designed to appeal to a large pop audience by discarding the high lonesome atmospherics of honky tonk and country western in favor of the silken aura of euphonious crooning with violin, not fiddle, accompaniment, no steel guitar, and a background of bleating, nonsense vocals. Big hits followed including "I Fall to Pieces" (1961), "Crazy" (1961), and "She's Got You" (1962), all of which soared very high on both the *Billboard* country and pop charts. A pair of albums, *Patsy Cline Showcase* and *Sentimentally Yours*, broadened her crossover repertoire and appeal. Cline's rise to stardom as a country singer with a pop sound was closely timed with the social transformations worked by 1950s prosperity and the rise of a new middle class defined by consumption. If whatever appeals to the widest audience and sells the most recordings is by definition popular music, as Jocelyn Neal argues herein, then Cline's success rested on the foundations of new class relations and a felt need by middle-class consumers to define themselves with a music detached from the working-class origins of traditional country. Or, put differently: by working-class consumers newly possessed of the means for a middle-class identity.

Perhaps the saddest, most poignant development surrounding Cline's tragic death in March 1963 was not just the recording and release dates for "Sweet Dreams" but an overpowering national grief that paralleled in strength the rise of the social class to which she most strongly appealed. The irrevocable loss of a timeless voice that spoke profoundly to so many men and women was deeply felt. Her recordings did well in the aftermath of the tragedy with posthumous releases all reaching the Top 10 and her *Greatest Hits* album launched in 1967 on its way to diamond status. But the memory of one of America's greatest singers appeared to be in decline during the next decade as no rereleases of Cline's hits charted well, and it took Loretta Lynn's tribute album, *I Remember Patsy* (1977), and Lynn's widely popular autobiography, *Coal Miner's Daughter* (1976), to keep Cline's memory alive.

The movie version of Lynn's story appearing in 1980, however, marked a turning point in the recovery of Cline's greatness. Several of the authors in this volume mark the following decade as crucial in the resurgence of her popularity. Overdubbed versions of Cline's "Always" and "Have You Ever Been Lonely" (the latter with Jim Reeves) reached the upper registers of the *Billboard* charts in the early eighties. And two serious biographies, one by Ellis Nassour (*Honky Tonk Angel*, 1981) and the other by Margaret Jones (*Patsy: The Life and Times of Patsy Cline*, 1994), in addition to two plays, *Always . . . Patsy Cline* and *A Closer Walk with Patsy Cline*, in the early 1990s conveyed the dual message that Cline was to be taken seriously again and that her fan base was growing rapidly.

*   *   *

No authors in this volume take on the question of why it took several decades for Cline to achieve celebrity status as a country music icon more directly than Jocelyn Neal and Joli Jensen. Both employ the tools of cultural studies and critical theory in deriving different but mutually reinforcing answers. Putting nothing off to the capricious nature of public opinion or popularity, Neal probes changes in American popular culture, reasoning that the resurgent interest in Cline and her music after 1980 owed less to her raw talent and more to a newfound expressionist meaning in her music. As country music moved from its roots in the displaced working classes of America's industrial cities and towns to a new mainstream musical status amid more conservative, suburbanized audiences by the 1980s and 1990s,

Cline came increasingly to stand for an authenticity lacking in the seemingly soulless new sound of corporate capitalism that exploited the genuine honesty of country culture to peddle a sonic commodity. The irony to
which Neal is so closely attuned lies in Cline's leading role in pioneering
the Nashville Sound during the late 1950s as a means of tapping rapidly
expanding middle-class markets. At that time fans for whom true country
meant nasal vocals, piercing fiddles, whining steel guitars, and a pounding
four-four beat rejected the Nashville Sound as selling out. But as Neal sees
it, Cline's undeniable struggle to make it in Music City as a working girl and
the reaffirming story of a poor, cut-off but immensely talented personality
repositioned her as the real thing amid the pop culture glitz that country
music had become in the years after her death. From selling out she was
reborn as true country.

To Joli Jensen, Cline's achievement of expansive celebrity status during
the last decades of the twentieth century established her as a cultural icon
not just of American music but of American culture writ large. Jensen's
article examines the long history of the imagery defining Cline, finding her
presentation in the 1993 postage stamp so universal that it embodied any
meaning perceivers attached to it. This universality, in fact, defines an icon
for Jensen—it becomes whatever can legitimately be seen in it. The postage-
stamp Cline means anything her audience wants it to mean. Thus even the
affectation of black curled hair and dark, bold, red lipstick can be genuine.
In this formula, much like Neal's, Cline's late posthumous popularity is
owing to the authenticity her audience beheld in her iconic image.

As person or icon—in life or afterlife—Cline has always been a woman of
her age. Her world is our world. Insofar as this book is an examination of
the world of Patsy Cline, she is the agent through which we can view certain
aspects of American life and culture from the post–World War II era to today.
Neal and Jensen root the contemporary Patsy Cline in our own present.

Bill Malone situates Cline in her own past and in the history of country
music's various social contexts. He reminds us that country music is not a
quaint survival of a timeless folk culture stranded in the hills and hollers of
Appalachia with origins in Elizabethan England or the ancient migrations of
Scots-Irish peoples. And he cautions us concerning the errancy of essentialist
arguments about the diffusion and persistence of pure Anglo-Saxon or Celtic
cultures surviving in country music. Country music from its origins in the
twentieth century reflected ever-changing adaptations by displaced peoples
to rapidly developing commercial technologies and to the mass audiences
developed by radio, recordings, film, and finally television among the labor-
ing classes in American urban environments. Country music entertained

hard-working men and women as it linked them to rural pasts and the home communities of their upbringing. Cline's evolution as a singer therefore "paralleled the major transformations that were reshaping the cultural moorings of her class and region." This was the experience that singer George Hamilton IV lived and sang to—and writes about in this volume—during a stint with Cline, Gay, Dean, and "the gang" in Washington during the 1950s. As he put it: "young folks—government workers—from the South, who were 'home sick' for their home towns . . . loved to go to the bars and dances to listen to the music they grew up on and loved."

The notion that Cline's character and career beat to deep rhythms of contemporaneous culture and its twentieth-century conversions informs the perspectives Warren Hofstra and Mike Foreman adopt in their reconstruction of the community that shaped her personal and artistic development. They suggest that however much country music may have ameliorated the emotional strains of separation and dislocation, the move of the Hensley family to Winchester in 1948 fulfilled the life patterns of country people seeking a better existence in towns throughout the South. Cline's indefatigable search after musical success, her irrepressible talent, her ebullient sexuality, and her restless ambition challenged the hoary certitudes of town life bound by taut lines of class, gender, and race. Insofar as Cline strove, in the words of the old country song, to get "above her raisin'," she peeled back the boundaries of expected behavior and laid bare the messy, often ugly, work of cultural restraint and repression. The result was a legacy of disputed expectations and thwarted recognition, the social discipline of sexual slander employed more powerfully and painfully than tradition or habit to suppress ambition, and an obsessive relationship between a town and its most famous personality. For these authors, however, it is this contested legacy—still expressed in the civic functions and public spaces of the town—that makes the world of Patsy Cline deeply resonant with meaning both for the shape of Cline's career and the shaping of the community out of which it developed.

Like Hofstra and Foreman, Beth Bailey sees the potential in deconstructing Cline's contested legacy for retrieving its cultural content, but Bailey zooms out from Winchester to the nation in modeling broader social processes. At work from her perspective is a novel set of class relationships governed by technological change and the new media of television. If the old world inherited by the men and women of the 1950s from the social and industrial struggles of the Great Depression was defined by the urban social dichotomy of common workers versus respectable owners or managers of property, then the new, expansive middle class fueled by socially diffusing economic growth, suburbanization, and consumption achieved an inclusive identity around a new national culture in which authority was divorced from the older tenets of social propriety. Television was critical to this development insofar as programming served the singular purpose of creating an audience for advertising consumer goods. Thus television relied upon selling sensationalism in the news and celebrity in the personages of people such as Arthur Godfrey or Patsy Cline. Although Cline's victory on *Talent Scouts* sold soap and aspirin for Godfrey's sponsors, success in the national media brought autonomy and agency to a young female singer and independence from a town where too much self-expression—especially by a working-class woman—was considered disrespectful. At stake was the social authority that ordered the town, keeping its suborned people productive and profitable while reassuring everyone that resulting inequities of wealth and power were inevitable and justifiable, if not just. Anxiety among the proprietary upper classes about the social ground shifting under their feet, with the rise of a consumerist middle class and a valueless national media feeding off its consumptive habits, gave powerful meaning to Cline's plainspoken behavior, her fervent music, and the persistence of her contested legacy.

Douglas Gomery draws ever tighter the nexus of television and celebrity in the career of Patsy Cline. As he argues in a detailed analysis of the nature and development of this media, television enabled Cline to move upward from a career as a regionally popular singer with a territory band to the status of a star with a national following and the capacity to shape musical tastes in the further pursuit of celebrity. This is precisely what Cline did in the genesis of the Nashville Sound and the ultimate achievement of iconic status.

If one implication of Beth Bailey's and Douglas Gomery's work is that Cline's rise to celebrity was a function of the new media of television and a new sonic culture powerfully appealing to middle-class consumers, then Kris McCusker applies this paradigm to the construction of Cline as a feminist—or protofeminist in the age of the feminine mystique. McCusker's foil is the oft-told story of a courageous woman battling sexism in a male-dominated artistic field and besting its triumphant musical masculinity. A reading of new sources such as fan magazines reveals a country music world in which women played varied and unexpected roles. A truer, recontextualized Patsy Cline, according to McCusker, "tears away" the veneer of the feminist Patsy Cline who by pluck and gruff fended off the barbs of sexual bigotry and opened a path for women in country music. McCusker instead resituates Cline in an industry and musical culture in the grip of deep change following the collapse of the barn dance radio paradigm with its down-home domesticity and its rituals of female subordination. Its replacement by a newer musical culture opening opportunities for women as singers and recording stars was owing to the rise of television, rock and roll, and Nashville at the center of the country music world. The confluence of all these developments according to McCusker better explains Patsy Cline's career as a female recording star—a performer much more than musician—in a new age of national media, the middle-class culture it spawned, and an original, urban sound playing so powerfully to this class. With McCusker's article we arrive full circle in the age of Cline's posthumous notoriety with which Neal and Jensen began this discussion.

* * *

A number of themes knit together all of the articles in this volume, and none is more paradoxical or productive than a common concern for authenticity in country music performance.[5] That Cline's posthumous popularity depended upon perceptions of her "real country" persona when in her own day the Nashville Sound signified a disingenuous compromise with popularity represents one of the many incongruities of her career. Exploring this paradox helps explain why Cline was more popular two to three decades after her death than at the time she passed away, seemingly at the peak of her career. According to Jocelyn Neal, it was Cline's struggle to maintain a traditional country music identity in the face of Nashville's anonymous popularization that enshrouded her with the aura of authenticity as country music engulfed the new pop mainstream in the 1980s. And as we have also already seen, it is Joli Jensen's contention that with Cline's iconization by the early 1990s in a postage-stamp image, her identity would be construed in whatever way pleased her audience. Cline as an icon, then, could be socially constructed as authentic country. Either way, authenticity governs Cline's self-constructed and socially constructed identity. This, too, is the point that Warren Hofstra and Mike Foreman make in exploring Cline's contested legacy among the people of her home community and in explaining the volatility of her reputation in the passion she evoked among men and women in the town's working classes, as well as the condemnation she simultaneously provoked among the "better" classes by appearing a bit too true to her upbringing. And to a large measure authenticity replaced respectability in Beth Bailey's account of how social authority shifted in the 1950s from a proprietary upper class within Cline's hometown to a national media culture where notoriety and celebrity supplanted moral virtue as the key to success. In the new world of television in which only a star's capacity to create an audience and sell commodities to middle-class consumers counted, authenticity among fans was all that remained to the self-respectability of someone like Cline.

The theme of gender threading through many of the articles in this volume also bears its own paradoxes.[6] According to George Hamilton, Cline "didn't 'open the doors' for women in country music; she 'kicked them down.'" But that Cline could be perceived as a standard bearer in confronting gender discrimination in the country music industry when, as Kris McCusker demonstrates, opportunities for women were in reality quite varied, underscores her observation that Cline did not take on the male-dominated country music establishment as a woman but as a performer contending with musicians. And to some degree what was contested in Cline's legacy according to Hofstra and Foreman was less her ambition than her sexuality. Just as hypersexualized black men lethally threatened the hegemony of white men over white women in the Jim Crow society of the South, so too did someone like Cline menace the confidence of all women in the fidelity of their men. But sexual attraction, so threatening locally, became a signal asset for a rising star in the national media of television with its audience of middle-class consumers among whom sex sold goods.

The paradoxes, however, that shaped Cline's character and career were also the contradictions of her age and her world. That Cline's life provides insight into the central tendencies of her times and that the deep changes defining these times shaped her music also represent primary themes in this volume that will be more fully reviewed in the book's Afterword. According to Bill Malone: Cline led her brief life "at one of the most important intersections of cultural and economic development in the South's history, when three centuries of rural dominance gave way to urban and industrial ascendancy." Cline lived this transformation as her first sixteen peripatetic years in various rural communities throughout the Shenandoah Valley evolved, on the eve of her adulthood, into a new life among working-class families in the town of Winchester. For Cline the male supremacy and domestic dependency of rural life gave way to a female-dominated home in which Cline herself labored for the wages of household independence.

If the move to Winchester signified the cultural shift from rural to urban life, then the early development of Cline's career tells Bill Malone's story about the power of country music to help southern people "find community and assert identity in a new environment that often seemed alien or forbidding." Singing in dance halls, wearing fetching cowgirl outfits her mother had so carefully crafted, consorting with honky-tonk bands, and socializing with working people over beer and good times on a Saturday night, this young woman no doubt spoke, as Malone describes, to "emotionally needy people, transporting them with their songs and stage personas to realms of romance but also speaking with clarity to them about their current problems and dreams."[7]

But Cline's life and career were also swept along by the spring tide of a rising middle class newly defined by consumption. Singing in cocktail dresses at dinner clubs, after all, had equally defined her development as a performer. Identity, for middle-class men and women, could be purchased not in the compensatory power of emotions but in the new, material world of consumer goods such as laborsaving appliances, high-speed automobiles, or contemporary suburban homes and the equipage of modern, outdoor living where progress was a most important product.[8] Thus the translation of rural into urban life that so deeply affected American men and women in the twentieth century was also mirrored no more symbolically among the signifiers of consumer culture than in the conversion of radio to television as the most powerful medium of popular culture in the 1950s. If radio had based its appeal on the replication and broadcast of rural entertainments, then television played more directly to urban audiences among whom television ownership was overwhelmingly concentrated and tastes tended more toward drama, public affairs, and celebrity appearances. In 1950 the second highest rate of television ownership in Virginia occurred in Winchester, which lay just outside metropolitan Washington, D.C., where four powerful stations had studios and transmission towers.[9] *Arthur Godfrey's Talent Scouts* clearly reached Winchester viewers, making the message of Cline's celebrity immediate and transformative.

In another theme of this book, therefore, the revolutionary medium of television helped create new national sources of cultural authority amid an emerging middle-class consumer culture.[10] Thus Cline knew precisely what she was doing when in 1954 she began singing on Connie B. Gay's country music roundup program in Washington, D.C. She knew her audience would be composed of displaced, white, working-class southerners. Although only regional, Gay's audience for country music provided a stepping-stone to the national recognition she craved. As Douglas Gomery artfully describes herein, Cline actively sought the opportunity to appear on the Arthur Godfrey show based on her media exposure in Washington and the hope of converting it into stardom. Shedding her cowgirl image and adopting, at the program's request, the persona of a southern chanteuse for its viewers, she sang "Walkin' After Midnight" onto the national charts and herself into celebrity.

Celebrity ultimately impelled Cline's move to Nashville, where working with producer Owen Bradley and Decca Records she emerged as one of the creators of the Nashville Sound. This sonic experience, crafted for middle-class tastes and consumption, represented her ticket to join the movement of millions of Americans in remaking the class structure of the nation. She bought the house in the Nashville suburbs, got the Cadillac, had two children—a boy and girl, of course—and became mother, housewife, and country music legend all in a piece.

Cline's untimely death was a genuine tragedy because it cut short the career of an immensely talented artist. In the tumultuous years of the 1960s that followed, her loss deprived the world of someone whose life and art might have conveyed the same consoling recompense with which her honky-tonk songs had relieved the hard lives of Winchester working people a decade earlier. The year of her death was also the year of President John F. Kennedy's assassination, an event that fractured the narrative of American history and initiated a long, national journey through social conflict, political confrontation, and racial violence, to deep cultural change. This was also the year before the British invasion of rock bands such as the Beatles and the Rolling Stones would shift the center of gravity in American music away from Nashville and middle-class consumption toward a cynical critique of this very culture upon which Cline had staked her stardom and success.

Insofar as the themes of this volume comport with Malone's assertion that Cline's life outlined the metamorphoses of her age, then the resurgence of her popularity in the 1980s coincided not only with new releases of songs, books, and movies by and about her but also with Ronald Reagan and a resurgent conservatism that adopted country music as the sound of traditional patriotism. Although the politicization of contemporary country dates at least to the Vietnam War era, Reagan's mantra of restoring national greatness after liberal distractions in the 1960s and 1970s resolved the New Left's ambivalence toward the genre. By appealing broadly throughout the same audience that had initially brought Cline to greatness and then defined a new conservatism, country music grew increasingly alien, if not hostile, to the Left.[11] But that her restored popularity had anything to do with Reagan conservatism is at odds with the luminary figure she became among gay and lesbian audiences. The political uses to which country music was put during this era nonetheless constitute undeniable evidence that this art form remains a living force in American life. The themes of authenticity, gender, sexuality, social class, media influence, cultural authority, rural tradition, and urban modernism that reverberate through Patsy Cline's story are the same themes that roil the deep currents of her world then as much as now.

Notes

1. In 1963 economic historian Harold G. Vatter wrote that the "remarkable capacity of the United States economy in 1960 represents the crossing of a great divide in the history of humanity. . . . The full significance for all mankind lies in

the possibility that poverty can be eliminated within the foreseeable future"; see Harold G. Vatter, *The U.S. Economy in the 1950's: An Economic History* (New York: Norton, 1963), 1. Various measures of extraordinary economic performance in postwar America are further substantiated in Robert J. Lampman, "Changes in the Share of Wealth Held by Top Wealth-Holders, 1922–1956," *Review of Economics and Statistics* (Cambridge: Harvard University Press, 1959); Lampman, *The Share of Top Wealth-Holders in National Wealth, 1922–56*, National Bureau of Economic Research 74 (Princeton: Princeton University Press, 1962); George Donelson Moss, *America in the Twentieth Century*, 4th ed. (Upper Saddle River, N.J.: Prentice Hall, 2000), 344–45; Thomas C. Reeves, *Twentieth-Century America: A Brief History* (New York and Oxford: Oxford University Press, 2000), 156; James D. Smith and Stephen D. Franklin, "The Concentration of Personal Wealth, 1922–1969," *American Economic Review* 64 (May 1974): 162–67; U.S. Bureau of the Census, Census of Housing, Historical Census Housing Tables, http://www.census.gov/hhes/www/housing/census/historic/owner.html (accessed July 2010); Vatter, *U.S. Economy in the 1950's*, 22, 36–38, 48, 225.

2. The argument here is not that an economy of consumption, and certainly not that the middle class, emerged in the 1950s for the first time in American history. Both consumption and the middle class have long histories, but it was in the 1950s that the former came to define the latter in ways more powerful and significant than ever before. That by the 1950s most Americans began calling themselves middle class regardless of income signified a class identity defined more by participation in a common marketplace of goods than by the traditional social markers of wealth, property, or manners. Appreciation for the power of consumption in an industrial economy indeed dates at least to the 1920s when advertising and various new forms of consumer credit democratized consumption. And a much earlier consumer revolution can be traced to the last half of the eighteenth century when improvements in manufacturing, finance, and transportation made an ocean of European goods readily available throughout the Atlantic world, affecting ordinary life in early America and helping to precipitate an American Revolution. Issues of social class identity and consumption are treated more fully by Warren Hofstra and Mike Foreman in chapter 2, but for works on the prosperity of the 1950s and its broadening distribution among a middle class defined more by relations to consumption than to the means of production, see Melanie Archer and Judith R. Blau, "Class Formation in Nineteenth-Century America: The Case of the Middle Class," *Annual Review of Sociology* 19 (1993): 17–41; Lizabeth Cohen, *A Consumers' Republic: The Politics of Mass Consumption in Postwar America* (New York: Alfred A. Knopf, 2003); John Kenneth Galbraith, *The Affluent Society* (Boston: Houghton Mifflin, 1958); Avner Offer, *The Challenge of Affluence: Self-Control and Well-Being in the United States and Britain since 1950* (New York: Oxford University Press, 2006).

3. Patsy Cline's life has provided a subject for a number of popular biographies, but not until Douglas Gomery's study of her life has it been a subject of academic scrutiny and extensive original research; see Gomery, *Patsy Cline: The Making of an Icon* (Bloomington, Ind.: Trafford Publishing, 2011). See also Mark Bego, *I*

Fall to Pieces: The Music and the Life of Patsy Cline (Holbrook, Mass.: Adams, 1995); Cindy Hazen and Mike Freeman, *Love Always, Patsy: Patsy Cline's Letters to a Friend* (New York: Berkley Books, 1999); Margaret Jones, *Patsy: The Life and Times of Patsy Cline* (New York: HarperCollins, 1994; New York: De Capo, 1999); Brian Mansfield, *Remembering Patsy* (Nashville: Rutledge Hill, 2002); Ellis Nassour, *Honky Tonk Angel: The Intimate Story of Patsy Cline* (New York: St. Martin's, 1993).

4. McCoy's own account of this incident can be found in John Douglas, *Joltin' Jim: Jim McCoy's Life in Country Music* (Berkeley Springs, W.Va.: Troubadour, 2007), 16–21.

5. If by virtue only of its overuse, the concept of authenticity in the culture of country music remains controversial and provocative. For various viewpoints on the subject, see Mark Fenster, "Buck Owens, Country Music, and the Struggle for Discursive Control," *Popular Music* 9 (October 1990): 275–90; Pamela Fox, "Recycled 'Trash': Gender and Authenticity in Country Music Autobiography," *American Quarterly* 50 (June 1998): 234–66; Pamela Fox and Barbara Ching, eds. *Old Roots, New Routes: The Cultural Politics of Alt.Country Music* (Ann Arbor: University of Michigan Press, 2008); Melissa Jane Hardie, "Torque: Dollywood, Pigeon Forge, and Authentic Feeling in the Smokey Mountains," in *The Themed Space: Locating Culture, Nation, and Self*, ed. Scott A. Lukas (Lanham, Md.: Lexington Books, 2007), 23–37; Allan Moore, "Authenticity as Authentication," *Popular Music* 21 (May 2002): 209–23.

6. The traditional narrative of talented, ambitious women struggling for a place in the masculine world of country music during much of the twentieth century has been rendered more complex and nuanced in recent scholarship on gender and the genre; see Mary A. Bufwack and Robert K. Oermann, *Finding Her Voice: Women in Country Music, 1800–2000* (Nashville: Country Music Foundation Press and Vanderbilt University Press, 2003); Pamela Fox, *Natural Acts: Gender, Race, and Rusticity in Country Music* (Ann Arbor: University of Michigan Press, 2009); Jewly Hight, *Right by Her Roots: Americana Women and Their Songs* (Waco, Tex.: Baylor University Press, 2011); Richard Leppert and George Lipsitz, "'Everybody's Lonesome for Somebody': Age, the Body and Experience in the Music of Hank Williams," *Popular Music* 9 (October 1990): 259–74; George H. Lewis, "Interpersonal Relations and Sex-Role Conflict in Modern American Country Music," *International Review of the Aesthetics and Sociology of Music* 20 (December 1989): 229–37; Kristine M. McCusker, *Lonesome Cowgirls and Honky-Tonk Angels: The Women of Barn Dance Radio* (Urbana: University of Illinois Press, 2008); Kristine M. McCusker and Diane Pecknold, eds. *A Boy Named Sue: Gender and Country Music* (Jackson: University of Mississippi Press, 2004); Charles K. Wolfe and James Edward Akenson, eds. *The Women of Country Music: A Reader* (Lexington: University of Kentucky Press, 2003).

7. Malone explores the connections between country music and urban working-class culture more fully in his other publications, most notably: Bill C. Malone, *Country Music, U.S.A.* 2nd ed. (Austin: University of Texas Press, 2002); Malone,

Don't Get above Your Raisin': Country Music and the Southern Working Class (Urbana and Chicago: University of Illinois Press, 2002).

8. The idea that the middle class came to be more powerfully identified in the material culture of modern suburban life and less in the habits and mannerisms of rural tradition is treated by a variety of authors; see Cohen, *A Consumers' Republic*; Matthew Hilton, "The Female Consumer and the Politics of Consumption in Twentieth-Century Britain," *Historical Journal* 45 (March 2002): 103–28; Shelley Nickles, "More Is Better: Mass Consumption, Gender, and Class Identity in Postwar America," *American Quarterly* 54 (December 2002): 581–622; Jan Whitaker, *Service and Style: How the American Department Store Fashioned the Middle Class* (New York: St. Martin's, 2006).

9. U.S. Bureau of the Census, *General Characteristics, Virginia: 1950 Housing Census Report*, prepared by the Population and Housing Division, Howard G. Brunsman, chief (Washington, D.C.: U.S. Government Printing Office, 1952), table 20, "Year Built, and Equipment for Standard Metropolitan Areas and Constituent Counties, Urbanized Areas, and Urban Places of 10,000 or more: 1950."

10. The influence of television on the development of country music has been much more fully explored for the era of Country Music Television and the rise of MTV in American popular culture during the 1980s than it has been for the earlier age of TV's initial development. The new medium, however, played a major role in launching Patsy Cline's career and has been treated elsewhere by Douglas Gomery in *A History of Broadcasting in the United States* (Malden, Mass.: Blackwell, 2008); and Gomery, *Patsy Cline*. See also William Boddy, *Fifties Television: The Industry and Its Critics* (Urbana: University of Illinois Press, 1990); Simon Frith, "Look! Hear! The Uneasy Relationship of Music and Television," *Popular Music* 21 (October 2002): 277–90.

11. As Jeffrey T. Manuel writes in the entry "Country Music" for the encyclopedia *Culture Wars*: "Country music achieved mainstream appeal throughout the nation in the last third of the twentieth century, but it retained a close connection with conservative political causes"; see Roger Chapman, *Culture Wars: An Encyclopedia of Issues, Viewpoints, and Voices* (Armonk, N.Y.: M. E. Sharpe, 2010), 122–23. See also Chris Willman, *Rednecks & Bluenecks: The Politics of Country Music* (New York: New Press, 2005); Peter La Chapelle, *Proud to Be an Okie: Cultural Politics, Country Music, and Migration to Southern California* (Berkeley: University of California Press, 2007); Kevin S. Fontenot, "'Dear Ivan': Country Music Perspectives on the Soviet Union and the Cold War," in *Country Music Goes to War*, eds. Charles K. Wolfe and James E. Akenson (Lexington: University Press of Kentucky, 2005), 143–51; James N. Gregory, *The Southern Diaspora: How the Great Migrations of Black and White Southerners Transformed America* (Chapel Hill: University of North Carolina Press, 2005); Rachel Rubin, "Sing Me Back Home: Nostalgia, Bakersfield, and Modern Country Music," in *American Popular Music: New Approaches to the Twentieth Century*, eds. Rachel Rubin and Jeffrey Melnick (Amherst: University of Massachusetts Press, 2001), 93–109.

CHAPTER 1

Patsy Cline
and the Transformation
of the Working-Class South

Bill C. Malone

The memory of Patsy Cline is much celebrated and honored today, but it has not always been the fate of working-class people to receive this kind of recognition. I do not mind telling you that this son of working-class Texas parents is thrilled to see Cline receive her due. It also seems appropriate that Cline's popularity today is greatest in urban areas throughout America and the world because country music really took shape in the towns and cities of the South, not in the remote hills and hollows of Appalachia or the far-off Western Plains that have always fired our romantic souls. It was the ever-developing technology of the cities—marked first by the emergence of radio and recording in the 1920s—that disseminated the grassroots styles of rural America. Without radio and recording, such music would never have coalesced into the commercially marketable entity now known as "country music." And the music was not even called "country" until as late as 1949 or 1950. The towns had the radio stations, the businesses, and other commercial entities that wanted their products hawked. Emerging urban centers had the movie houses that provided glimpses of exotic sounds and dances (such as the ones done by Shirley Temple that so thrilled the very young Patsy Cline); automobiles that quickened the pace of change; and the department stores that peddled sheet music, instruments, Edison cylinders, Victrolas, and the old 78 rpm records, long before real music stores came into existence.

Working-class southerners, black and white, had persistently cast their lot with the newly developing towns that emerged in the South in the late nineteenth century in the wake of railroad expansion and industrial development of all kinds. These newcomers provided the core audience for the hillbilly bands that emerged on local radio stations throughout the region and who played in country schoolhouses, churches, tents, and movie theaters in an ever-widening arc of personal appearances. The radio hillbillies brought diversion and entertainment into the lives of hard-working people, provided an important security link to the past that they had so recently abandoned, and helped them to find community and assert identity in a new environment that often seemed alien or forbidding. The musicians, in short, brought both fantasy and reality into the lives of emotionally needy people, transporting them with their songs and stage personas to realms of romance but also speaking with clarity to them about their current problems and dreams.

Patsy Cline grew up in one of these hard-working but fractured families and, in fact, had to leave school to become a wage worker when she was still a very young teenager. This is a major key to understanding her drive and ambition. The contours of her life, and her evolution as a singer, paralleled the major transformations that were reshaping the cultural moorings of her class and region. Just as we should reject any romantic notions about country music's alleged origins in the remote and pristine hollers of Appalachia, or in the distant and lonely western plains, we should also reject the equally fanciful belief that its musicians and fans were nothing more than yokels or remnants of some pure Anglo-Saxon or Celtic culture. "Purity" was not their defining element, and although many of them had been farmers, it is not far fetched to argue that a substantial number of them embraced life and labor in the city, along with the fruits that a capitalistic consumer culture offered. Patsy Cline's all-too-brief life took place at one of the most important intersections of cultural and economic development in the South's history, when three centuries of rural dominance gave way to urban and industrial ascendancy. She was born in 1932 in Winchester, Virginia, at one of the low points of the Great Depression. She died at the age of thirty, in 1963, at a time of great expectations for herself and for her country. She could hardly have been born at a more propitious time for a strong woman, sure that her talents would take her further than her humble origins might have suggested.

The major catalyst for change, World War II, had no less than revolutionary consequences for the South and its people. *Movement*, both economic and geographic, became the crucial fact of their lives. Many thousands went into America's armed forces. Many moved north or west to industrial centers outside the South. Countless others remained within the South, but moved from the farms into nearby villages, and from there to bigger cities. Though less heroic than the idea of a migration from the Deep South to Chicago, or from Appalachian Kentucky to the hillbilly ghettos of Detroit, these shorter internal moves within the South—say, from the East Texas farms to Houston or from the small rural town of Georgia to Atlanta—tell us more about the South's postwar history. The geographical relocations of southern working people took them away from the land, from agriculture to blue-collar work in mines, mills, oil camps, and defense factories and shipyards. Their children and grandchildren have moved persistently into white-collar, service, and technical occupations. Like many of the South's working folk, Patsy's family made a tentative step toward relocation, going first to tiny Gore and then to Winchester. Patsy and her family moved about nineteen times by the time she was fourteen years old. Of course, her own career took her much further—to places like Nashville and that "overgrown southern country town, Washington, D.C."

People responded, or adjusted, to change in various ways, depending on age, gender, race, ethnicity, education, income, and other variables. Most people who moved expected or hoped for an economically better way of life. At least in the beginning, many may have assumed that, otherwise, nothing much would change. That is, the old social hierarchies that had promoted the illusion, if not the fact, of stability and promised security in their departed communities would remain intact: masculine dominance, white supremacy, the unquestioned obedience of youth. But in spite of such expectations, all of these assumptions had been challenged, implicitly or explicitly, by the moves to town, the growing availability of money, the beckonings of the consumer culture, and all of the loosened restraints promoted by the war. The Old Order, of course, did not readily surrender. The resulting conflicts between old and new, emerging dramatically in the late 1950s and 1960s, wrought major consequences for the South and the nation. The South that we now know was born in the crucible of those years running roughly from 1946 to 1963: the Black Revolution; the politicization of religious fundamentalism; militant stirrings among both women and youth, as well as the emergence of a youth consumer culture; and, of course, the rise to hegemony in the region of the Republican Party (at least as expressed in national politics).

While it may be legitimate to speak of the long-term consequences that came to the South in the wake of the social upheavals of the 1940s, we should nevertheless be aware that clean breaks with the past almost never occur, and unqualified embraces of the new do not come easily or immediately. Residences and occupations changed, but cultural attitudes often lagged far behind, allowing people to fall back on traditional supports as coping mechanisms: individualism, the family, religion, politics, and, as we have seen, music. But not even these traditional forces remained unchanged by the movement to the city. All of them had long been in transition, or even under assault by the forces of modernism, but as we have seen in the case of evangelical religion, "traditional" movements have exhibited a wondrous facility for coping with change. The first generation or two who moved to town built a culture that was a composite of old and new.

Let's return to music. As we all know, Patsy Cline's music has transcended most categories, and some have argued that "country" is too limiting a description to affix to her. I meet people all the time who adore Patsy's music, but yet express surprise that anyone would call her "country." But though she had a voice that reached far beyond the "traditional" country audience, country music is the music that Patsy grew up with, and she considered herself to be a country singer. Along with the music of the church, with which it was intimately intertwined, country was the form most accessible to her—on local radio stations, in honky tonks, on jukeboxes, and in occasional public appearances, including the "package" shows such as the popular one headed by gospel impresario, Wally Fowler. Country music was "folk" in just about every sense of the word, not only because it frequently drew upon traditional or inherited songs, but also because it could be performed by regular folk down at the local VFW hall or church pie supper as well as by seasoned professionals on radio or television.

Patsy began to launch her campaign to win country music acclaim during the era that many would call its "golden age," the period from 1946 to the mid-1950s when it broke free from the constraints of scarcity and rationing imposed by the war to become a thriving commercial form with audiences found increasingly across the world. Radio stations everywhere, large and small, began featuring country music. Popular, too, were Saturday night barn dances such as the *Big D Jamboree*, *Saturday Night Shindig*, *Cowtown Jamboree*, *Wheeling Jamboree*, *Crossroads Follies*, *Mid-Day Merry Go Round*, and many more. Later on in this volume you will read George Hamilton IV's description of Connie B. Gay and the important Washington, D. C., scene. Radio transcriptions permitted musicians to roam freely from their home stations. Disk jockeys built a close community among themselves, the musicians, and their fans. Small record labels proliferated. Over four hundred thousand jukeboxes, with chrome, neon, and their clever and openly displayed record-changing mechanisms were an intimate accompaniment for dances and casual get-togethers and an example of capitalistic ingenuity. Sophisticated booking agencies and managers bolstered a burgeoning network of personal appearances.

This was the era of Eddy Arnold, Hank Williams and all the other Hanks, Lefty Frizzell, Red Foley, Slim Whitman, Carl Smith, Webb Pierce, and other legendary acts. Patsy's unyielding ambition would have been heightened by the visibility and acclaim won by her working-class contemporaries, and she would have been further emboldened by the emergence of women who were beginning to compete with men on more than equal terms. Although it is true that many of these women often performed with supporting groups (as in the case of Rose Maddox and her brothers), and that well into the 1950s one still heard female vocalists referred to as "girl singers" on whatever show to which they were attached, women were building identities of their own. Although Kitty Wells never truly broke free from the image of a housewife who sang only during her spare time and who in fact always deferred to the stage leadership of her husband, Johnny Wright, Kitty nevertheless evoked pride among Patsy and other women who hoped for careers of their own. Patsy and her "sisters" in country music strived to emulate Kitty's success without standing in anyone else's shadow. Liberation in country music, however, has generally come in small steps. And I will leave it to other authors in this volume to determine how well Patsy controlled her own career during her dealings with Owen Bradley.

Like the working-class culture that had produced and sustained Patsy's ambitions, country music was torn by contradictions and often-competing interests. One foot in the past, and one in the present. A fusion of old and new. Its stylistic diversity far outstripped anything heard today in the music, and certainly on Top Forty. Fans did not distinguish among the styles that they heard on radio or saw on personal appearances. Whether performed by Bob Wills and his Texas Playboys, Gene Autry and the Cass County Boys, Bill Monroe and his Blue Grass Boys, Hank Williams and the Drifting Cowboys, or Hank Snow and the Rainbow Ranch Boys, to name only a few of the very disparate country groups who played during the period, the music was generally described as "hillbilly" or "country." Not until the late 1950s and after did fans, merchandisers, and others begin to affix such labels as Western Swing, Bluegrass, Honky Tonk, and Hard Country to styles that they thought were "purer" or more "authentic" than others.

This, then, was the world of country music that witnessed Patsy's remarkable ascent to fame. It was a body of music, and a business, strongly shaped by its working-class origins, but desperately determined to succeed in an increasingly urban and middle-class society. Older listeners sought the security of what they already knew; younger fans sought innovation and excitement. Owen Bradley's "compromise" sought to win both of these audiences while also winning new converts to the music who had never listened to it before. Patsy Cline was exhibit A in his experiment. But her immense gifts—and untimely death—created a legacy that grew beyond compromise and became the legend and promise that inspired Loretta Lynn and the many young women who have succeeded to shape their own "sweet dreams."

CHAPTER 2

LEGACY AND LEGEND

The Cultural World of Patsy Cline's Winchester

Warren R. Hofstra and Mike Foreman

On a spring evening in 1961, Patsy Cline climbed to the top of the projection booth of the Winchester Drive-In where *King of the Wild Stallions*—"gun-hot death on Wild Horse Mesa"—had just finished running and the crowd was awaiting *Young Jesse James*. Cline had donned her cowgirl regalia. According to her friend Joltin' Jim McCoy, local country music singer, who had arranged the event:

> Here's Patsy singing, and the women—it was never the men, that's one thing I want to clarify—the women started blowing the horns and booing her. Now she already started to get a name for herself; I guess she was working the Opry then. Here's these women booing and carrying on. Now how do you feel? Here's a girl singing her heart out, has already made it and you got these idiots out there making fun of her and booing her. She started crying so bad. This guy, the manager, he had a trailer that he used as an office. We just took her over there, and I'll never forget it: she said, "Why do people in Winchester treat me like this?"[1]

What this incident betrays is the contested legacy of Patsy Cline. She was already at age twenty-eight a well-known vocal artist with a national following—her song "I Fall to Pieces" would peak later that summer at number one on the *Billboard* country charts. At the same time, she was subject to condemnation, often with the crudest sexual slander, by many people of her own community. It broke her heart, but her plight tells us something quite important about how social class, race, gender, and country music interacted in the identity of Patsy Cline, her legacy, and its function in the cultural history of a small town in the upper South during the 1950s.[2] Ultimately this legacy would join a patchwork of sites, structures, places, processes, and rituals wherein the necessary cultural work was performed that brought order, stability, and security to this community out of which Patsy Cline arose first as a country music star in the 1950s and eventually as a national icon several decades later.

Cline's tragic death in a private plane crash barely two years after her Winchester Drive-In performance added poignancy to this contested legacy. Her greatest hits album, released in 1967, has sold more than ten million copies and has stayed on the charts longer than any other record by a female vocalist. Several plays and numerous books have been written about this country music diva. Her iconic hit "Crazy" was declared the number one jukebox single of all time in 1997. She was admitted to the Country Music Hall of Fame in 1973 and received a star on the Hollywood Walk of Fame twenty-six years later. In 2002 Country Music Television placed her number one among the "Forty Greatest Women in Country Music." Within three years her humble home on Kent Street in Winchester appeared on the National Register of Historic Places.[3]

Yet before her death she lamented, "I don't know what's wrong with this town. It's like they don't want a person to make anything of herself."[4] More tourists visit Winchester for Patsy Cline than out of interests in the Civil War or George Washington, who slept there often during sojourns in the late 1740s and throughout the 1750s as both surveyor and soldier.[5] Yet a museum project interpreting Cline's story struggled for years to raise enough money to open her girlhood home in Winchester to the public in 2011, while another museum dedicated to decorative arts and the colonial history of the town opened a decade earlier with a multimillion dollar endowment.

Explaining this contradiction is the familiar cultural script of a poor girl who makes good in Hollywood or Nashville but never escapes her origins. Unpacking this script to reveal the workings of class and gender in the town leads us into its vernacular spaces and places in which music joined other behaviors in the social process of rendering a deeply divided social world tolerable, if not acceptable, to a hard-bitten people and the privileged few who benefited disproportionately from their labor. The question of Cline's contested legacy begins to make sense only when we understand how profoundly different the town was in the 1950s—how much it is to us today a foreign country.[6]

For much of the late eighteenth and nineteenth centuries, Winchester functioned as a market town serving the highly productive agricultural region of the lower Shenandoah Valley (see fig. 2.1). Most townspeople—rich and poor, black and white—made their living exchanging goods and services with local farmers. Wheat, the local staple, and flour, a global commodity,

Figure 2.1: Bird's eye map of the City of Winchester, 1926 (drawn by William Woods, created by W. A. Ryan, G3884. W6A3 1926.W6, Geography and Map Division, Library of Congress, Washington, D.C.).

generated a complex regional economy of primary (agriculture), secondary (flour manufacturing and related industries: iron, tanning, lumber, and so forth), and tertiary economic activities (merchant, financial, and artisan services). But it was Main Street (Loudoun Street) in Winchester that integrated all three sectors. Here residence and work comingled as merchants and artisans often lived above the shop with clerks or apprentices in lofts and slaves or free blacks in various back-lot structures. Social control among classes and races enjoying disproportionately the prodigious wealth of the local grain economy was immediate, personal, and based on face-to-face relationships among proprietors and workers as codified in the laws of contract, apprenticeship, and slavery.[7]

Change in this social system came in the twentieth century with the rise of the commercial apple industry throughout the lower Shenandoah Valley. Orchards had been part of the farm landscape of the Valley since the region was first occupied by Europeans during the second third of the eighteenth century. Apples, cider, sauce, and vinegar were consumed as critical commodities in the subsistence economy and local trade of farm families. By the end of the nineteenth century, however, these commodities fed a burgeoning demand in East Coast cities. Large commercial ventures joined farm orchards in the landscape. Families such as the Byrds, Harry and Tom, and the Glaizes, Fred and Philip, as well as partnerships like Moore and Dorsey made fortunes in apple production. Under the direction of Harry Byrd, Virginia governor in the late 1920s and member of the U.S. Senate from the 1930s onward for more than thirty years, the Byrd orchards, eleven in all engrossing five thousand acres, produced one and one-half million bushels of apples in 1955. As second largest, Moore and Dorsey produced about half that number. The Glaize brothers combined apple production with a lumber and millwork business in addition to other concerns supplying water tanks and spraying equipment locally. By the early twentieth century Frederick County was leading Virginia in apple production, and apples were a big business.[8]

But it was not until the era of Patsy Cline in Winchester that apples came to clearly dominate the agricultural economy of the region surrounding the town. Between 1949 and 1954 the percent that fruit production contributed to the value of farm products sold in Frederick Country increased from 39 to 66 as the total value of the apple yield more than tripled. As the economic value of apples soared, nonorchard areas witnessed the interconnected decline of wheat and flour and a transition to a farm economy based on livestock and hay. The disappearance of the grain economy was dramatic. Wheat production dropped by almost 24 percent in the 1940s and exceeded 36 percent during the next decade. Meanwhile stocks of beef cattle increased by more than 90 percent during the 1950s, and pasturelands grew in excess of 40 percent. Anyone living through the decades following World War II would have seen a landscape transformed by the decay of the old farm infrastructure of growing, harvesting, storing, and grinding grains; the conversion of cropland to pasture; the adaptation of bank barns as feeding stations; and the construction of miles and miles of new wire fencing along roadways. But it was the orchards in both a real and symbolic sense that came to dominate the countryside.[9]

Although the market-town social world created by wheat and flour persisted, cast upon it was a new urban economy of apple processing and an emerging working class of industrial laborers. Winchester grew as the regional center for storing, packing, and shipping apples in addition to processing various apple products (see fig. 2.2). The National Fruit Product Company, established at Alexandria, Virginia, in 1908, inaugurated Winchester operations with a vinegar plant in 1915 and a cannery three years later. In 1938 company offices relocated to the town. By the 1950s National Fruit with its White House brand of apple products employed 325 people year-round and close to seven hundred additional workers during the fall apple-picking and packing season. In 1931 Zeropack, an Ohio frozen food

Figure 2.2: Packing apples (736-417 thl, Stewart Bell Jr. Archives, Handley Regional Library, Winchester, Virginia).

processor, set up in Winchester and by Patsy Cline's era processed thirty-one million pounds of apples annually, employing as many as four hundred people at the peak of the apple season. It was joined by three additional cold storage plants, including the largest apple storage facility in the world. By this time as well, an H. J. Heinz vinegar plant was in its third decade of making this famous company's signature products consuming fifty million pounds of apples annually.[10]

It was in this economic context that textile mills located in the town during the era of World War I, and various light industries producing auto parts, rubber heals, records, plastic ware, and other goods, during the half century thereafter (see fig. 2.3). The Winchester Knitting Mills and the Virginia Woolen Company constructed large commercial mills in Winchester to take advantage of local wool production and the national trend of relocating the textile industry from New England to the South where white labor was cheap and abundant. Both mills were locally owned, and the latter employed more than five hundred workers and operatives before it closed in 1956. O'Sullivan Rubber Corporation moved to Winchester from Massachusetts in the depression year of 1932 and thirty years later was employing six hundred laborers. Proclaimed as the "public policy of Virginia that the right of persons to work shall not be denied or abridged on account of membership or nonmembership in any labor union or labor organization," Virginia's right-to-work law, passed in 1947 in the wake of the Taft-Hartley Act, ensured a low-wage, nonunionized, dependent work force in the town.[11] That same year American Brake Shoe opened its Winchester operations and within ten years was employing more than 580 people. By 1950, 51 percent of Winchester workers were employed in manufacturing, construction, and other basic economic activities, and more than three quarters (78.2 percent) of the town's labor force held working-class jobs.[12] Industrialists and manufacturers joined the older merchant class, but the size, residential segregation, and class identity of the workers significantly weakened the personal mechanisms of traditional social control. Winchester had become a working-class town, or perhaps more correctly, a traditional market town with a large working class. Class divided the town at the same time that the culture of class distinction worked in varied and complex ways to provide stability and community in a world in which some people lived better off the labor of others.[13]

Change in the economic, employment, and class system of the town during the 1950s and the decades before Patsy Cline launched her career there added to social stresses. Tensions in the town with the rise of industry and an industrial working class reflected regional changes traceable to at least

Figure 2.3: Virginia Woolen Company, North Kent Street, Winchester, 1926 (C. Frederick Barr, photographer, 106-119 wfchs, C. Fred Barr Collection, Stewart Bell Jr. Archives, Handley Regional Library, Winchester, Virginia).

the 1920s (see figs. 2.4 and 2.5). For that decade within a four-county area (Frederick, Shenandoah, Warren, and Page) including Winchester, agricultural income exceeded wages in manufacturing and trade by nearly 20 percent. By 1940 farm earnings constituted only 58 percent of income from these more urban sources. Ten years later, in Patsy Cline's era, this percentage had dropped to 42, and by the time she was famous and living in Nashville, farm production constituted only 20 percent of the regional economy. Trade, both wholesale and retail, was the big winner in these changes, not manufacturing. From 1940 to 1950 manufacturing jobs in Winchester increased by only 3 percent while employment in trade and the service economy grew by more than half. The trend away from manufacturing employment accelerated during the 1950s when Winchester's largest industrial employer, the Virginia Woolen Company, shuttered its doors. Between 1954 and 1958 employment in manufacturing dropped from 2,156 workers to 1,529, while the retail trade gained five establishments and more than 250 jobs.[14] Clearly work in service industries was replacing male-dominated factory labor, and the high percentage of women (54 percent in 1950) compared to men in the population may have been a result.[15]

Figure 2.4: Workers at Winchester Cold Storage, North Loudoun Street, Winchester, 1917 (738-1 thl, Winchester Cold Storage Collection, Stewart Bell Jr. Archives, Handley Regional Library, Winchester, Virginia).

Figure 2.5: Workers at the Jones Knitting Mill, North Kent Street, 1920 (601-1498 wfchs, Stewart Bell Jr. Archives, Handley Regional Library, Winchester, Virginia).

These changes also affected the income and status of those who owned or managed stores, shops, and various businesses. Throughout the lower Shenandoah Valley region in 1929, total income from wages and salaries about equaled the income of business proprietors and the money they earned by rents and investments. By 1950 the proprietors' share of total earnings had slipped to one-third while the far more numerous workers were collectively taking home almost three-fifths of the pie. Ten years later workers earned about two-thirds of the total to the proprietors' one-quarter.[16] These figures suggest that the Shenandoah Valley region was following national trends in which the rich were growing poorer by comparison and workers were becoming middle class in the 1950s. In Winchester the share of total income deriving from businesses, property rental, and other investments fell from 29 to 22 percent between 1950 and 1955, while the cut going to wages and salaries increased 43 percent.[17] This does not mean that the town's better-off citizens were suffering or manning barricades on well-heeled Washington Street, where many of the region's powerful apple families lived. Individually, the people of Patsy Cline's Kent Street still earned much less, but these developments must have unsettled some local bluebloods and entrenched class lines.

Asked today, most Americans will identify themselves as middle class, livelihood or income notwithstanding. Consumption defines this class—you are what you buy, and anyone can buy anything with the anonymity of money and the inclusiveness of mass marketing and advertising. Suburbanization and the new urbanism shape its social geography.[18] By comparison Patsy Cline's Winchester was, indeed, still a foreign country. Although elements of a consumerist middle class were emerging, for the most part a two-class system shaped life in a town with only a few suburbanlike developments and a retail trade governed by petty proprietors—grocers, pharmacists, clothiers, and merchants of shoes, hardware, furniture, or housewares. National chains controlled only two of thirteen groceries. Penney's and Ward's were on Main Street, but they competed with separate shops for every commodity they sold, and marketing on the scale of today's Lowe's, Home Depot, Target, or Walmart was inconceivable. Shopping was personal and often negotiated directly with a clerk over a counter. Black people could buy shoes but not try them on; pharmacists intimidated teenagers seeking "personal" items; and classy shops discomforted working people.

Dependence, far more than money, delineated the working class. According to author Joe Bageant, who grew up as working class in 1950s Winchester, "Working class might best be defined like this: You do not have power over your work. You do not control when you work, how much you get paid, how fast you work, or whether you will be cut loose from your job at the first shiver on Wall Street" (see fig. 2.6).[19] Similarly ownership or control over

Figure 2.6: Winchester and Western Railroad Workers, 1936 (E. E. Bayliss Jr. Collection, 735–764, Stewart Bell Jr. Archives, Handley Regional Library, Winchester, Virginia).

property, not money alone, identified a class of owners and managers of business and industry better described as a proprietary class than an upper class (see fig. 2.7). Whenever significant disparities of power and wealth exist in a society where personal control is inadequate for maintaining social order, powerful cultural mechanisms develop, first, to identify and distinguish social classes; second, to allow men and women of different classes to live separately but regularly encounter and engage one another peacefully and respectfully in workplaces and public spaces; and, in the final analysis, to justify themselves to each other—to rationalize the disparity of privilege.[20] Change would gather momentum in the 1950s. The rise of a national middle class around a mass media and the consumption of consumer goods it promoted would advance Patsy Cline's celebrity. The smooth, crooning Nashville Sound of her blockbuster hits such as "Crazy" came to signify a more homogeneous middle-class world in which the old mechanisms of identification, separation, and engagement gave way to the signs and symbols of a national pop culture of diminished class distinction and middle-class respectability.[21]

The complexity of this situation and the nuanced relationships among people of different classes—as well as races and genders—was evident in the seemingly contradictory statements Cline's contemporaries made about

Figure 2.7: Stockholders and officers of the Winchester and Western Railroad standing before the company's new engine, 1952 (69-1515 wfchs, Stewart Bell Jr. Archives, Handley Regional Library, Winchester, Virginia).

the realities of their social world. Sharply delineated by urban space from a surrounding countryside of farms and hamlets, the town, itself, constituted a distinct but insulated site wherein class relations played out in the geography of wealth and power. Society divided east and west along Main Street, a Winchester surrogate for the proverbial railroad tracks (see fig. 2.8). The "best" families lived to the west on Washington Street, conscious of the rich symbolism and influence of this name. Only four blocks eastward on the other side of Main, Kent Street lay at the center of the working-class world: North Kent was predominantly black, and South Kent, white, although there were significant islands of interracial residence (see fig. 2.9).[22] In a three-block area of South Kent Street that included Patsy Cline's home, the *Winchester City Directory* for 1955–1956 showed a total of forty-two homes. Only three were owner occupied; the remainder were rentals. No residents in Cline's block owned their own homes. Renters toiled as drivers, waitresses, cooks, or workers at American Brake Shoe. One homeowner on Kent worked as a foreman at the Winchester Knitting Mills. A parallel stretch of three blocks on Washington Street contained only twenty homes

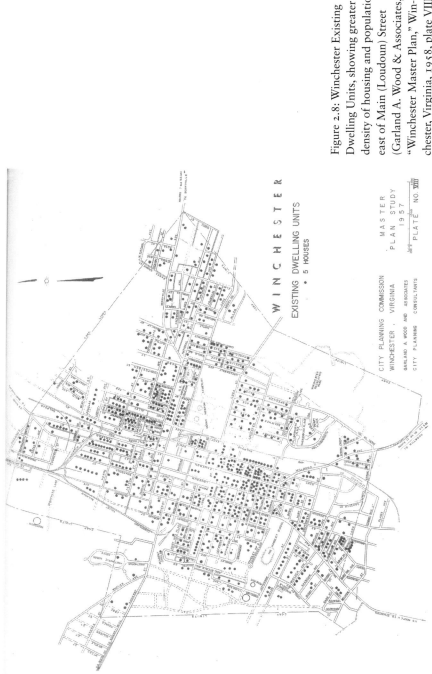

Figure 2.8: Winchester Existing Dwelling Units, showing greater density of housing and population east of Main (Loudoun) Street (Garland A. Wood & Associates, "Winchester Master Plan," Winchester, Virginia, 1958, plate VIII).

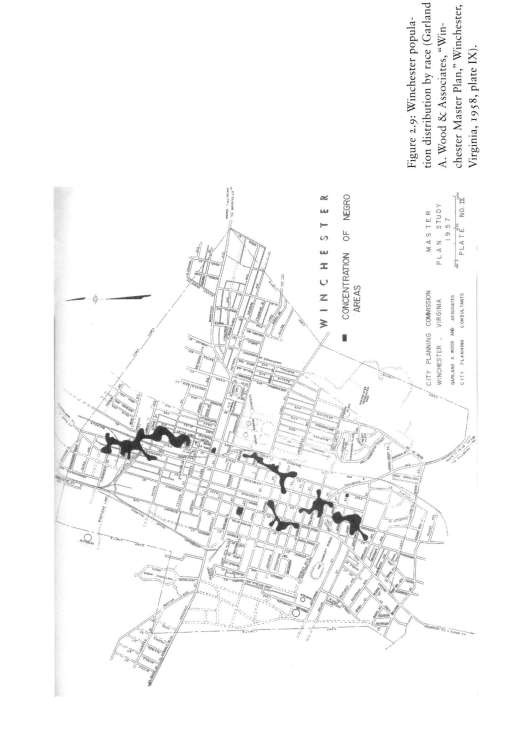

Figure 2.9: Winchester population distribution by race (Garland A. Wood & Associates, "Winchester Master Plan," Winchester, Virginia, 1958, plate IX).

on large lots. Fifteen were owner occupied, and an additional two served as parsonages for ministers. The lone renter worked as a salesman for the local power company. Homeowners included two physicians, a bank vice president, three retirees, two orchardists, two businessmen, and a manager of a knitting mill. The two orchardists were among the largest apple growers in the leading apple-producing region of Virginia.[23]

Not surprisingly, Winchester overall had an extraordinarily high rate of rental housing. Only two in five residents owned their own home. Most homeowners lived west of Main Street. Many of them also invested in rental housing on streets like Kent. Blunting this potentially exploitive relationship was a high rate of rental homes that in 1950 had plumbing and stood in good condition. Blight in working-class neighborhoods was not as significant a factor in class relations as was the dependence of renters on landlords.[24]

Within this self-contained, larger community, architecture and architectural space distinguished neighborhoods. Neoclassical, colonial revival, Italianate, and other high styles of revival architecture in brick and stone graced Washington Street where porticoes, yawning lawns, high hedges, and meticulous landscaping insulated private from public space (see fig. 2.10). A few blocks away on Kent Street the wood-framed I-house (two

Figure 2.10: Elegant colonial revival home on South Washington Street (126-265 wfchs, E. E. Bayliss Collection, Stewart Bell Jr. Archives, Handley Regional Library, Winchester, Virginia).

rooms up, two down, three window/door bays) and derivative vernacular styles dominated the cheek-by-jowl street line. Porches built directly into sidewalks enmeshed family with neighborhood life in a lively street scene (see fig. 2.11). This workaday landscape was interwoven on North Kent in the African American community with various shotgun houses and a more developed infrastructure of shops, corner markets, sandwich shops, and even a juke joint or two as befitted a neighborhood insulated by race and segregation.[25] Sharp differences in household income, home value, population density, and educational attainment divided east and west Winchester.[26]

Figure 2.11: View of South Kent Street; Patsy Cline's home is the third house from the left with a concrete apron to the street (133-83 wfchs, Stewart Bell Jr. Archives, Handley Regional Library, Winchester, Virginia).

Contemporaries of Patsy Cline growing up in Winchester during the 1950s recognized and acknowledged the geographical divide of class and wealth. As one put it: "If you had money, made or inherited, you lived on the west side. If you were working (middle) class you lived everywhere else. . . . Let's face it, if you lived on Washington, Stewart, Amherst, Briarmont Drive, Tennyson, etc.; you were doing good."[27] Or as one east-sider observed: "The upper class was almost entirely on Washington, Stewart, around Handley [High School] or behind the hospital or as my mother would say the rich lived on 'snob hill.'"[28] But another when asked "What do you feel were the social and economic differences between kids who lived on the west side of Winchester and the east side?" pointed to deeper nuances of class distinction in admitting that "I can't really answer this question, and I would say that the fact that I can't answer it is an answer itself. I don't ever remember feeling that where somebody lived was important."[29]

For many residents on both sides of the class and geographical divide, one way of ameliorating the disparity of wealth and comfort was to ignore it or deny it in deference to social democracy. Not talking about class was one of the ways that *class* worked in this society. Another resident commented: "As an east-side kid, I was aware of the economic differences but blind to any divisive social differences. Families from both sides of the 'track' went to the same schools, churches, athletic and social events, and the differences in social class were mollified and diminished by those commonalities. . . . Aside from the fact that many of the west side kids' families were better off financially, I can't think of any other major difference. Dress? Never noticed if someone was wearing a Ralph Lauren shirt or blouse or a no-name brand from Sears. Language? I think we all spoke a common language. Interests? Similar if not identical." But then came the admission: "Clubs? Aside from the Winchester C[ountry] C[lub], can't recall anywhere 'they' could go that 'we' couldn't."[30] Many affirmations that class did not matter came with just this type of qualification accompanied by deeper signifiers that it did matter, but not overtly. This ambiguity, if not irony, surfaces in comments by one white east side resident who grew up on the fringes of the African American Kent Street neighborhood: Social classes were a "way of life in the '50s and I don't think there was much resentment. The fifties followed two wars and the Great Depression, so people appreciated jobs, kids going to school, the start of buying homes and cars in Winchester. My parents always talked respectfully and supportive of their boss and business owners around Winchester. They didn't want to cause trouble or 'rock' the boat." This kind of compliancy, however, was not universal. "I grew up in

Winchester and went through 12 years of school there, including Handley High School," writes one Winchester émigré. "My father carried mail in the city for 33 years, and he used to relate stories about his mail route and the small-town snobs on it. In addition, no one there will ever let me forget that my father was a 'blue-collar postman.'"[31]

The ambiguity of social class was no more evident than in education. The people of Winchester had been the beneficiaries of a nineteenth-century legacy from a Scranton, Pennsylvania, judge who left the town a major endowment for a public library and a public school. All white children attended the John Handley High School, a site of intense class-making behavior named for its benefactor (see fig. 2.12). One poor student awestruck by the imposing neoclassical structure completed in 1923 proclaimed "This isn't a high school; it's like a college. It's overwhelming."[32] That was the precise intention of its planners, a group of local worthies charged with implementing the Handley trust. Independent of any statewide program, students were tracked in academic, general, and commercial programs. College-bound students took an academic degree emphasizing the same classical cultures embodied in the school's architecture. But acceptance in the academic program required passing a semester-long "Latin tryout" course. Commented one student: "None of my friends from Liberty Ave. [on the

Figure 2.12: John Handley High School (1196-12 thl, Stewart Bell Jr. Archives, Handley Regional Library, Winchester, Virginia).

east side] took the academic course. Since I came from the V[irgini]a Ave. School, most of those kids took the non-academic courses. . . . The east side kids were generally not viewed as good academic students, and the west side kids were good at everything . . . studies clubs, sports." As exclusive as Virginia's constitution, which conferred the franchise on only those able to interpret a passage from it, "Latin tryout" excluded many working-class students from the opportunities of a college education. This same student, however, "loved" Handley High because "it was the first time in my life that I realized it didn't matter where I lived and that I could be successful if I just tried hard and did the right things."[33] Evidently social class and class prejudice did matter apart from this student's high school experience.

If this message was insufficiently clear, the school's principal and super-intendent of schools rendered it explicit in 1956 by announcing to the as-sembled student body that new state laws designed to implement "massive resistance" to school desegregation had repealed mandatory high school at-tendance requirements. "If you do not wish to be here," Garland R. Quarles announced pointing to the rear of the auditorium, "then there's the door." Patsy Cline's younger bother Sam joined the group of students turning their backs that very day on a high school education and likely consigning them-selves to a lifetime of low-wage employment.[34] Other students nonetheless affirmed that they were "treated equally" by the educators, but "different social groups hung with their class of people." Differences in "attire and social graces" might distinguish social classes, but according to one student there were "no resentments" between them: "It just was what it was."[35]

The public use of Main Street was scripted similarly to mask social ten-sions and allow for ongoing interaction of people from different classes, genders, and races (see fig. 2.13). Like members of the same animal spe-cies, such as house cats occupying a common territory but utilizing its resources in varying ways at different times in alternative spaces, access to Main Street was self-regulated to prevent overt competition and conflict. At the same time, commercial space functioned to maintain class identity and difference. Country people from the county and white, working people from Kent Street thronged the streets and shops on Saturdays when stores stayed open until 8:00 or 9:00 P.M. After completing their marketing, many people would alternate a sidewalk stroll with an evening sitting in their parked car as a kind of mobile front porch engaging whoever passed by in conversation.[36] There were "definitely" different shops for different folks.[37] As one Winchester resident commented: "Main Street had shopping for everybody but there was the Workingman's Store, Penny's and nickel dime

Figure 2.13: Main Street (Loudoun Street), 1954 (69-1532 wfchs, Stewart Bell Jr. Archives, Handley Regional Library, Winchester, Virginia).

stores for the working class. Upper class shopped the better retail stores or drove to the Washington, DC area."[38] One person growing up working class remembered that "we were able to shop at an upper-class shop because my Mother worked there and we got discounts."[39] In one example, Swimley's furniture store and Patton's Furniture were known as being more expensive and catering to Washington Street tastes, while stores owned by the Groves or the Shewels sold cheaper furniture such as chrome kitchen table sets or Naugahyde couches. As for restaurants: "The working class that I knew didn't eat out at all," commented one east side resident.[40] In other examples people from the working and proprietary classes occupied the same restaurant spaces in different ways: "The upper class families may have ordered a more expensive entrée . . . for example, or paid twice as much as someone from the working class for a pair of shoes at Kinney's, but we shopped and ate at the same stores/restaurants."[41]

Among Washington Street society, most of the men owned or managed the stores, and the women shopped during weekdays as semiformal occasions with white gloves, hats, friends, and most likely lunch at the George Washington Hotel.[42] The social symbolism of a hotel named for Washington may have escaped residents of the eponymous street, but not so with an evening at the Capitol Theater, a half-block off Main Street prominently facing the stately county courthouse (see fig. 2.14).[43] The Capitol had opened in 1913 under ownership by eminent local citizens, most notably William H. Baker, a wealthy manufacturer of chocolate and president of the Shenandoah Valley National Bank. Baker had constructed one of the largest homes on Washington Street, a fantasy of architectural accretion incorporating numerous historical styles featuring minarets, balconies, towers, and shingling. Warner Studios acquired the theater in the late 1920s, booked movie runs from its New York offices, and brought America's most popular cinema to town from Hollywood's premier studios, including Paramount, RKO, and MGM, in addition to its own. The Capitol catered to a dressy crowd. Mike Foreman remembers as a teenager dressing in coat and tie for Saturday night dates at the Capitol. Anyone entering the

Figure 2.14: Capitol Theater, 1932; note the painting of George Washington and the people of Winchester in the arch above the stage (photographer C. Frederick Barr, 69-1047 wfchs, Stewart Bell Jr. Archives, Handley Regional Library, Winchester, Virginia).

THE PEOPLE OF WINCHESTER APPEALING TO WASHINGTON

NEW YORK G.P. PUTNAM & CO.

Figure 2.15: The People of Winchester Appealing to George Washington (engraving by Darley-Hall studio of G. Putnam, 1859, 69-348 wfchs, Stewart Bell Jr. Archives, Handley Regional Library, Winchester, Virginia).

theater could not help but notice the painting in the arch above the screen entitled "The People of Winchester Appealing to George Washington for Protection from the Indians" (see fig. 2.15).[44]

Nearby but squarely on Main Street stood the less stately, seven-hundred-seat Palace Theater, designed as a Spanish courtyard with a balcony for African American patrons (see fig. 2.16). It was owned by Herman Hable whose Jewish, German-immigrant grandfather, Solomon Hable, had operated a mens clothing store in Winchester as early as 1872. Faced with competition, the powerful Warner Brothers studio blocked major new movies from showing at the Palace until reaching an agreement granting Hable access to Fox pictures. Still excluded from many of the most popular movies, Hable labored to attract a working-class audience with live vaudeville, minstrel, country music, and local variety shows. Country music artists including many stars from Nashville's *Grand Ole Opry* such as Roy Acuff, Grandpa Jones, T. Texas Tyler, Cowboy Copas, and Wally Fowler and His Oak Ridge Quartet made frequent appearances at the Palace. It was there

Figure 2.16: Palace Theater (1406-91 thl, Stewart Bell Jr. Archives, Handley Regional Library, Winchester, Virginia).

that a young Patsy Cline would dash on a Saturday afternoon from a job flipping burgers down the street and win—often—the ten dollar prize.[45]

Society luncheons, banquets, and dances took place in the (Lord) Fairfax Dining Room and the grand ballroom of the George Washington Hotel (see fig. 2.17). Set in the stripped classicism of contemporary civic architecture by New York architect William Lee Stoddard, it was the center of social life for nearby Washington Street. In its elegant facilities three all-male civic clubs—Rotary, Lions, and Kiwanis—held weekly luncheons, and the Women's Civic League convened monthly. The ballroom also accommodated various society dances such as the "Ladies Night" events of the service organizations and the New Year's Eve ball of the Women's Auxiliary of the Winchester Memorial Hospital. The hotel proved highly popular for wedding receptions and dances. Dancers swayed to the imitative big band sounds of ensembles such as the Bob Riley Orchestra or the Les Arnold Band.[46] Below the dance floor, however, was a Howard Johnson's Restaurant serving more pedestrian fare to tourists and working people looking for a cheap meal or an ice cream treat on an evening. And organizations of working people such as the Winchester policemen occasionally held celebratory events in the upstairs facilities.[47] But African Americans at the hotel were always veiled behind the screen of

Figure 2.17: George Washington Hotel in the early 1950s (Marken & Bielfeld, Frederick, Maryland, 830-1 wfchs, Stewart Bell Jr. Archives, Handley Regional Library, Winchester, Virginia).

service employment and its segregated spaces. As with the high school, Main Street, and other places throughout the town, the George Washington Hotel, even with the elitist pretensions of its name, its architecture, and its social affiliations, provided a single, spatially segregated structure utilized by people of varied classes and races in different, highly scripted ways. As a setting for dances and dance bands, the hotel also segregated the aural experience of music, its venues for performance and consumption, and its social culture.

As a site for dining, dancing, and socializing among the proprietary classes, the George Washington Hotel certainly had its counterparts in the Winchester Country Club and the York Inn (see fig. 2.18). Founded as an exclusive, private, membership-only organization in 1923, the club provided the sole facility combining golfing, swimming, and tennis in Winchester. For many years the country club also maintained one of the best and most exclusive restaurants in town.[48] The York Inn was also a favorite spot for dinner and dancing. Despite its rustic, log architecture, it catered to a crowd from Washington Street and up-and-coming younger professionals. Later demolished for a bank drive-through, the Chanticleer Inn located in one of the grand Washington Street homes near downtown offered some of the best food in town with an all-black service staff. One patron commented that diners would have been uncomfortable with white servers.[49]

Figure 2.18: Party at the York Inn, c. 1948 (69-1510 wfchs, Stewart Bell Jr. Archives, Handley Regional Library, Winchester, Virginia).

If society music and the big band sound appealed to upper-class tastes, then country music was clearly the choice of working people. As country music historian Bill Malone observes in this volume, industrial development and railroad expansion stimulated a migration of southern country people to American cities in the late nineteenth and twentieth centuries. They became the principal audience for country music heard live in varied urban venues, including beer joints and dance halls, on the radio, or through records played at home or on jukeboxes. Entertaining and transporting, the music connected displaced working people to rural pasts and eased adjustments to city life by conferring upon them a coherent, respectable working-class identity.[50]

Winchester's oldest residents remember beer joints at many intersections in the town during the 1950s. Although Virginia law forbade liquor by the drink at that time, beer could be sold and consumed on the premises of small establishments that additionally offered companionship, camaraderie, and consolation to friends and neighbors in working-class communities (see fig. 2.19). With catchy names such as the Mel Max, Little Corner, Daisey and Reds, Lucky Inn, Steve's Rest, and Red Star, they offered music—live

Figure 2.19: Rustic Tavern on the right adjoining the Seventh-Day Adventist Church and *Shenandoah Valley News* on West Cork Street in the 1930s (69-1542 wfchs, Stewart Bell Jr.Archives, Handley Regional Library, Winchester, Virginia).

occasionally, but always on jukeboxes. Mixing country music with pop, top-forty sounds, jukeboxes brought the latest country artists and honky-tonk singers such as Hank Williams, George Jones, Kitty Wells, and Ernest Tubb into the lives of working people. Their songs about home, family, love, loss, betrayal, and trust stitched a fabric of meaning and emotion into the otherwise tattered cloth of hard work, low income, economic dependence, and personal vulnerability. In 1968 Virginia amended its alcoholic beverage laws to forbid the sale of beer or wine unless consumed with meals. Restaurants, in other words, wiped out the beer joints.[51]

Dance halls, no less familiar than beer joints, could be found in both black and white communities, but many were spread around the countryside on rural roads. Working-class people gathered on Saturday evenings for dancing, drinking, and conversation as well as romancing and occasionally brawling in these large open spaces with a stage at one end and tables or a bar along the sides and back. Most popular in Winchester was Patton's Dance Hall on the lower end of Main Street where Don Patton and His Swingsters carried on during many weekend evenings. In surrounding communities were the Shamrock, the Rainbow Inn, the Orchard Inn, and the Mountainside Inn.

Music by the Kountry Krackers, Sonny Frye and the Playboys, the Mountainside Ramblers, the Dixie Night Hawks, or the Esquires brought these halls alive. Organizations such as the American Legion, the VFW, and various social lodges such as the Moose, the Elks, and the Eagles often sponsored dances at their own halls. In Winchester the National Guard Armory was a favored spot for weekend dances, often alternating Friday nights for African Americans with Saturdays for white dancers. On one Christmas weekend in 1955 Patsy Cline appeared with the Kountry Krackers on a Friday night at the American Legion Hall in nearby Berryville followed by a Christmas Eve dance the next night with the same band at the Winchester Armory.[52]

The national media of radio and, increasingly during the 1950s, television penetrated the musical culture of Winchester and shaped social tastes. Even before Winchester's local station, WINC, began broadcasting in 1941, powerful clear channel stations such as WSM in Nashville or WLS from Chicago reached listeners in the Shenandoah Valley, bringing live programming into most homes. On Saturday evenings the *Grand Ole Opry* or the *National Barn Dance* entertained local listeners with folksy variety shows featuring country music stars and comedy routines borrowed from vaudeville.[53] On network broadcasts from WINC, people in Winchester could hear a mixture of music, news, religion, sports, variety, drama, and comedy any afternoon or evening of the week with programs such as the *Grand Ole Opry*'s competitors, *Broadway's My Beat* and the *Guy Lombardo Show*, or other broadcasts including *Bob and Ray*, *Gene Autry*, *Our Miss Brooks*, *Twenty Questions*, *Hopalong Cassidy*, *Amos and Andy*, and the *Shadow*, to name just a few.[54]

In 1950 televisions appeared in Winchester homes more commonly than any other Virginia community except suburban areas such as Alexandria.[55] Proximity to four network stations in Washington, D.C., brought this new national medium into peoples' lives in Patsy Cline's hometown sooner than it appeared in most communities. Television programming in its early days largely mimicked or usurped radio shows, and country music performers often got star billing on variety programs such as Ed Sullivan's or Steve Allen's along with opera divas, Broadway stars, ballet dancers, and classical musicians. Radio and television, in other words, during the era before format stations took over the airwaves and long in advance of specialty cable stations, provided a common but varied media space in which people from throughout town could fulfill quite separate tastes in music and entertainment. The first televisions may, by reason of expense alone, have been more available in homes west of Winchester's Main Street, but television viewing in the 1950s was much more a public or community activity than it is today. Neighbors and acquaintances would frequently gather for a favorite program in the home of the only television owner on a block, thus broadening the impact of a rapidly developing, media-driven, national consumer culture. The socially interactive but segregated spaces of the Handley High School, Main Street, or the George Washington Hotel thus had their virtual counterpart in what the people of Winchester saw and heard on television.[56]

Identifying with the music of the working class thus came easily and naturally for Patsy Cline. Her father, Sam Hensley, a gifted gospel singer but a man troubled by alcohol and violence, left the family shortly after moving to Winchester and 608 South Kent Street in 1948. Patsy abandoned Handley High School to support her mother and siblings by working first in a chicken factory and then at a neighborhood drugstore soda fountain. But singing was her passion. Radio and local performance shaped her tastes, and her first opportunities to sing publicly came through Joltin' Jim McCoy's live Saturday morning broadcast on local WINC radio and a country music performance at the Palace Theater with Wally Fowler. She cut demonstration disks at the recording studio above G & M Music to send to come-ons in newspaper ads promising instant stardom for a dollar or two. Bigger breaks came with Bill Peer and the Melody Boys beginning in 1953 and first place in a regional country music championship in summer 1954, landing her a regular spot on Connie B. Gay's *Town and Country Time*, a barn dance show like the *Opry* in Washington, D.C. Her career took off in 1957 when she won Arthur Godfrey's talent scout competition on January 21, singing "Walkin' After Midnight," soon a top hit on both the *Billboard* pop and country charts. Then came a move to Nashville, a Decca Record contract in 1961, and acceptance on the *Opry* the same year, followed soon thereafter by monster hits "I Fall to Pieces" and "Crazy." But significantly, she always called Winchester home, visiting her mother there regularly, and proclaiming "One of these days I'm going to come to Winchester and draw one hell of a crowd. One hell of a crowd!"[57]

Although her untimely death precluded this satisfaction, she always preferred the cowgirl outfits her mother made and singing in the roadhouses and honky tonks of working-class people. In her own hometown, her music and her personality remained a subversive force. Appearing with her hair in rollers on Main Street on a Saturday afternoon or in short-shorts with bare midriff at a yard party could be affronting, as was her signature bright red lipstick that painted her in the minds of some as a trollop.[58] Calling everyone "Hoss" as a term of mixed endearment and belittlement, she had a reputation for gruffness and blunt language. "If you crossed her up she'd tell you off," said friend Johnny Anderson. "Oh, I heard her cuss people out, hell yeah."[59] As one member of a prominent Winchester family put it:

"Social class didn't matter in old Winchester. We treated everybody equally. But you know what Patsy Cline's problem was? Country music. Nobody liked country music."[60] Nobody, of course, but Patsy Cline's people. According to Skeeter Knee, who grew up with Cline, "Country music had a little something to do with it, when it started. . . . Here's a class of people we are and we're going to sing about it. We're going to sing about, you know, the taverns and the drinking and everything . . . that attracted the people that felt that they were in that group." Although Cline was "probably as good as will ever come along," Knee continued, working people "took to her just like one of the people that were there [at dance halls]. She was just like everyone else that was there. She was, she was just one of the people that were there for the dance, or the fight, or whatever broke out."[61]

As an attractive outspoken woman, however, Cline was not just like everybody else. She challenged conventional notions of sexuality prevalent in the 1950s and especially potent in small southern communities like Winchester where sex and race had long been compounded in the social powder keg of class relations. Since its inception, Jim Crow segregation had been justified throughout the South, in part as a barricade necessary to shield white women from black men. Southern fears of interracial mixing were pathological.[62] In racial integrity legislation passed in the 1920s, Virginia had outlawed interracial marriage as well as racial intermixing in theaters and public places, proclaiming the "one-drop rule" defining blackness and premised upon the horror that the stock of one black ancestor, however distant, impregnated in the white race would degrade its presumed superiority forever.[63] Phobia about sexual attraction as a vindication for white supremacy had justified the lynching of thousands of black men in the South since the 1880s when the barriers of Jim Crow segregation were first erected. Broaching them could be deadly, as Howard Walker, a black man in Winchester, discovered when he was accused of rape, tried, and executed all within sixty days in 1946 for what had in fact been consensual relations with a prominent white woman.[64]

Patsy Cline was no Howard Walker, but she was possessed of an instinctive sensuality that could menace class barriers and ensnare vulnerable white men in a way equally provocative. According to Rosanne Cash, Johnny Cash's daughter, Cline was "rooted in her body like a redwood in the earth . . . in command of a startling sexuality that infuses everything." A photo of Cline singing at a party on Fairmont Street (an extension of Washington Street) sporting short-shorts and a bare midriff reveals an allure that was as forthright as it was socially subversive.[65] This was the same seductiveness that beguiled white men from that side of town into slumming it for an evening at a low-class strip show once a year when a carnival set up on the eastern edge of town. Their duplicity, however, was sanctioned as a transient upending of approved morality in a momentary release of class tension. Cline's appeal was not. This chanteuse doubled as a siren, debasing family values and unsettling the social geography premised upon them. Thus she became the target of sexual slander. The woman in a photograph sitting nude in the back seat of a car on a Saturday night—her head clipped from the image and her body too plump to be Cline—nonetheless became Cline by transposition as the image passed from hand to hand at the National Guard Armory in nearby Martinsburg, West Virginia. Stories about Cline's affairs with married men were rife. People reveled in the tale of Cline seducing a strapping young Mountie she stumbled upon in a hotel lobby during a Canadian tour.[66] The truth of these stories was doubtful, at best, but irrelevant. Their importance lay in the cultural work performed in scapegoating a young woman for the iniquities moving deep beneath the barriers of race and class within her community.[67]

In 1955 Cline and her band crashed the Apple Blossom parade in Winchester. Apple Blossom is a three-day spring festival first held in 1926 to celebrate the apple industry and its economic benefits. Organizing the annual event lay firmly in the grasp of the town's proprietary class. Men and women from the west side of town constituted the committees that planned the luncheons, the balls, and most notably the two parades bracketing the festival. Ruling not only the festival but metaphorically the people of her apple kingdom were a queen and her court of princesses representing other communities throughout Virginia. The queen's coronation was—and still is—the highlight of the festival. Each year during the 1950s Handley High School principal, Garland Quarles, composed an august new ceremony set in an imaginary but sublimely regal world drawing on themes from mythology, ancient civilizations, medieval life, chivalry, romantic literature, and aristocratic fantasy over which people wept, marveled, and transferred the emotions of a benighted people to the virtual splendor of a royal court. Few, however, saw the event as a classic ritual of cultural reversal in which women disempowered in the 1950s by female subordination and gendered stereotypes of happy homemaker, obeisant wife, and selfless mother were ritually mollified by feigned, if only temporary, deference for a queen (see fig. 2.20). Arguably the experience went far in ameliorating the disparities, not only of gender but class as well, in mutual fealty for an idol in whom the tensions and transgressions of the community could not only be sacrificed but also forfeited and foreclosed. So it was, too, with prominent merchants, bankers, lawyers, and doctors who slummed it for an afternoon at a "stag lunch" eating fried chicken, sitting on overturned apple crates in the bay of a cold storage plant, and drinking whiskey from a soda can (see fig. 2.21).[68]

Figure 2.20: Apple Blossom Queen with members of her court in the Apple Blossom Parade, 1951 (46-37g thl, Stewart Bell Jr. Archives, Handley Regional Library, Winchester, Virginia).

Figure 2.21: Stag lunch for men only at Glaize Packing Shed, Apple Blossom Festival, 1959 (1406-93 thh, Stewart Bell Jr. Archives, Handley Regional Library, Winchester, Virginia).

Parades have long been recognized as ritualized expressions of community order. Staged to recognize cyclical events in religious or political calendars, commemorations such as the signing of the Declaration of Independence or extraordinary moments including delivery from a flood or drought, victory in war, or the ratification of the Constitution, these marches laid bare the structure of society in long processions of people organized by trade and profession in a front-to-back hierarchy of civic culture. Parades, too, are popular entertainments in which meaning and often social coherence or reassurance arises from the association of marchers and onlookers. Thus the annual fireman's parade of the Winchester Apple Blossom Festival reinforced the community's sense of the collective security provided by fire companies against one of the greatest threats to life and property. Composing those companies were predominantly the working people of the town for whom being a fireman was itself a masculine ritual of military competence and community adulation. If the Apple Blossom Festival provided a segregated space in which working people could celebrate their contributions to community order, then it was the street over which fire companies marched, their engines roaring with blaring horns and wailing sirens.[69]

The grand feature parade was something else. Composed of local luminaries—often the organizers of the festival itself, joined by prominent politicians and leaders in various civic organizations—and national celebrities drawn from the worlds of sports and popular culture, including singers and movie stars, the parade accentuated for its audiences the magnitude of civic pride and the magnanimity of civic leaders. But in 1955 when Cline was denied a spot in the grand parade, she tagged along anyway in an unofficial car with cowgirl gear causing no small stir among partygoers at homes lining the Washington Street parade route. "On certain streets they would holler and applaud," commented one observer, "then in the ritzy sections they would just absolutely ignore her as she went by. It was so still and quiet, you could hear the noise the crepe paper was making. . . . It was that extreme." According to a parade official: "One of the marching bands was positioned after her car and the comment I heard was, 'I would rather follow the horses.'"[70] Here was no ritual reversal of poor girl as heroine, but an affront, an outrage, a subversive act by an outcast.

One year later, due to her rising notoriety with television appearances in Washington, D.C., Cline joined the parade as an official participant with a properly designated car. Victory as a Godfrey "Talent" landed her star billing in the 1957 parade. That she could so quickly go from Apple Blossom renegade to public idol signifies the volatility of her reputation and the complex, controversial nature of her public image. As festival celebrity she was entitled to an escort, or chauffeur, for sanctioned events. Festival organizer, Tom Baldridge, secured a convertible on this occasion from an Oldsmobile dealership in Warrenton, Virginia. The dealer insisted that his driver bring it to Winchester, drive it in the parade, and return it to Warrenton. As one story told about the occasion circulated, however, Baldridge could find no man in Winchester willing to be associated with Cline as escort and had to hire an anonymous stand-in from a considerable distance.[71]

Volatility remained at the center of Cline's legacy. The funeral procession at her burial in 1963 stretched for miles to her grave located significantly outside the town, and the grief over her passing was by all accounts profound, universal, and genuine. But a little more than twenty years later, a proposal to rename the innocuous "Pleasant Valley Road" in her honor provoked a local uproar. A petition drive timed with the anniversary of her March 5 death yielded sufficient support among fans to place the matter on the city council's agenda in early 1986. While the council waited until May to take up the matter, a war raged among the townfolk. A sizable number were "very pleased about the belated recognition some concerned citizens of Winchester are trying to bring about to honor the late, great Patsy Cline." With a partially veiled reference to George Washington, another advocate penetrated to the heart of the social ironies shaping the debate by characterizing Cline as a "gutsy, shoot-from-the-hip individual who knew what she wanted and didn't let small-town mentality get in her way. These other individuals so honored with streets named after them have built fortunes doing exactly the same thing." Another supporter queried, "How many other Winchester gals have sung at Carnegie Hall? It should be with pride that we make this change." More poignant and suggestive was the assertion that "they say Patsy Cline had a 'reputation.' They say Kent Street has a 'reputation.' Let's change the name of Kent Street to Patsy Cline Boulevard and fight for the reputation and dignity of both."[72] At the session in which council members considered the name change, supporters presented petitions with close to 900 signatures, but opponents countered with 546 names on their petition. The resolution of the thousand-member First Assembly of God Church must have helped sway the council into an eleven-to-one vote against memorializing Cline.[73] More bluntly, one resident testified: "Ask anybody in this town and they'll tell you. Patsy Cline was nothin' but a whore."[74] When the town finally did get around to naming a street for her, it was only an access road to Lowe's Hardware. A sign in the parking lot read with evident intent: "No Exit to Pasty [sic] Cline Blvd."[75]

With less apparent controversy, the auditorium at the much revered John Handley High School was renamed the Patsy Cline Theatre in 2009. On

September 11, school officials made this announcement with the news that Willie Nelson had agreed to give a dedication concert planned for October 29.[76] No petitions for or against this stunning development circulated among the townspeople. No angry, or even skeptical, protest letters appeared in the local newspapers even though the venerable old building had become the object of considerable tension over the city's recent expenditure of sixty-five million dollars for its restoration. Yet the event was laden with numerous ironies resonating with the depth to which Cline's contested legacy had become embedded in the culture of the community.

Poverty and paternal abandonment had robbed Cline of the opportunity of attending Handley as a high school student, so the town could not claim its now-legendary citizen as an alumna of its most prized civic institution. The man most responsible for renaming the auditorium and organizing the dedication concert—a retired state senator and gubernatorial candidate—had himself originated in the humblest circumstances on the east side of town. When Cline was fifteen she had performed at a talent contest sponsored by the American Legion on the self-same stage of the "theatre" so newly named for her. Now the front row of center-section seats had all been dedicated in honor of local worthies, and Cline's memorial seat stood side by side with the one commemorating Judge Handley himself. One Washington Street resident, a teacher who had devoted her career to Handley High, recalled with evident disgust that after the talent show performance long ago, the budding country music star had stripped a garter from her leg and tossed it to the audience. And now from that very stage one of country music's contemporary superstars would sing Cline's signature song "Crazy," a number he had in fact composed. As one of Austin, Texas's musical "Outlaws," Nelson was something of a renegade himself and a refugee from the music business of Nashville that Cline had helped create with the crooning sound that gave "Crazy" its compelling yet enigmatic quality.

Attending Nelson's concert were people from all across Winchester and from each of its neighborhoods. Everyone cheered together, and even some of Winchester's most prominent citizens appeared wearing Willie Nelson headbands. Restored as it appeared in the 1950s, the old high school still provided a site for the commingling of all townspeople even if the scripted segregation of social classes was now articulated in new rituals of cultural reversal. If Cline's legacy seemed less contested on the occasion, it was because her memory had become as culturally capacious and complex as the symbol of the school she had never attended and as equally accommodating of the multiple meanings that justify an otherwise disparate people one to another among themselves.

NOTES

1. Margaret Jones interview with Jim McCoy, March 5, 1991, in Jones, *Patsy: The Life and Times of Patsy Cline* (New York: HarperCollins, 1994; New York: De Capo, 1999), 205–6. See also: Mark Bego, *I Fall to Pieces: The Music and the Life of Patsy Cline* (Holbrook, Mass.: Adams Publishing, 1995), 131–32; Ellis Nassour, *Honky Tonk Angel: The Intimate Story of Patsy Cline* (New York: St. Martin's, 1993), 147–48. No claim is made here that Winchester by virtue of class, race, gender, or the particular cultural context out of which arose the contested legacy of Patsy Cline was in any way unique among towns of its size and type in the 1950s South. The rejection of Cline by certain elements in the social structure of the town was indicative, in fact, not of the community's peculiarity but its quotidian ordinariness and the manner in which it represented small-town life throughout its region, if not the nation.

2. It is not the contention of this chapter that any accusations regarding Cline were either true or untrue, but that their use reveals how conventions of race, class, and gender functioned within communities such as Winchester, Virginia, in the 1950s. That these accusations usually lack substantiation is indicative of their role as stories or cultural scripts that reinforce social conventions often at the expense of individual freedoms and reputations. For more on towns in Cline's era and before, see Pete Daniel, *Lost Revolutions: The South in the 1950s* (Chapel Hill: University of North Carolina Press for the Smithsonian National Museum of American History, 2000); Don H. Doyle, *New Men, New Cities, New South: Atlanta, Nashville, Charleston, Mobile, 1860–1910* (Chapel Hill: University of North Carolina Press, 1990); Robert R. Dykstra, "Town-Country Conflict: A Hidden Dimension in American Social History," *Agricultural History* 38 (October 1964): 195–204; Douglas Flamming, *Creating the Modern South: Millhands and Managers in Dalton, Georgia, 1884–1984* (Chapel Hill: University of North Carolina Press, 1992); David R. Goldfield, *Region, Race, and Cities: Interpreting the Urban South* (Baton Rouge: Louisiana State University Press, 1997); Mary P. Ryan, *Civic Wars: Democracy and Public Life in the American City during the Nineteenth Century* (Berkeley: University of California Press, 1997); Christopher Silver and John V. Moeser, *The Separate City: Black Communities in the Urban South, 1940–1968* (Lexington: University Press of Kentucky, 1995).

3. The resurgence of Patsy Cline's celebrity and her achievement of iconic status in American popular culture is the subject of Joli Jensen, *Nashville Sound: Authenticity, Commercialization, and Country Music* (Nashville: Country Music Foundation Press and Vanderbilt University Press, 1998), 89–118.

4. Jones, *Patsy*, xi.

5. *Winchester Star*, October 13, 2011.

6. The concept of the past as a foreign country is owing to the beginning sentence in L. P. Hartley's 1953 novel *The Go-Between*: "The past is a foreign country: they do things differently there" (London: H. Hamilton, 1953; New York: New York Review of Books, 2002), 17. Although Winchester may not be significantly distinguished

from towns of its size and type throughout the mid-twentieth-century South, this chapter is premised on the argument that the values and functions of race, class, and gender in the community during the 1950s render it foreign to twentieth-first–century investigators.

7. On the development of Winchester as a market town, see Christopher E. Hendricks, *The Backcountry Towns of Colonial Virginia* (Knoxville: University of Tennessee Press, 2006); Warren R. Hofstra, *The Planting of New Virginia: Settlement and Landscape in the Shenandoah Valley* (Baltimore: Johns Hopkins University Press, 2004), 236–325; Robert D. Mitchell, *Commercialization and Frontier: Perspectives on the Shenandoah Valley* (Charlottesville: University Press of Virginia, 1977), 7–14, 152–60, 188–201; Mitchell, "The Settlement Fabric of the Shenandoah Valley, 1790–1860," in *After the Backcountry: Rural Life in the Great Valley of Virginia, 1800–1900*, eds. Kenneth E. Koons and Warren R. Hofstra (Knoxville: University of Tennessee Press, 2000), 34–47. On the question of social control in rural and market-town societies, see Thomas Perkins Abernethy, "Social Relations and Political Control in the Old Southwest," *Mississippi Valley Historical Review* 16 (March 1930): 529–37; Douglas Greenberg, "Crime, Law Enforcement, and Social Control in Colonial America," *American Journal of Legal History* 26 (October 1982): 293–325; Pippa Holloway, *Sexuality, Politics, and Social Control in Virginia, 1920–1945* (Chapel Hill: University of North Carolina Press, 2006); Lawrence Frederick Kohl, "The Concept of Social Control and the History of Jacksonian America," *Journal of the Early Republic* 5 (Spring 1985): 21–34; Charles David Phillips, "Exploring Relations among Forms of Social Control: The Lynching and Execution of Blacks in North Carolina, 1889–1918," *Law & Society Review* 21 (1987): 361–74.

8. Winchester–Frederick County Chamber of Commerce, "Industry in Winchester," *Virginia Record* 78 (April 1956): 14.

9. Virginia Department of Agriculture, Division of Statistics, "Frequency County, Farm Statistics, 1910–60" (Richmond, 1962).

10. Ibid., 14–16; "Industry in Winchester," 14–16, 32–34.

11. Code of Virginia, title 40.1.58–69. Formally Taft-Hartley was the Labor-Management Relations Act of 1947.

12. "Industry in Winchester," 14–16, 32–34; Garland A. Wood & Associates, "Winchester Master Plan" (Winchester, Va., 1958), 7–10, table IV.

13. Much of the literature on class relations in industrial towns focuses on one-industry, company towns. Diverse agricultural processing and textile industries in Winchester during the first half of the twentieth century, nonetheless, affected the lives of working-class people much as cotton factories or steel mills did in towns throughout both the South and the North. Class relations and cultural politics in Winchester beginning in Patsy Cline's era is the subject of Joe Bageant's, *Deer Hunting with Jesus: Dispatches from America's Class War* (New York: Crown, 2007). Additionally, see Margaret Crawford, *Building the Workingman's Paradise: The Design of American Company Towns* (London: Verso, 1995); Hardy Green, *The Company Town: The Industrial Edens and Satanic Mills that Shaped the American*

Economy (New York: Basic Books, 2010); John C. Hudson, "The Other America: Changes in Rural America during the 20th Century," in *North America: The Historical Geography of a Changing Continent*, eds. Thomas F. McIlwraith and Edward K. Muller (Lanham, Md.: Rowman and Littlefield, 2001), 409–21.

14. Bureau of Population and Economic Research, Graduate School of Business Administration, University of Virginia, "Income Estimates: Virginia: Standard Metropolitan and Other Economic Areas, Selected Years, 1929 to 1968," 33–35, table 7: Personal Income by Major Sources; Frederick County and Winchester: Economic Survey, 1961, 7–8, Virginia Historical Society, Richmond, Va. For more on the textile industry in the twentieth-century Shenandoah Valley, see Wilbur S. Johnston, *Weaving a Common Thread: A History of the Woolen Industry in the Top of the Shenandoah Valley* (Winchester, Va.: Winchester–Frederick County Historical Society, 1990).

15. According to city planners, the high percentage of women in the population was "possibly because the males of that age are moving out of Winchester to work," Wood & Associates, "Winchester Master Plan," 35–36. For a discussion of the retail trade in Winchester, see ibid., 17–21. Nationally, the number of workers in the service sector doubled from 1950 to 1970, and between 1900 and 1950 the number of workers engaged in trade went from less than half the number in manufacturing to more than the total number of manufacturing workers; see James R. Green, *The World of the Worker: Labor in Twentieth-Century America* (New York: Hill and Wang, 1980; Urbana: University of Illinois Press, 1998), 226; Joseph G. Rayback, *A History of American Labor* (New York: Free Press, 1966), 193; Melvyn Dubofsky and Foster Rhea Dulles, *Labor in America: A History*, 8th ed. (Wheeling, Ill.: Harlan Davidson, 2010).

16. Bureau of Population and Economic Research, "Income Estimates," 38–40, table 9. Again, these figures mirror national trends in which for 1948 wages and salaries constituted 65 percent of total personal income, and proprietary and property income amounted to 30 percent; see Harold G. Vatter, *The U.S. Economy in the 1950's: An Economic History* (New York: W. W. Norton, 1963), 69.

17. Wood & Associates, "Winchester Master Plan," 16, table 9.

18. On the subject of middle-class identity, the historian Burton Bledstein comments: "Indeed, in the twentieth century a large body of Americans—a majority in most polling data since the 1930s—have identified themselves as somewhere in the middle of the class structure, neither rich nor poor, neither upper nor lower, closer to being typical than not, striving to be in the center—the middle," in Burton J. Bledstein and Robert D. Johnston, eds. *The Middling Sorts: Explorations in the History of the American Middle Class* (New York: Routledge, 2001), 1. Social science polling confirms Bledstein's point. According to Robert W. Hodge and Paul M. Siegal: "When asked simply 'What social class are you a member of?' or when forced to choose between membership in the 'upper,' 'middle,' or 'lower' class, 80 to 90 per cent of a national sample—at least in the United States—will place themselves squarely in the middle, with negligible proportions electing the extremes or disavowing the existence of social classes." See Hodge and Siegal, "Social Stratification: The

Measurement of Social Class," in *International Encyclopedia of the Social Sciences*, ed. David L. Sills, 17 vols. (New York: Macmillan and Free Press, 1972), 15:317–18; Richard Centers, *The Psychology of Social Classes: A Study of Class Consciousness* (Princeton: Princeton University Press, 1949; New York: Russell & Russell, 1961). When presented with the option of identifying as working class, however, with the following question "If you were asked to use one of four names for your social class, which would you say you belong in: the lower class, the working class, the middle class, or the upper class?" this 90 percent in the middle divides about equally between working and middle classes. For polling on this question since the 1970s, see Tom W. Smith; Peter V. Marsden; Michael Hout; Jibum Kim, *General Social Surveys, 1972–2010* [machine-readable data file]. Principal Investigator, Tom W. Smith; Co-Principal Investigators, Peter V. Marsden and Michael Hout, NORC ed. Chicago: National Opinion Research Center, producer, 2005; Storrs, Conn.: The Roper Center for Public Opinion Research, University of Connecticut, distributor, 1 data file (55,087 logical records) and 1 codebook (3,610 pp). When asked a similar question on a 2005 *New York Times* poll, however, a clear plurality of respondents called themselves middle class; see *Class Matters* (New York: Henry Holt, 2005), 253. On consumption and class identity, see Gabrielle Esperdy, *Modernizing Main Street: Architecture and Consumer Culture in the New Deal* (Chicago: University of Chicago Press, 2008); Arthur Kornhauser, "Public Opinion and Social Class," *American Journal of Sociology* 55 (January 1950): 333–45; Carol A. O'Connor, "Sorting Out the Suburbs: Patterns of Land Use, Class, and Culture," *American Quarterly* 37 (1985): 382–94.

19. Bageant, *Deer Hunting*, 11.

20. Because social stratification is a foundational concept in sociology and fundamental to understanding social change in American history, the subject is vast, but basic principles are laid out in Daniel W. Rossides, *Social Stratification: The Interplay of Class, Race, and Gender*, 2nd ed. (Upper Saddle River, N.J.: Prentice Hall, 1997); Melvin M. Tumin, *Social Stratification: The Forms and Functions of Inequality*, 2nd ed. (Englewood Cliffs, N.J.: Prentice Hall, 1985).

21. Social scientists debate the nature of change in and the power of class identity in American life, but Janny Scott and David Leonhardt clearly associate consumption with "diminished class distinction" in claiming: "Today, the country has gone a long way toward an appearance of classlessness. Americans of all sorts are awash in luxuries that would have dazzled their grandparents. Social diversity has erased many of the old markers. It has become harder to read people's status in the clothes they wear, the cars they drive, the votes they cast, the god they worship, the color of their skin. The contours of class have blurred; some say they have disappeared"; see Scott and Leonhardt, "Shadowy Lines That Still Divide," in *NYT, Class Matters*, 2. On the "changing cultural meanings of the country [music] business" and the implication that Cline's "commercial success" can be viewed as both a "country tradition" and a ticket to respectability, see Diane Pecknold, *The Selling Sound: The Rise of the Country Music Industry* (Durham: Duke University Press, 2007), quotes on 8,10;

Beth Bailey, *Sex in the Heartland* (Cambridge: Harvard University Press, 1999). The rise of a national middle class during the 1950s defined by universal consumption and supplanting the polarized class system of the older manufacturing economy is treated in Margo Anderson, "The Language of Class in Twentieth-Century America," *Social Science History* 12 (Winter 1988): 349–75; Lizabeth Cohen, *A Consumers' Republic: The Politics of Mass Consumption in Postwar America* (New York: Alfred A. Knopf, 2003); Matthew Hilton, "The Female Consumer and the Politics of Consumption in Twentieth-Century Britain," *Historical Journal* 45 (March 2002): 103–28; Shelley Nickles, "More Is Better: Mass Consumption, Gender, and Class Identity in Postwar America," *American Quarterly* 54 (December 2002): 581–622; Mary Louise Roberts, "Gender, Consumption, and Commodity Culture," *American Historical Review* 103 (June 1998): 817–44; Jan Whitaker, *Service and Style: How the American Department Store Fashioned the Middle Class* (New York: St. Martin's Press, 2006). On issues of class, consumption, country music, and pop culture, see Curtis W. Ellison, *Country Music Culture: From Hard Times to Heaven* (Jackson: University Press of Mississippi, 1995); Richard A. Peterson, *Creating Country Music: Fabricating Identity* (Chicago and London: University of Chicago Press, 1997); David Suisman, *Selling Sounds: The Commercial Revolution in American Music* (Cambridge: Harvard University Press, 2009).

22. On the geography of social class in American towns and cities, see the special issue of *Social Science History* on "The Working Classes and Urban Public Space," 24 (Spring 2000).

23. Wood & Associates, "Winchester Master Plan," plate, IX; *Winchester City Directory, 1955–56*, vol. 14 (Ashville, North Carolina: Southern Directory Co., 1955). See also: *Winchester, Virginia, Con Survey City Directory* (Chillicothe, Ohio: Mullin-Kille Co., 1952).

24. Frederick County and Winchester: Economic Survey, 2.

25. The analysis of social class and material culture plays a prominent role in vernacular architecture studies. For an introduction to this broad subject, see Thomas Carter and Elizabeth Collins Cromley, *Invitation to Vernacular Architecture: A Guide to the Study of Ordinary Buildings and Landscapes* (Knoxville: University of Tennessee Press, 2005); Henry Glassie, *Vernacular Architecture* (Bloomington: Indiana University Press, 2000); Paul Groth, "Making New Connections in Vernacular Architecture," *Journal of the Society of Architectural Historians* 58 (September 1999): 444–51.

26. Although detailed census statistics are not available for the 1950s, the demographic portrait of the city in the 2000 census year reflects the stark remnants of the earlier era. Districts east of Main Street were up to two and one-half times more crowded than western districts where median household income and rates of homeownership could be almost twice as great and the median value of homes more than two times home values in the North Kent Street community. Educational attainment measured by the percentage of people with bachelor's degrees was up to four times greater along Washington Street than on Kent. See U.S. Bureau of the

Census, Winchester City–Census Tract, "GCT-PH1. Population, Housing Units, Area, and Density: 2000"; "GCT-P14. Income and Poverty in 1999: 2000"; "GCT-H6. Occupied Housing Characteristics: 2000"; "GCT-H9. Financial Housing Characteristics: 2000"; "GCT-P11. Language, School Enrollment, and Educational Attainment: 2000," http://factfinder.census.gov/home/saff/main.html (accessed July 2010). Higher densities of population and housing east of Main Street than west of it for the 1950s is confirmed in the demographic studies conducted for the 1958 city master plan. See Wood & Associates, "Winchester Master Plan," plates, IV, VIII, and p. 42.

27. Jerry Weatherholtz, questionnaire completed for authors, August 14, 2008.

28. Larry Boppe, questionnaire, August 14, 2008.

29. Shanda Kiser Rowe, questionnaire, October 17, 2008.

30. G. W. Lanahan, questionnaire, July 29, 2008.

31. Boppe, questionnaire, August 14, 2008; Jr. and John A. Haines, "Small-Town Boy," *Washingtoncitypaper.com*, April 28, 1995.

32. Mike Foreman, personal communication, March 31, 2009.

33. Boppe, questionnaire, August 14, 2008.

34. Mike Foreman, personal communication, January 28, 2008. On the issue of racial performance and architectural space, see Steven Hoelscher, "Making Place, Making Race: Performances of Whiteness in the Jim Crow South," *Annals of the Association of American Geographers* 93 (September 2003): 657–86; Robert R. Weyeneth, "The Architecture of Racial Segregation: The Challenges of Preserving the Problematical Past," *Public Historian* 27 (Fall 2005): 11–44.

35. Bev Bailey, questionnaire, August 12, 2008.

36. On the history and cultural significance of Main Street in American social history, see Wayne K. Durrill, "A Tale of Two Courthouses: Civic Space, Political Power, and Capitalist Development in a New South Community, 1843–1940," *Journal of Social History* 35 (Spring 2002): 659–81; Richard V. Francaviglia, *Main Street Revisited: Time, Space, and Image Building in Small-Town America* (Iowa City: University of Iowa Press, 1996); Richard Longstreth, *The Buildings of Main Street: A Guide to American Commercial Architecture* (Walnut Creek, Calif.: AltaMira Press, 2000).

37. Rowe, questionnaire, October 17, 2008.

38. Boppe, questionnaire, August 14, 2008.

39. Bailey, questionnaire, August 12, 2008.

40. Jerry Weatherholtz, questionnaire, August 14, 2008.

41. Lanahan, questionnaire, July 29, 2008.

42. On the history of shopping and the social culture of consumerism, see Dorothy Davis, *A History of Shopping* (London: Routledge and K. Paul; Toronto: Toronto University Press, 1966); Lizabeth Cohen, "From Town Center to Shopping Center: The Reconfiguration of Community Marketplaces in Postwar America," *American Historical Review* 101 (October 1996): 1050–81; Kenneth T. Jackson, "All the World's a Mall: Reflections on the Social and Economic Consequences of the American Shopping Center," *American Historical Review* 101 (October 1996): 1111–21; William R. Leach, "Transformations in a Culture of Consumption: Women and

Department Stores, 1890–1925," *Journal of American History* 71 (September 1984): 319–42; Richard Longstreth, "The Neighborhood Shopping Center in Washington, D.C., 1930–1941," *Journal of the Society of Architectural Historians* 51 (March 1992): 5–34; Longstreth, "The Mixed Blessings of Success: The Hecht Company and Department Store Branch Development after World War II," in *Perspectives in Vernacular Architecture*, vol. 6, *Shaping Communities*, eds. Carter L. Hudgins and Elizabeth Collins Cromley (Knoxville: University of Tennessee Press, 1997), 244–62; Laura Byrne Paquet, *The Urge to Splurge: A Social History of Shopping* (Toronto, Ont.: ECW Press, 2003); Whitaker, *Service and Style*.

43. The best recent works on architecture and building culture of American hotels are John A. Jakle and Keith A. Sculle, *America's Main Street Hotels: Transiency and Community in the Early Auto Age* (Knoxville: University of Tennessee Press, 2009); A. K. Sandoval-Strausz, *Hotel: An American History* (New Haven: Yale University Press, 2007).

44. Douglas Gomery, "Moviegoing in the Shenandoah Valley of Virginia: A Case Study of Place, Transportation, Audiences, Racism, Censorship & Blue Laws" (paper presented at the Shenandoah Valley Regional Studies Seminar, James Madison University, March 21, 2003), 2, 9. See also Gomery, *Shared Pleasures: A History of Movie Presentation in the United States* (Madison: University of Wisconsin Press, 1992); Peter Lev, *Transforming the Screen, 1950–1959* (New York: Charles Scribner's Sons, 2003); Richard Maltby, Melvyn Stokes, and Robert C. Allen, *Going to the Movies: Hollywood and the Social Experience of the Cinema* (Exeter, England: University of Exeter Press, 2008); Craig Morrison, *Theaters* (New York: W. W. Norton, 2005; Washington, D.C.: Library of Congress, 2006); Gregory A. Waller, *Main Street Amusements: Movies and Commercial Entertainment in a Southern City, 1896–1930* (Washington, D.C.: Smithsonian Institution Press, 1995).

45. Gomery, "Moviegoing in the Shenandoah Valley," 9. On the subject of social class and the moviegoing experience, see Richard Butsch, "American Movie Audiences of the 1930s," *International Labor and Working-Class History* 59 (Spring 2001): 106–20.

46. Issues of gender and public space in hotels are treated in Carolyn Brucken, "In the Public Eye: Women and the American Luxury Hotel," *Winterthur Portfolio* 31 (Winter 1996): 203–20.

47. For more on Howard Johnson's and its cultural associations, see Warren Belasco, "Toward a Culinary Common Denominator: The Rise of Howard Johnson's, 1925–1940," *Journal of American Culture* 2 (Fall 1979): 503–18; Andrew Hurley, "From Hash House to Family Restaurant: The Transformation of the Diner and Post–World War II Consumer Culture," *Journal of American History* 83 (March 1997): 1282–1308. See also Jakle and Sculle, *America's Main Street Hotels*; Sandoval-Strausz, *Hotel*.

48. On the construction of class, gender, and race in the social space of country clubs, see Marvin P. Dawkins and Graham C. Kinloch, *African American Golfers during the Jim Crow Era* (Westport, Conn.: Praeger, 2000); M. Mikell Johnson, *The African American Woman Golfer: Her Legacy* (Westport, Conn.: Praeger, 2008);

George B. Kirsch, *Golf in America* (Urbana: University of Illinois Press, 2009); James M. Mayo, *The American Country Club: Its Origins and Development* (New Brunswick, N.J.: Rutgers University Press, 1998); Richard J. Moss, *Golf and the American Country Club* (Urbana: University of Illinois Press, 2001).

49. Restaurants provide widely varied venues for the performance of social class in taste, presentation, interior design, dress, and many other manifestations of culture; see Andrew P. Haley, *Turning the Tables: Restaurants and the Rise of the American Middle Class, 1880–1920* (Chapel Hill: University of North Carolina Press, 2011); Alan Warde, *Consumption, Food, and Taste: Culinary Antinomies and Commodity Culture* (London: Sage Publications, 1997).

50. On country music and class identity, see Pete Daniel, "Rhythm of the Land," *Agricultural History* 68 (Autumn 1994): 1–22; Aaron A. Fox, *Real Country: Music and Language in Working-Class Culture* (Durham: Duke University Press, 2004; Pamela Grundy, "'We Always Tried to Be Good People': Respectability, Crazy Water Crystals, and Hillbilly Music on the Air, 1933–1935," *Journal of American History* 81 (March 1995): 1591–1620; Bill C. Malone, *Don't Get above Your Raisin': Country Music and the Southern Working Class* (Urbana: University of Illinois Press, 2002); Pecknold, *Selling Sound*, 23–35, 44–46.

51. See *Acts and Joint Resolutions of the General Assembly of the Commonwealth of Virginia, Regular Session, 1968* (Richmond: Department of Purchases and Supply, Commonwealth of Virginia, 1968), 8–14.

52. *Winchester Evening Star*, December 23, 1955. For more on dance halls although not in the Winchester area, see Randy D. McBee, *Dance Hall Days: Intimacy and Leisure among Working-Class Immigrants in the United States* (New York: New York University Press, 2000); Jocelyn R. Neal, "Dancing Together: The Rhythms of Gender in the Country Dance Hall," in *A Boy Named Sue: Gender and Country Music*, eds. Kristine M. McCusker and Diane Pecknold (Jackson: University of Mississippi Press, 2004), 132–54.

53. The close alliance between the development of radio and the evolution of country music especially through the broadcast of barn dance programs has produced a sizeable literature; see Steve Craig, "'The More They Listen, the More They Buy': Radio and the Modernizing of Rural America, 1930–1939," *Agricultural History* 80 (Winter 2006): 1–16; Tracey E. W. Laird, *Louisiana Hayride: Radio and Roots Music along the Red River* (Oxford: Oxford University Press, 2005); Kip Lornell, "Early Country Music and the Mass Media in Roanoke, Virginia," *American Music* 5 (Winter 1987): 403–16; Malone, *Don't Get above Your Raisin'*, 61–69; Kristine M. McCusker, *Lonesome Cowgirls and Honky-Tonk Angels: The Women of Barn Dance Radio* (Urbana: University of Illinois Press, 2008); Pecknold, *Selling Sound*; Suisman, *Selling Sounds*; Peterson, *Creating Country Music*.

54. For this particular selection of programs, see *Winchester Evening Star*, December 29, 1951.

55. Although close to a third of the households in Alexandria claimed a television set in 1950, Winchester stood second in Virginia in television ownership—several percentage points ahead of other, larger urban areas including Richmond. See U.S.

Bureau of the Census, *General Characteristics, Virginia: 1950 Housing Census Report*, prepared by the Population and Housing Division, Howard G. Brunsman, chief (Washington, D.C.: U.S. Government Printing Office, 1952), table 20, "Year Built, and Equipment for Standard Metropolitan Areas and Constituent Counties, Urbanized Areas, and Urban Places of 10,000 or more: 1950."

56. On the interrelated subjects of television, popular music, and American society in the 1950s, see Paul C. Adams, "Television as Gathering Place," *Annals of the Association of American Geographers* 82 (March 1992): 117–35; William Boddy, *Fifties Television: The Industry and Its Critics* (Urbana: University of Illinois Press, 1990); Simon Frith, "Look! Hear! The Uneasy Relationship of Music and Television," *Popular Music* 21 (October 2002): 277–90; Douglas Gomery, *A History of Broadcasting in the United States* (Malden, Mass.: Blackwell, 2008); Donna Halper, *Invisible Stars: A Social History of Women in American Broadcasting* (Armonk, N.Y.: M. E. Sharpe, 2001).

57. Jones, *Patsy*, xii [quote]. On Patsy Cline's upbringing and rising career, see Bego, *I Fall to Pieces*, 1–102; Gomery, *Patsy Cline: The Making of an Icon* (Bloomington, Ind.: Trafford Publishing, 2011), 33–149; Jones, *Patsy*, 1–140; Nassour, *Honky Tonk Angel*, 3–93.

58. The question of Cline's preference for cowgirl outfits over sleek, cocktail dresses, although she wore both, is the stuff of legend about the performer. Biographer Ellis Nassour quotes Cline as complaining to her manager Randy Hughes about a booking on the Las Vegas strip: "Hoss, that's too uptown for me. I don't wanna wear fancy gowns. I want to wear my cowgirl outfits"; see Nassour, *Honky Tonk Angel*, 208. On Cline appearing in public with her hair in rollers, see Margaret Jones interview with Johnny Anderson, May 24, 1991, in Jones, *Patsy*, 48.

59. Margaret Jones interviews with Johnny Anderson, May 22 and 24, 1991, in Jones, *Patsy*, 27.

60. Personal communication, July 23, 2009.

61. Skeeter Knee, interview, July 16, 2007.

62. On sexuality, racism, and violence in the South, see Kevin Boyle, "The Kiss: Racial and Gender Conflict in a 1950s Automobile Factory," *Journal of American History* 84 (September 1997): 496–523; W. Fitzhugh Brundage, *Lynching in the New South: Georgia and Virginia, 1880–1930* (Urbana: University of Illinois Press, 1993); Marybeth Hamilton, "Sexuality, Authenticity and the Making of the Blues Tradition," *Past & Present* 169 (November 2000): 132–60; Paula S. Rothenberg, *Race, Class, and Gender in the United States: An Integrated Study*, 8th ed. (New York: St. Martin's Press, 1992; New York: Worth Publishers, 2009); Whitney Strub, "Black and White and Banned All Over: Race, Censorship and Obscenity in Postwar Memphis," *Journal of Social History* 40 (Spring 2007): 685–715.

63. On the issue of racial integrity in Virginia, see Gregory Michael Dorr, *Segregation's Science: Eugenics and Society in Virginia* (Charlottesville: University of Virginia Press, 2008); Richard B. Sherman, "'The Last Stand': The Fight for Racial Integrity in Virginia in the 1920s," *Journal of Southern History* 54 (February 1988): 69–92; J. Douglas Smith, "The Campaign for Racial Purity and the Erosion of

Paternalism in Virginia, 1922–1930: 'Nominally White, Biologically Mixed, and Legally Negro,'" *Journal of Southern History* 68 (February 2002): 65–106; Smith, *Managing White Supremacy: Race, Politics, and Citizenship in Jim Crow Virginia* (Chapel Hill: University of North Carolina Press, 2002). Issues of race and popular music in the 1950s are covered brilliantly by Michael T. Bertrand in *Race, Rock, and Elvis* (Urbana: University of Illinois Press, 2000).

64. On the case of Howard Walker, see the case file at the Winchester Circuit Court, file 2626, Winchester–Frederick County Joint Judicial Center, Winchester, Virginia; and newspaper articles in the *Winchester Evening Star*, March 10, 15, 18, May 27, 1944.

65. The image of Patsy Cline in short-shorts can be viewed in Stuart E. Brown Jr. and Lorraine F. Myers, *Patsy Cline: Singing Girl from the Shenandoah Valley* (Berryville, Va.: Chesapeake Book Company, 1996), 41. Unfortunately, rights to reproduce this photograph in this book could not be secured.

66. Margaret Jones interview with Jimmy Dean, May 19, 1992, in Jones, *Patsy*, 255. See also Nassour, *Honky Tonk Angel*, 49; and Bego, *I Fall to Pieces*, 163–64, both of whom rely on separate testimony for this story from Dean, who was a notorious storyteller and not always friendly with Cline.

67. Rosanne Cash, "Honky-Tonk Angel," *New York Times Magazine*, November 24, 1996. Numerous other contemporaries and later biographers commented on Cline's latent sexual powers. Brian Mansfield, for instance, observed that Cline was a "saucy, strong-willed brunette from Virginia with the voice that could do almost anything. They admired her straightforwardness, her vitality, and her raw sensuality"; see Mansfield *Remembering Patsy* (Nashville: Rutledge Hill, 2002), 5; also Ellis Nassour, who quotes Faron Young on his attraction to Cline: "When she moved, the earth shaked. I couldn't take my eyes off her body. Ah she had a figure like an hourglass"; see Nassour, *Honky Tonk Angel*, 113. On young women, feminism, and sexuality in the 1950s, see Beth Bailey, *From Front Porch to Back Seat: Courtship in Twentieth-Century America* (Baltimore: Johns Hopkins University Press, 1989); Bailey, *Sex in the Heartland*; Wini Breines, *Young, White, and Miserable: Growing Up Female in the Fifties* (Chicago: University of Chicago Press, 2001); Susan K. Cahn, *Sexual Reckonings: Southern Girls in a Troubling Age* (Cambridge: Harvard University Press, 2007); Stephanie Coontz, *The Way We Never Were: American Families and the Nostalgia Trap* (New York: Basic Books, 1992); Susan J. Douglas, *Where the Girls Are: Growing Up Female with the Mass Media* (New York: Three Rivers Press, 1995); Carolyn Johnston, *Sexual Power: Feminism and the Family in America* (Tuscaloosa: University of Alabama Press, 1992); Patricia McDaniel, "Shrinking Violets and Caspar Milquetoasts: Shyness and Heterosexuality from the Roles of the Fifties to *The Rules* of the Nineties," *Journal of Social History* 34 (Spring 2001): 547–68; Elaine Tyler May, *Homeward Bound: American Families in the Cold War Era* (New York: Basic Books, 1988).

68. Although it would provide an excellent subject for a critical study by a cultural theorist, the Shenandoah Apple Blossom Festival is documented only in locally published volumes; see David Lee Brill, *The Trail of Pink Petals: The Official History of*

the Shenandoah Apple Blossom Festival (Winchester, Va.: Shenandoah Apple Blossom Festival, 2001); Helen Lee Fletcher, *Shenandoah Apple Blossom Festival* (Charleston, S.C.: Acadia, 1999); Katherine Glass Greene, Philip Williams, and W. W. Glass, *Winchester, Frederick County, and the Shenandoah Apple Blossom Festival,* reprinted from J. Julian Pickeral and Gordon Fogg, *An Economic and Social Survey of Frederick County,* University of Virginia Record Extension Series 15, no. 2 (August 1930).

69. For more on parades and the ritualization of power arrangements within communities, see Jean Harvey Baker, "Politics, Paradigms, and Public Culture," *Journal of American History* 84 (December 1997): 894–99; William O. Beeman, "The Anthropology of Theater and Spectacle," *Annual Review of Anthropology* 22 (1993): 369–93; Susan G. Davis, *Parades and Power: Street Theatre in Nineteenth-Century Philadelphia* (Philadelphia: Temple University Press, 1986); Sallie A. Marston, "Public Rituals and Community Power: St. Patrick's Day Parades in Lowell, Massachusetts, 1841–1874," *Political Geography Quarterly* 8 (July 1989): 255–69; Simon P. Newman, *Parades and the Politics of the Street: Festive Culture in the Early American Republic* (Philadelphia: University of Pennsylvania Press, 1997); Dell Upton, *Another City: Urban Life and Urban Spaces in the New American Republic* (New Haven and London: Yale University Press, 2008), 310–16.

70. Eddie Dean, "Nobody's Patsy," *Washington City Paper,* April 7, 1995, http://www. washingtoncitypaper.com (accessed April 2010).

71. Mary Nelson Edens to Mike Foreman, personal communication. Edens was a part-time Apple Blossom volunteer working for Baldridge. This story raises many questions about masculinity in the culture of the 1950s; see Jesse Berrett, "Feeding the Organization Man: Diet and Masculinity in Postwar America," *Journal of Social History* 30 (Summer 1997): 805–25; K. A. Cuordileone, "'Politics in an Age of Anxiety': Cold War Political Culture and the Crisis in American Masculinity, 1949–1960," *Journal of American History* 87 (September 2000): 515–45; Leigh H. Edwards, *Johnny Cash and the Paradox of American Identity* (Bloomington: Indiana University Press, 2009); Craig Thompson Friend, *Southern Masculinity: Perspectives on Manhood in the South since Reconstruction* (Athens: University of Georgia Press, 2009); James Gilbert, *Men in the Middle: Searching for Masculinity in the 1950s* (Chicago: University of Chicago Press, 2005); Susan Nanes, "Maturity and Masculinity: Frank Sinatra in the 1950s," in *America under Construction: Boundaries and Identities in Popular Culture,* eds. Kristi S. Long and Matthew Nadelhaft (New York: Garland, 1997), 19–40; Trent Watts, ed. *White Masculinity in the Recent South* (Baton Rouge: Louisiana State University Press, 2008); Stephen M. Whitehead, *Men and Masculinities: Key Themes and New Directions* (Malden, Mass.: Polity Press, 2002).

72. Teresa J. Bowers to the *Winchester Star,* March 21, 1986; Laurel Stevens to ibid.; M. J. Dick to ibid., March 11, 1986; L. R. Pierce to ibid., March 4, 1986.

73. Terresa Lazazzera, "City Rejects 'Cline Blvd.': How to Memorialize Patsy," *Winchester Star,* May 14, 1986.

74. Mike D'Orso, "Bittersweet Dreams," *Virginian Pilot and Ledger-Star,* January 3, 1988; Jones, *Patsy,* 297.

75. Jones, *Patsy*, 298.

76. This account of the naming and dedication of the Patsy Cline Theatre at the Handley High School is based on *Winchester Star*, September 11, 2009; *Northern Virginia Daily*, September 11, 2009; Mike Foreman, personal communication, November 17, 2009; March 26, 2010. The story of Winchester's reconciling with the legacy of Patsy Cline can be traced in Matthew Barakat, "Hometown Finally Embraces Cline," Associated Press, April 25, 2001; Hank Stuever, "Winchester Is Crazy about Patsy, Now," *Winchester Star*, July 10, 2004.

PATSY CLINE AND THE PROBLEM OF RESPECTABILITY

Beth Bailey

In early 1955, Patsy Cline's life was the stuff of soap opera—though with censorship regulations that banned the use of the word "pregnant" (much less the truck driver's vocabulary Cline regularly employed) and restricted married couples to twin beds, no television show could approach the private complications and public scandal that surrounded her as she moved toward her first Nashville recording session that spring. Patsy's two-year-old marriage to Gerald Cline, as she told her sidemen in explicit detail, was not "satisfying." In the interest of her career, she had taken back up with her manager, Bill Peer—a married man with two young children, eleven years older than Patsy—soon after her wedding. And Gerald, described as both "phlegmatic" and "dull," was not waiting at home. He had begun running around with other women. Gerald knew about Patsy and Bill's affair; most of the time he ignored it. Patsy's mother also knew about the affair, as did Bill Peer's wife and much of the population of Winchester, Virginia.[1] People talked. It was small-town gossip, to be sure, but not a difficult story to believe about a woman whose reputation had never been her strong point. Thus when Patsy turned up in Winchester's Apple Blossom Parade that April decked out in a black cowgirl outfit with long white fringe and riding atop a Cadillac Coupe deVille driven by Bill Peer, few people bought into the local-girl-makes-good narrative that Patsy was trying to create. While in retrospect the story is of elitist, narrow-minded hypocrites who refused to recognize the remarkable talent of one of their own, the tensions surrounding Patsy's ride through the heart of Winchester go beyond hypocrisy, and they extend beyond the class politics of this small Virginia town.

Patsy Cline was an exceptional musician. She was a woman driven by ambition who managed, despite the odds, to succeed in the male-dominated world of country music. She was the product of a troubled family, born into and continuing a long history of economic struggles and poor choices and domestic violence, even though her circumstances were leavened by an abundance of mother-love. The tales of her spunk and determination and generosity to those she cared about are a powerful legacy, second only to the music she left behind. But her story also moves beyond the individual, illuminating a question that bedeviled American society in the postwar era: who belongs, and on what terms? Patsy Cline, unknowingly, helped change the answer to that question.

This essay looks at Patsy Cline in relation to two broad themes: the importance of respectability in postwar American society, and the growing reach and power of national culture and the market economy in the postwar era. World War II and the economic boom that followed it unsettled the meaning of class in America. More and more Americans, no matter whether they worked in offices or factories, graduated from high school or college or not at all, began to see themselves as part of a broad and increasingly inclusive middle-class culture. Belonging—especially for those who came of age after World War II—often seemed to depend more on the ability to participate in a national, mainstream culture than on the specifics of family background and circumstance. But inclusion was not automatic. Race was a clear barrier in most of the United States. And so were more intangible qualities. Many of those who meant to act as gatekeepers, from educational institutions to advice columnists in popular magazines, tried to hold the line, insisting that inclusion in the new middle class required observance of middle-class values and behaviors. Chief among these, during the 1950s, was respectability.

It is difficult, in an era when the mainstream press chronicles celebrity hookups and births by unmarried women raise scarcely an eyebrow, to convey how important respectability and reputation were in 1950s American society, most particularly for women. A great many Americans saw respectable behavior as the foundation of a moral, civil, and legitimate social order. And a great many Americans saw respectability as the *natural* price of admission to the expanding American middle class. It is crucial to understand that this commitment to respectability was not universal and was often more honored in the breach than in the observance. A great many Americans behaved in ways that were not, strictly speaking, respectable—especially when it came to sex.

By and large, in mid-1950s America, those who broke the rules fell into one of two camps. The first—those who lived outside the boundaries of respectable society, openly rejecting its tenets—inhabited the margins of American society. Many of them were poor people, both black and white, who fell outside the broadening "mainstream." Their sexual misbehavior, whether actual or assumed, seemed to provide further evidence that they deserved to be excluded from the world of those who "count." Into the same group fell the small but visible number of Americans who purposely violated rules and rejected mainstream conventions for a world of cultural and artistic freedom. Into the other camp fell those who belonged securely to the growing middle-class mainstream society and endorsed the rules of respectability and the importance of reputation, while at the same time eroding their margins or violating their principles. Rules were quite often observed in the breach, but breaking (or bending) rules is not the same thing as openly defying them. Despite the profound tensions between behavior and convention in post–World War II America, the bottom line is clear: very few people directly and openly challenged the rules *and* at the same time expected to be welcomed into the emerging middle-class culture.[2]

However, as a growing national culture opened and eroded class boundaries, it also disrupted various forms of authority. That happened on the local level, as the increasing importance of national culture created spaces in which some were able to circumvent the power of local elites (those that Hofstra and Foreman call Winchester's "proprietary class") to claim new forms of success and visibility. It also happened on the national level, as traditional cultural authorities confronted the increasing power of a much broader population of those who mattered, if only because they made up a powerful market force. No matter how powerfully old local elites tried to maintain the traditional boundaries of class, no matter how vehemently the defenders of high "art and culture" made their exclusionary case, no matter how uniformly those who claimed authority in the new middle-class culture insisted that middle-class *values* defined the middle class, the growing force of national culture and market economy continued to undermine boundaries. Those who did not fit easily into the emerging middle class—those who did not embrace "middle-class values," who lacked education, who were geographically isolated, or provincial, or living close to the edge—still spent money. And on the national level, who "counts" increasingly depended on the ability of different groups to make their presence felt in the consumer marketplace. The growing visibility of "hillbilly" or country music—the music of poor whites—both on the charts and on national television and radio during the postwar era was a sign of the change already underway. Patsy Cline was one of those who, on the local level, took advantage of the new opportunities for success and visibility that her defiance of respectability would otherwise have precluded.

*   *   *

Respectability took two interlinked forms in postwar American society. For women, in particular, respectability was linked to sex—not only to sexual behavior, but also to appearance and self-presentation. At a time when employment ads were segregated into "male" and "female" categories, with lower-paying jobs vastly overrepresented in the female column, a woman's economic security, quality of life, and class status depended heavily on the husband she was able to attract. And while entire forests perished to provide paper on which to print the advice books and women's magazines devoted to the art of winning a good husband, one thing was clear in those many pages: Reputation was key; respectability mattered.

The argument that a woman must maintain both her virginity and her reputation as a "good girl" went beyond the moral argument to a logic best described as economic. Sex was posited as an act in which men and women had very different interests. Men, according to this understanding, wanted sex—nothing more. Women, conversely, wanted marriage. In this system, marriage became the price for sex. But this highly gendered exchange works only if there is a sexual trust, only if virtually all women play by the same rules. Both advice literature and the casual slang of the time drove home that point, using the language of the market to reinforce the economic argument. Slang defined girls who were too "free" with their affections as "cheap." "Your clothes can cost a lot," advised one columnist, "yet you'll look cheap with that toss of the head. . . . Reprice your line. . . . Make yourself scarce and watch your value go up." Yet another asked, ominously: "Who wants second-hand goods?"[3]

Though women and girls policed the boundaries of respectability, using gossip and exclusion to marginalize those who went "too far," men were still key. Most girls and young women tried to walk the fine line between sexual attractiveness and appeal, petting enough to demonstrate that they were neither prudish nor "frigid" while maintaining "standards"—and thus their reputations. For no matter whom they dated, middle-class boys and men made clear, they expected to marry a virgin. It was not so difficult for a young woman to ruin her reputation—because young men boast, because an unintended pregnancy was a disaster for a "respectable" girl—and so lessen her value in the middle-class marriage market. A "lost" reputation in high school could, according to widespread beliefs of the time, ruin a girl's entire future.

Respectability, during this era, was also clearly linked to class. Those whose middle-class status was most secure could push the boundaries more, but those with any vulnerability—at least among those who sought to "count" in the emerging middle-class mainstream—had to demonstrate that they belonged. Respectability, for example, was critically important to the civil rights movement of the 1950s and early 1960s. Rosa Parks, the civil rights activist whose refusal to give up her seat to a white passenger began what became the Montgomery bus boycott, was an eminently respectable woman; other black women had been arrested for similar acts, but the NAACP had not seen them as proper candidates around which to organize. And many of the most powerful confrontations in the civil rights struggle were staged to emphasize the contrast between well-mannered, neatly dressed, obviously respectable black people and their vulgar, uncouth white opponents.[4]

In another example, during the 1960s, the parents of young people who openly violated the rules of respectability—having sex outside marriage, using vulgar language, rejecting all the trappings of propriety—were not simply stodgy old people who had forgotten the joys of youth. Parents who had worked hard to become middle class could not believe that their children could so blatantly reject respectability without destroying their lives. They feared that this generation, those who had so much potential and who had been given so much, were throwing it all away. In the experience of adults who had lived through the Great Depression and sought the stability of a comfortable middle-class existence, respectability was necessary—for a steady job and economic security, for a woman's marriage to a good provider, for belonging to America's broad middle-class culture.

During the 1950s, no matter what tensions were roiling beneath the surface, respectability was key to middle-class identity. Respectability did not guarantee entrance to the middle class. Those from the wrong side of the tracks or with the wrong skin color might well be denied entrance, no matter how circumspect their behavior. But for those who attempted the move, who wanted to be accepted, respectability was key. There was little tolerance for missteps.

And Patsy Cline was not respectable.[5]

She had not been born to respectability. Patsy—Virginia Patterson Hensley—was the product of a shotgun wedding. Her parents, Hilda Patterson and Sam Hensley, were married in the Frederick County Courthouse in Winchester on September 2, 1932. Hilda was nine months pregnant. She was also sixteen, which made her twenty-seven years younger than her baby's father. Sam Hensley was dragged in front of the judge by Hilda's stepfather, a former prison guard. He was determined that his stepdaughter's child be "legitimate," if only by a margin of six days.[6]

Sam and Hilda, Patsy's parents, came from different worlds. Hilda's family had a scrap of land, just enough to allow them to scrape by on subsistence farming and seasonal day labor so long as nothing went badly wrong. But when Hilda was a baby her father fell from a roof; that accident left him with only one leg. Bad luck, but it would get worse. Soon thereafter James Patterson died in the flu epidemic of 1918—along with more than fifty million people worldwide. His wife, Goldie, was left alone with three small children. Hilda, at two, was the youngest. Goldie struggled to feed her children. She went to work in the National Fruit Company plant in Winchester, where the local apple crop was processed, and eventually met and married Frank Allanson, with whom she had five more children. It was never better than hard work and struggle, but their lives were typical of many families in the rural South—people with few options, always just one bad break away from disaster.

Samuel Lawrence Hensley, Patsy's father, was the son of a well-off family from Elkton, Virginia, for whom things had gone badly wrong. He was a handsome young man with a beautiful singing voice, a master blacksmith in line to inherit a thousand acres of prime farmland. Sam was fond of flashy cars and big cigars. In his late twenties and still unmarried, he enjoyed the company of women. But in 1917, when the United States joined the belligerents in the Great War, he enlisted. Hensley fought in the Battle of the Argonne Forest, one of the bloodiest battles in U.S. history. He returned with a streak of violent anger and a new tendency to drink heavily. Marriage seemed to calm him, but an automobile accident claimed the life of his pregnant wife, leaving him alone with two young children. Other troubles followed. Sam's father got a local fifteen-year-old girl pregnant. He paid off the girl's family—with a substantial sum—but the scandal was public, and it did Sam's family no good. The stock market crash and the Great Depression followed. Sam's father began selling off the land that would have been Sam's inheritance, and at cut-rate prices. Abandoning his two children (somewhat inexplicably) to the care of their music teacher, Sam took to the road. He was working in a sand mine not far from Winchester when he met Hilda. He never intended to marry her.

If Patsy lacked proper family background and respectable parentage, her upbringing offered nothing different: she was bred to respectability no more than she was born to it. Ginny (as Patsy was called as a child) and her family moved nineteen times as she was growing up, from one big, empty, abandoned—and often isolated—house to another. Sam lived beyond their means, and rent was a low priority. The Hensleys were evicted from one place, and then another. Patsy rarely went to the same school for more than a year, and in an era in which skipping grades was common, she repeated them instead. She earned D minuses in all her eighth-grade classes except one; school was not Patsy's refuge from the turmoil of the rest of her life. Sam was an overbearing husband and father; Hilda often fought back. Their struggles were not concealed behind a facade of respectability: one time Sam turned up at a church picnic with a shotgun to order his wife home. Patsy's father was a mean drunk and everyone knew it. What everyone didn't know—though some may have suspected—is that Sam was sexually abusing his daughter.[7]

With neither proper lineage nor upbringing, Patsy was never positioned for respectability in Winchester, where her family moved in 1948. Their new home was a broken-down duplex on Kent Street, definitely on the wrong side of the tracks. Sixteen-year-old Patsy enrolled in ninth grade, but within a few weeks she stopped turning up. Quitting school in ninth grade was not matter-of-course in 1948; though graduating from high school had been unusual for those in her parents' generation, it was more-or-less expected by the late 1940s. Sam left his family soon thereafter—for good—and Patsy took a job butchering chickens in a local processing plant to help support her younger brother and sister.

Patsy's own behavior also put her firmly on the wrong side of middle-class respectability. Sex was part of it, especially in her adult life, but she also violated middle-class standards of taste and propriety. Teenaged Patsy went to the movies in Winchester with her hair in rollers, a minor but nonetheless significant act that, as one friend later recalled, "was considered loose in those days."[8] And as Patsy struggled to launch her career, she sang at almost any place that would have her: gin mills and dance halls and other rough places, as well as the York Inn, where she wore the sexy costume of an old-fashioned cigarette girl and acted as hostess before taking the stage later in the evening. Not all of Patsy's costumes were sexy, but all exceeded the boundaries of tasteful restraint. Hilda made most of her daughter's costumes—in a repeated act of motherly devotion—hand-sewing thousands of sequins or rhinestones and acres of fringe onto increasingly flamboyant cowgirl outfits. Writing to the president of her fan club in 1956, Patsy described one of her favorites: "This is my blue suit with white stars in rhinestones on it. I think it's pretty." In 1957, she wrote of one "made princess style," with "4 in. leather fringe in silver off the neck line and around the bottom of the skirt with music notes in silver all over it with rhinestones around fringe and notes."[9]

Patsy's fringe and rhinestones appeared vulgar to many on the other side of the class divide. Her taste was always on the loud side: when she bought the house of her dreams for herself and second husband Charlie Dick and their two children, a thirty-thousand-dollar red brick ranch about fifteen miles outside Nashville, she decided money was no object in making it her own. She bought an artificial magnolia tree, attached dozens of artificial songbirds to it, and placed it in front of the living room's picture window. The bar in the music room was made of red padded Naugahyde with metal studs spelling out "Patsy and Charlie." The evaluating eyes of middle-class respectability would find little elegant or restrained about Patsy's house.[10]

Though Patsy's enthusiastic rejection of restraint when it came to fashion, home furnishing, or vocabulary violated the local norms of propriety, it was her sexy outfits that caused the most talk. Twenty-two-year-old Patsy performed in D.C. "hillbilly dives" wearing what biographer Margaret Jones calls "The Outfit." "It consisted," Jones writes, "of a pair of fringed short-shorts that emphasized Patsy's bodacious fanny, a fringed décolleté top that bared her midriff, broad wrist cuffs, a dashing white scarf tied flush around her neck and the usual white cowboy boots." In a time when a "morality survey" of college students found that a greater percentage of women believed "wearing short-shorts in town" was morally or ethically wrong than the percentage that condemned cheating on an exam, Patsy's willingness to use all her assets to get ahead put her significantly outside the narrow boundaries of propriety, most especially in the small southern town of Winchester.[11]

And, finally, Patsy's sexual behavior mattered a great deal. Though she was not in love with her manager Bill Peer—and turned him away after his wife divorced him—she carried on an affair with him for years. That fact became too difficult for anyone to ignore after the concierge at a New York hotel returned Patsy's coat to Bill's wife with a polite note letting "Mrs. Peer" know that the hotel maid had found the coat she had left in her room. The editors of a collection of Patsy's letters to the founder of her fan club describe Patsy's 1953 affair with a twenty-year-old sailor who was based in Norfolk, Virginia. All of her biographers repeat Jimmy Dean's 1962 story about Patsy and the Canadian Mountie, the "big, good-looking son of a bitch" that Patsy spotted in a hotel lobby and vowed that she would "screw the boots off him tonight." She "did what she said she was going to do," recalled Dean, who also volunteered that he had never slept with Patsy, but that he "might be one of the few" who hadn't.[12] "Patsy flirted with anything in pants," one of the *Town and Country Jamboree* band members recalled. "Sometimes you just had to pull her off you." A female friend from Winchester allowed that "Pat had a reputation for being a bit loose."[13] And while Patsy loved second husband Charlie Dick to distraction, he was given to drink, and Charlie and Patsy's fights were legendary.[14] The stories of Patsy's misconduct multiplied, and whether they were based on the indisputable affair with Bill Peer or on the boasts of men, the jealousy of women, or simply salacious gossip, Patsy's reputation suffered. And she did nothing to change that fact.[15]

It is not that Patsy could have won over Winchester simply by curbing her tongue, reforming her behavior, and replacing the fringe and rhinestones with cashmere twinsets. Her family background and disreputable childhood were just too big a hurdle in a small southern town so focused on lineage and with quite narrow parameters of acceptable behavior, appearance, and taste—at least for those who "mattered." As Harold Madagan, the pharmacist at Gaunt's Drugs where Patsy once worked, told a reporter in 1995, it wasn't easy to "cross over" in Winchester. He had also grown up on the wrong side of the tracks, he said, but "I worked my ass off to make it over here and get accepted." Madagan was a huge fan of Patsy Cline; he devoted a full wall of the drugstore to Patsy photographs and memorabilia. But he was clear: "Patsy didn't try to cross over. . . . Now, maybe she wasn't accepted, but maybe she didn't try very hard to be accepted. She was a bit crude and rude at times; even today you wouldn't do the crazy things she did. . . . She'd say, 'Hoss, this is the way I got started, this is the way I'm gonna finish. . . . I got here by being what I am, and I'm not going to change.'"[16]

Patsy Cline wanted to be accepted by her hometown—not only by those who went to the dives and the beer joints, or by the already large audience for "hillbilly" or country music, but by those who lived on the right side of the tracks, the ones who belonged in the Apple Blossom Festival. Every snub hurt; every rejection by those with power and status fueled her desire to make it, if only to "show" the "sonsabitches."[17] But Patsy wanted acceptance on her own terms. She was not going to play by rules that were not hers. She was not going to put on the false trappings of respectability. She despised the need to compromise. As she argued when trying to get out of recording "Walkin' After Midnight"—a song she "hated," but which would give her the big break she had been chasing for years—"doing something I don't believe in makes me feel like a whore."[18]

Patsy Cline was not respectable. She would not have been respectable in virtually any part of the United States at that moment, much less in Winchester, Virginia. She was not alone. Millions of Americans fell outside—or put themselves outside—the boundaries of respectability, especially those drawn so tightly that wearing curlers in public was a violation. But in her hometown, the fact that Patsy was breaking the rules really should not have mattered. She was from the wrong side of the tracks, ill educated, vulgar, promiscuous, lower class. She should have been irrelevant to the "good people" of Winchester, those who belonged to the adamantly respectable middle class and the town's elite. No matter how many times she popped up (only to be squashed), no matter how many times she inserted herself into the Winchester Apple Blossom Parade, she should have remained irrelevant. She should not have mattered.

But she did. Why? Because she became famous. Patsy Cline became famous because of her talent. She made it through grit and persistence and single-minded determination. But she also became famous because there were new spaces for people like her, spaces that ignored the rules and restrictions of the immediate local communities, spaces in which those without wealth, status, or even the trappings of respectability had a voice, if only because of the money they spent. Patsy Cline became famous in national culture, in the midst of a massive demographic transformation that shifted cultural power toward those who had previously been all-but-invisible to those who "counted."

The story of the rise and consolidation of national culture, in the form of national media, is too large and complicated to recount here. What is crucial, in relation to my argument about Patsy Cline, is that the growing national media system had a paradox at its heart. National media exposed Americans to new and different styles and cultures and ideas and forms. And national media led—at least for several decades—toward homogenization.

From the earliest days, little Ginny Hensley's aspirations were shaped by national media. When she was no more than four, Ginny was imitating child movie star Shirley Temple, even winning a minor talent show with a tap-dancing routine people figured she must have copied from the movies. Movie star and singer Patsy Montana, the yodeling cowgirl, was a longer-lasting influence. Hollywood film in the 1930s and 1940s was full of singing cowboys and western themes; Patsy Montana's recording of "I Want to Be a Cowboy's Sweetheart" had sold more than a million copies in 1936 and in addition to her movie roles she was a regular on radio barn dance shows through the 1940s. Teenage Ginny Hensley practiced her own yodel and adopted Montana's full cowgirl garb and spunky attitude.[19]

Of course there were other institutions that influenced Patsy's musical development. She sang gospel music in the Pentecostal church. And she sang at her many homes, with her family—her parents even gave her an old piano for her eighth birthday, when they were living near Elkton. And like virtually everyone in America during the hard years of the depression and the world war that followed, Patsy listened to the radio. Radio, during its "golden age" in the 1930s and 1940s, was a mixture of national networks and regional networks, powerful stations with enormous broadcast range and low-wattage stations that were profoundly local. Winchester and its surroundings were within range of, among others, WRVA in Richmond, WLS in Chicago, and

Nashville's fifty-thousand-watt WSM, which carried the *Grand Ole Opry* to listeners in thirty states before affiliation with NBC brought a national audience in 1939. On the other hand, Patsy's first radio performance was in 1948 on Winchester's own WINC, broadcasting at two hundred and fifty watts. WINC relied heavily on "electrical transcriptions" of dramas and variety shows and current popular music produced for a national audience, but like most small, low-wattage stations, it also broadcast a great deal of live, local material. Saturday mornings were devoted to "hillbilly music," and local bands who could find a sponsor willing to pay five dollars for half an hour of airtime filled the three-hour slot from nine to noon. Sixteen-year-old Patsy simply screwed up her courage and walked into the studio, asking the leader of the Melody Playboys if he would let her sing with them.[20] This mix of possibilities was critical to Patsy: she saw the stars of Hollywood films; she heard the music broadcast to a growing regional—and then national—audience, and she took advantage of the chaotic and unpredictable world of local live radio as she tried to find her big break.

It was television, however, that made Patsy famous (as other chapters in the volume explore more fully). She had her first shot at the big-time world of national television in 1954, with an audition for *Arthur Godfrey's Talent Scouts*. It did not go well: New York City made Patsy anxious—and thus both difficult and oversensitive; the backup band had not quite jelled; the producer's businesslike manner seemed, when interpreted through the norms of the working-class South, both condescending and dismissive. Offered the chance to try again the following day, Patsy simply did not show. Instead, she found her way in the informal, chaotic world of regional television much closer to home.

In 1946, soon after the end of World War II, a country music entrepreneur named Connie B. Gay (of Lizard Lick, North Carolina) saw an opportunity. The war had put Americans into motion, not only the young men sent off to war, but also a flood of rural southerners moving to defense factories in places like Detroit and Los Angeles, finding work in urban centers of the South and the mid-Atlantic. By the end of the war, the area in and around Washington, D.C., had gained a huge new population of people from the southern hill country. Gay, who had worked for the Agriculture Department during the war writing slogans promoting Victory Gardens, saw the potential of this new audience. He pitched a "hillbilly" radio show to WARL, the new one-thousand-watt station that broadcast from Arlington, Virginia: "Let's Be Gay with Connie B. Gay." It was a huge success, growing from its original half-hour slot to a weekly three-hour broadcast titled *Town and Country Time*. Gay parlayed that success into a regional *Town and Country* radio network, buying small local stations (including D.C.'s WGAY). He controlled the country music scene in and around D.C.—not only the radio shows, but most of the acts that appeared in the clubs and bars that drew the displaced southerners who made up his initial audience. In the early 1950s, he was producing shows: a *Hillbilly Moonlight Cruise* on the Potomac and a regular *Hillbilly Air Show* that combined music with airplane stunts. By 1954, he had moved into television. His *Town and Country Time*, hosted by the popular Jimmy Dean, was broadcast live daily, with a three-hour weekly *Town and Country Jamboree* broadcast from D.C.'s major wrestling arena on Saturday nights, with a live audience of four thousand. By 1956, the *Jamboree* had a regional television audience of half a million—including, sometimes, Arthur Godfrey, who watched from his country house in Leesburg, Virginia, about forty miles northwest of Washington, D.C.[21]

Patsy had fallen into Gay's orbit in the early 1950s. By 1954 she was the "girl singer" for Jimmy Dean and the Texas Wildcats and a regular "guest" on the *Town and Country Time* show that aired every weeknight at 6:30 P.M. Her second audition for *Arthur Godfrey's Talent Scouts* came in late 1956. Though Godfrey was drawn by what he called the "innocence" and "honesty" of her performance, it had been carefully managed. Appearing on *Arthur Godfrey's Talent Scouts* in January 1957, Patsy performed the song she hated: "Walkin' After Midnight" scored in a pop arrangement. Instead of her beloved cowgirl outfits, she wore a simple blue linen sheath. And she won by a landslide.[22]

"Walkin' After Midnight" hit hard: by late February it had risen to number twelve on the pop charts; soon thereafter it peaked at number two on the country charts. "Miss Cline has cracked New York, Philadelphia, Baltimore, Washington and other East Coast cities, as well as Southern and Midwestern key markets," *Billboard* reported. But her crossover hit also won her an invitation to appear at the *Grand Ole Opry*.[23]

Patsy had made it. It is not that her subsequent career was smooth. Like many musicians, she signed contracts that left her with little financial payoff despite her enormous popularity and a frantic schedule of performing and recording. Her personal life was sometimes rocky; her ability to navigate the politics of the music industry and the oversize egos of many inside it was never the best. Nonetheless, when Patsy Cline died in the crash of a small airplane in the mountains of Tennessee, only thirty years old, she was a star, and she would not be forgotten.

Patsy had benefited from the possibilities offered by a medium that had yet to find a stable form. She rose through Gay's country music empire, an intertwined mixture of radio and live performances and promotions (the air shows and cruises) and television programming that moved from local to regional to syndication in forty markets, and then on to the national stage through *Arthur Godfrey's Talent Scouts* that aired in prime time on CBS. Just as was true in Washington, D.C., her popularity had to do with the changing demographics of the nation. It also demonstrates how the emergence and consolidation of the new medium—television—altered the cultural landscape of the nation.

By 1957, when Patsy performed on *Arthur Godfrey's Talent Scouts*, there were televisions in forty-one million of the approximately forty-eight million American households. (Television ownership hit 90 percent in 1960, when more American households owned television sets than either washing machines or electric irons.) By 1957, with only three networks available during prime time, a single show might attract up to 70 percent of all viewers. Compare that to the early twenty-first century, when a wildly popular show might attract up to 12 percent of TV viewers—a total figure that continues to drop as more and more of the potential audience watch favorite shows at their own convenience, whether online or on DVR or DVD.[24]

Broadcast television, before the rise of cable in the 1980s, was a powerfully homogenizing force. With only three channels broadcasting in the late 1950s, there were no prime-time niche markets, no women-oriented Lifetime or African American–oriented BET, no channels devoted to movie classics or science fiction. Television programming was aimed at broadly conceived audiences.

In the United States, television was developed in a powerfully capitalist framework. The point of television programming was not to entertain the public. It certainly was not to uplift them. The point of television programming was to produce audiences for advertising. And because, given the technologies of the time, those audiences could not be carefully targeted, that meant that television frequently aimed to draw the broadest possible audience—which meant, at least for those who agreed with Federal Communications Commission chairman Newton Minow's condemnation of television programming as a "vast cultural wasteland" in 1961, that it appealed to the lowest common denominator.

Television, which was surpassing radio and film and newspapers as the medium of choice, upset reigning notions of cultural authority in the nation. For my argument, this works in two ways. First of all, though television programming was shaped by fear of offending sponsors, as well as by fear of audience boycotts of "objectionable" material such as "inappropriate" interactions between the races, sexually charged images, or a long list of forbidden words, the prime concern was selling products. The bottom line was revenue, and early television was concerned with enforcing conventional notions of morality and respectability only to the point of avoiding federal action or loss of sponsors.

Thus the respectability of the performer was often beside the point, so long as nothing inappropriate appeared on the air. There were those who found that disturbing. In early 1957, just as Winchester's scandal-ridden Patsy Cline was making her appearance on *Arthur Godfrey's Talent Scouts*, Ingrid Bergman—movie star and admitted adulteress—was a guest on NBC's popular *Steve Allen Show*. Thirty-one-year-old conservative critic William Buckley was outraged. "The point," he wrote, "is that once upon a time there was a thing called the public morality. Quite apart from Christian doctrine, certain prescriptions have grown out of a consensus of the people as to the requirements of social existence . . . not compounded out of superstition or prudery." Thus, he argued, it was necessary to maintain "social sanctions against the violator," and those who scorned the codes of public morality should not be given platforms on national television.[25] His argument made no difference. It did not matter that Ingrid Bergman or Patsy Cline—or Liberace, for that matter—did not fit the prevailing notions of respectability, so long as they did nothing inappropriate on the air. It did not matter that many respectable people in Patsy's hometown of Winchester saw her as willfully violating basic standards of social conduct. Patsy Cline was talented; she had presence; she was valuable in the capitalist arena of television.

She was valuable, in part, because more people had started to "count." There were more people in postwar America with disposable income, more people who thus had a "voice" in the capitalist marketplace of popular culture. That did not sit well with many of those who saw themselves as the cultural arbiters of the nation. Both the *New York Times* and the *Wall Street Journal* tried to come to terms with the popularity of "hillbilly" music during the 1950s, and both mixed a condescending-to-downright-insulting tone with amazement at the "business merits" of country music. Journalist McCandlish Phillips responded to the popular *Jimmy Dean Show*, launched on CBS in 1957, with a *New York Times* profile of Dean's patron and packager, Connie B. Gay. "Anyone who has ever, in the democracy of war," Phillips wrote, "shared barracks with a knot of fiddle-scraping wahoos from the swamp country will probably not be an instant admirer of Connie B. Gay, . . . the cultural shepherd of that considerable proportion of the American public whose appetite for country music cannot be gratified in any merely twenty-four-hour period." Phillips, who described Gay as self-confessedly "pretty nearly tone deaf"—a fact he believed offered no surprise to "the average music listener"—and noted that "successive mouthfuls of spaghetti stood between Mr. Gay and lucidity the other day," made a larger point about class and American culture. Although he was not sure about Gay's argument that World War II had "done a great deal for country music," he could not get past the larger point: country music earned Gay a million dollars a year.[26]

The *Wall Street Journal*'s investigation of why "rural rhythms and hill town tunes" so appealed to "sophisticated advertisers" made a similar point in an article that mentioned Patsy Cline. "Some 50 million hillbilly records were sold last year in the United States," the 1957 article informed *WSJ* readers. "That means that four out of every ten popular music records sold were the tunes known to the trade as country music." With corporations such as General Motors, Bristol Meyers, and Phillips Petroleum turning to country music programming to sell their wares to the American public, and a waiting list of corporations hoping to get in on the action, music formerly below the notice of America's cultural elites could not be ignored.[27]

Some still had difficulty believing that country music appealed. In 1958, Vance Packard, author of *The Hidden Persuaders*, testified to Congress that broadcasters were "manipulating" the tastes of their audiences to maximize their own profit. His prime example was the prevalence of "cheaply-mined" music "in the hillbilly field," which led to "a gross degradation in the quality of music supplied to the public over the airwaves." Al Gore Sr., senator from the state that hosted the *Grand Ole Opry*, arrived in the hearing room soon thereafter. After reading a telegram from the governor of Tennessee condemning Packard's "gratuitous insult to thousands of our fellow Tennesseans," Gore noted, in a somewhat awkward endorsement, that while "some renditions are not pleasing," the "language of the music expresses the hopes and aspirations" of people from the mountains of Tennessee, "people of pioneer stock," some of whom "still speak English of the Elizabethan age." "I would not," he concluded, "like to see all country music branded intellectually cheap."[28]

By 1958, however, country music was no longer the province of isolated residents of Appalachia who presumably spoke the language of Elizabethan England. And any people who remained so isolated in the hills and valleys of the region would likely not have recognized what the "hillbilly" music of their youth had become in the homogenizing world of 1950s popular culture. Attempts to appeal to a broad national audience during television's prime-time hours undoubtedly moved authentic "hillbilly" music closer to pop, smoothing out some of the twang, helping to standardize the field of "country" that Gay characterized as somewhere between the Model T of "hillbilly music" and the Cadillac of pop. Gay's "vehicular metaphor" offered country music as an Oldsmobile—a perfect car for a broad range of the American middle class.[29] So while it was still possible for *New York Journal-American* columnist

Dorothy Kilgallen to make fun of the "hicks from the sticks" scheduled to appear at Carnegie Hall in 1961 in a piece that missed the irony that the *Grand Old Opry*'s concert was to raise money for an organization that aided retired classical musicians, the more important point is that Carnegie Hall sold out. "We made 'em show their true colors," Patsy told an Atlanta audience a few days later. "They sittin' up there stompin' their feet and yellin' just like a bunch of hillbillies, just like we do."[30]

During the postwar era, more Americans than ever were visible; more, through an expanding economy and a system that "enfranchised" those with money to spend, helped to shape the nation's public, popular culture. That process unsettled previous models of authority, whether of local elites in small towns across the nation or of sophisticated commentators who saw themselves as the arbiters of national culture. It also brought the music of "outsiders"—of African Americans, of white "hillbillies"—into the expanding world of the white middle class. Patsy Cline played an important role in that transformation.

Despite her national fame—and even her tragic death, leaving behind two young children—Cline was never accepted by Winchester's elite or by many of its respectable middling class. As residents banded together to resist naming a street for Winchester's most famous citizen almost thirty years after her death, one testified in oft-quoted words: "Ask anybody in this town and they'll tell you. Patsy Cline was nothin' but a whore."[31] Neither Patsy's fame nor her accomplishments changed the minds of those who saw themselves as guardians of respectability in Winchester, Virginia. But her ability to succeed in ways beyond their control made it impossible for them to simply ignore her.

Thus the story of Patsy Cline and the problem of respectability has two endings. Patsy never surmounted the hurdles of respectability in her hometown, and its continued reluctance to embrace their homegrown star took an enormous emotional toll on her. But Patsy's rise through the new spaces created in a growing national culture demonstrates the importance of freedoms and different opportunities, as a growing mass-market culture made new portions of the American public "count," if only because they had money to spend.

NOTES

1. As a cultural historian of the period in which Patsy Cline rose to fame—but not an expert on either Cline or on country music—I want to emphasize my indebtedness to those who are. In particular, I have relied heavily on Patsy Cline's biographers,

especially Margaret Jones, in writing this chapter. Her exhaustive research and many interviews with those who knew Patsy Cline furnish the information about her life I have used to create my argument. Because all published works on Patsy Cline rely heavily on interviews, both quotes from Cline and anecdotes I use in this piece are often as recalled by those who knew her; in each case I cite the specific source. For more on Patsy Cline's life, please see the following works: Margaret Jones, *Patsy: The Life and Times of Patsy Cline* (New York: HarperCollins, 1994; New York: De Capo, 1999); Ellis Nassour, *Honky Tonk Angel: The Intimate Story of Patsy Cline* (New York: St. Martin's Press, 1993); Mark Bego, *I Fall to Pieces: The Music and the Life of Patsy Cline* (Holbrook, Mass.: Adams Publishing, 1996); and Cindy Hazen and Mark Freeman, eds. *Love Always, Patsy: Patsy Cline's Letters to a Friend* (Darby, Pa.: Diane Publishing Company, 1999). For broader context, see Bill C. Malone, *Country Music, U.S.A.* (Austin: University of Texas Press, 2002), and James C. Cobb, "From Muskogee to Luckenbach: Country Music and the 'Southernization' of America," *Journal of Popular Culture* 16 (Winter 1982): 81–91. For "dull" and "phlegmatic": Jones, *Patsy*, 44, 43. Winchester, Virginia, is located in the far northwestern portion of the state, in the Shenandoah Valley between the Blue Ridge and Appalachian mountains. It is approximately seventy-five miles from Washington, D.C.

2. My arguments about the importance of respectability and the significance of national culture are developed in more detail in *Sex in the Heartland* (Cambridge: Harvard University Press, 1999) and *From Front Porch to Back Seat: Courtship in Twentieth-Century America* (Baltimore: Johns Hopkins University Press, 1988). For discussions of manners, respectability, race, and class in the South, see Patrick Huber, "A Short History of *Redneck*: The Fashioning of a Southern White Masculine Identity," in *Southern Cultures: The Fifteenth Anniversary Reader*, eds. Harry L. Watson and Larry J. Griffin (Chapel Hill: University of North Carolina Press, 2008), 303–27; and Ted Ownby, ed. *Manners and Southern History* (Oxford: University of Mississippi Press, 2007).

3. For a more complete version of this argument, see Bailey, *From Front Porch*, especially chapter 5. Quotes are from Elizabeth Woodward, "Sub-deb: Bargain Buys," *Ladies Home Journal*, May 1942, 8; Gay Head, column, *Senior Scholastic*, 1945 (from clipping, full date missing), 28.

4. For a discussion of respectability in the African American civil rights movement, see Marisa Chappell, Jenny Hutchinson, and Brian Ward, "'Dress neatly . . . as if you were going to church': Respectability, Class and Gender in the Montgomery Bus Boycott and the Early Civil Rights Movement," in Peter John Ling and Sharon Monteith, eds. *Gender and the Civil Rights Movement* (New Brunswick, N.J.: Rutgers University Press, 2004), 69.

5. I want to stress that I mean that Patsy Cline was not respectable by the narrow standards of the 1950s; this statement is not my personal judgment of Patsy Cline, and I am arguing that standards of respectability are historically specific and often worked to exclude those who did not play by a fairly narrow set of rules.

6. On Patsy Cline's childhood and family background, see Jones, *Patsy*, 1–14. Nassour, in *Honky Tonk Angel*, 10–14, offers a less detailed account that does not fully correspond with Jones; I have followed the more exhaustively researched work.

7. I rely here on the evidence presented by Jones, *Patsy*, 10–12, including statements made by Loretta Lynn in an interview with Jones, March 3, 1992, and Jones's interviews with Don Hecht, June 15, 1992; with Mae Boren Axton, July 31, 1992; and with Bernard Schwartz, August 15, 1991, particularly his account of what Cline's mother told him as he prepared to make the biographical film *Sweet Dreams*.

8. Margaret Jones interview with Pat Smallwood Miller, March 8, 1991, in Jones, *Patsy*, 25.

9. For cigarette girl and venues, Jones, *Patsy*, 26–27; for costumes, Hazen and Freeman, *Love Always*, letters from Patsy dated May 14, 1956, and March 7, 1957.

10. Nassour, *Honky Tonk Angel*, 194–95; Bego, *I Fall to Pieces*, 164; Jones, *Patsy*, 260–61.

11. Jones, *Patsy*, 47–48; "Morality Survey" is the heading on the "Associated Women Students Survey for 'Roles of Women' Committee," 1964, University of Kansas Archives, Lawrence, Kans.

12. Coat story from Nassour, *Honky Tonk Angel*, 52–53; sailor from Hazen and Freeman, *Love Always*, 26–27, and Nassour, *Honky Tonk Angel*, 40; for Dean's account, see Nassour, *Honky Tonk Angel*, 49; the story also appears in Jones, *Patsy*, 255, and Bego, *I Fall to Pieces*, 163.

13. Nassour, *Honky Tonk Angel*, 47, 43. The female friend is Fay Crutchley.

14. Characterizations of Charlie Dick's drinking and of Patsy and Charlie's fights appear in Margaret Jones's interview with Johnny Anderson, May 24, 1991, and Billy Grammer, May 11, 1992, in Jones, *Patsy*, 112, 117; see also Nassour, *Honky Tonk Angel*, 125.

15. As I believe I have made clear in the text, it is difficult to know whether one individual story or another was strictly true; jealousy and male sexual boasting may account for some of the stories that circulated. Nonetheless, Patsy had definitely crossed the line in both her affair with Peer and in her own straightforward sexual comments, and the stories—whether fully accurate or not—helped to cement that position.

16. Eddie Dean, "Nobody's Patsy," *Washington City Paper*, April 7, 1995, http://www.washingtoncitypaper.com (accessed September 2012).

17. Margaret Jones interview with John Reid, May 21, 1991, in Jones, *Patsy*, xvi.

18. Nassour, *Honky Tonk Angel*, 65 (there is no original written or recorded source for this statement; Don Hecht supplied the quote in his interview with Nassour).

19. Jones, *Patsy*, 8, 15–16; Nassour, *Honky Tonk Angel*, 6–7.

20. Jones, *Patsy*, 15–17, 20–21; Radio Hall of Fame, http://www.radiohof.org/music/grandoleopry.html (accessed September 2012).

21. On Gay's empire, see Jones, *Patsy*, 64–68; McCandlish Phillips, "Country Stylist," *New York Times*, September 8, 1957; Eric Charles May, "Country Music

Promoter Connie B. Gay Dies at 75," *Washington Post*, December 5, 1989; Nassour, *Honky Tonk Angel*, 45–46.

22. See Nassour, *Honky Tonk Angel*, 76–77.

23. Jones, *Patsy*, 128–31.

24. For general information on the history of television, see Gary R. Edgerton, *The Columbia History of Modern Television* (New York: Columbia University Press, 2007).

25. Buckley's quote from "It's Not So Simple," *National Review*, February 2, 1957, 103.

26. Phillips, "Country Stylist."

27. Clarence B. Newman, "Homespun Harmony," *Wall Street Journal*, May 3, 1957.

28. Val Adams, "Hillbilly Tunes Praised In House," *New York Times*, March 13, 1958.

29. Phillips, "Country Stylist."

30. Kilgallen and Cline quotes from Jones, *Patsy*, 230, 232.

31. Quoted in Mike D'Orso, "Bittersweet Dreams," *Virginian Pilot and Ledger-Star*, January 3, 1988, and Jones, *Patsy*, 297.

CHAPTER 4

CULTURAL SCRIPTS AND PATSY CLINE'S CAREER IN THE 1950S

Kristine M. McCusker

Perhaps one of the most enduring narratives in country music scholarship is the scarcity of women in the country music industry; that is, until feminist revolutionaries like Patsy Cline, Loretta Lynn, Tammy Wynette, and Dolly Parton broke it wide open, beginning in the early 1960s. When this narrative began is unclear, although the emergence of a feminist critique of male-only histories in the 1970s and 1980s was most likely one catalyst. What is clear is that it has had a central place in some of the best country music scholarship. Writing about country radio barn dances in the 1930s, Bill C. Malone in *Country Music, U.S.A.* (1984) reported that, "Although women made important breakthroughs in the thirties, they still had very far to go. Negative images still clung to women who would forsake their 'traditional' roles and venture into an area formerly reserved for men."[1] It is a narrative that is repeated in more recent scholarship. Peter La Chapelle's excellent 2004 analysis of Los Angeles fan culture argued that a new "and more conservative gender politics" forced women out of the fan magazine business in the 1950s and named *Country Song Roundup*, *Country Music Life*, and *Country Music Report* as examples of magazines at which editorial boards replaced female writers and reporters with male ones. To prove his point, La Chapelle highlighted a *Country Song Roundup* feature, "Meet the Mrs.," in which journalists "assessed the homemaking skills" of famous musical men's wives, as evidence that the 1950s were especially difficult years for women who wanted to work.[2]

In Cline's case, discussions of her earthy and assertive nature imply her personality and success were not rooted in her working-class background, but in an openly feminist attempt to succeed in an industry that had no use for female artists. In Cline biographer Margaret Jones's words, "Girl singers were rare and girl soloists were an anomaly."[3] This trend is, in part, music journalists' and scholars' tendency to reify and repeat assumptions about musicians from every genre, divorced from the context that produced them: blues musician Robert Johnson sold his soul to the devil; Patsy Cline was a feminist.[4] Neither exists in a time and place that opened or closed musical and professional choices, but rather in an imaginary world inhabited by fantasy people. But the "Patsy equals Feminist" trend also includes assumptions endemic to country music scholarship in which mere existence in the industry tends to rest almost exclusively with those who had commercial success or were musical innovators. Few women had the *financial* or *musical* success that Cline did; therefore, few women must have been performers. The lack of primary source material, outside of recorded music, tends to reinforce this assumption. In either case, the feminist label, which assumes that she refused to bow to men's exploitation (one need think only of the contract she signed with Bill McCall of 4 Star Records to disprove that), that she was always bold and assertive, and that she had a consciousness of herself as a woman needing to break open the industry for other women hides more than it reveals. In doing so, Cline's success seems more dramatic and bold rather than a natural outcome of a generation's work and innovation.

This essay examines a different Patsy Cline, one in which both she and her female peers were welcomed with opened arms, narratively speaking, to the post–World War II country music industry, a different Patsy who will seem less bold, more of a performer than a musician, and certainly welcomed to the country music industry in an era of significant change. The industry did this because women had been crucial to its development in the 1920s, 1930s, and 1940s, especially on radio barn dances that featured a mixture of southern and western performers on large urban radio stations in Chicago, Detroit, Nashville, and other places. As I have argued elsewhere, producers such as WLS Chicago's John Lair of *National Barn Dance* discovered that women who donned costumes and musical repertoires evoking a southern mountain home or a western range were particularly popular with audiences. Whether she was 1936's Radio Queen Lulu Belle Wiseman or Western performer Patsy Montana, whose recording of "I Wanna Be A Cowboy's Sweetheart" sold a million copies during the Great Depression, southern and western women soothed an audience disturbed by depressions and world wars. The fact that a pretty face sold well did not hurt either, because producers and musicians linked women's sexuality to the commercial production of music. Women made barn dance music commercially viable, and as it reinvented itself as country and western music in the 1950s, these assumptions carried over. It was that context that Patsy Cline navigated, managing various tensions and trends on her way to stardom.[5]

This chapter, then, tears away the image of a feminist Patsy Cline and locates her in that industry on the verge of a reinvention precipitated by the collapse of barn dance radio, the emergence of television and rock and roll, and the relocation of country music's geographic center to Nashville, Tennessee.[6] How were women incorporated into the new social and musical relationships being forged? The answer was quite clear early on: industry insiders assumed that women were essential to making southern and western music in various, though limited, ways. One of the main places where this welcome was apparent was in fan magazines that supported, promoted, and touted the famous star and the up-and-comer novice alike. The most significant was *Country Song Roundup*. Published in Derby, Connecticut, beginning in July 1949, the magazine featured women in diverse roles that evolved over time to account for new musical trends and artists. While *Country Song Roundup* defined success as the million-selling record, it never ignored "girl" singers and other women in its pages. But it also closed roles for women (and men)—narratively speaking, at least—leaving the assumption that if the magazine could not imagine someone in a role, the industry could not either. *Country Song Roundup* thus helped shape the expectations of producers and other recording executives for the potential of Cline and other women. Moreover, it was a public forum that hid profound behind-the-scenes tensions whereby men claimed the most powerful roles such as producer as in the case of Owen Bradley, instrumentalist as in the case of Chet Akins, businessman as in the case of Bill McCall, and Nashville star as in the case of Eddie Arnold, thus relegating women to important, but still less powerful, places in the industry.

The public welcome female performers like Patsy Cline received should make us reconsider the image of the feminist Patsy battling her way through sexist men who were eager to exploit and dominate her. The full run of *Country Song Roundup*, archived at the Country Music Hall of Fame and Museum, locates Cline in a context that allows us to reassess the "Patsy equals Feminist" image. Therefore, I end this essay with a reassessment of three core assumptions that naturally emanate: that Patsy did not allow men to exploit her or, alternatively, that Nashville was out to exploit only women and Cline would have nothing to do with it; that the infamous battles between Cline and Owen Bradley were examples of her willingness to stand up to exploitive men; and that her adherence to western costuming and repertoire on stage was another example of her assertiveness, even when the image became passé. Recontextualizing Patsy Cline with *Country Song Roundup* journalism makes a more substantial, eminently human, Patsy possible.

* * *

Journalists and country music have a long history together, beginning in the barn dance radio heyday of the 1930s. In 1927, the *Prairie Farmer* newspaper purchased WLS Chicago, home of the popular *National Barn Dance*, and began publishing a fan magazine called *Stand By!* that promoted both the program and its stars in 1935. *Stand By!* nurtured the careers of Lulu Belle Wiseman, Patsy Montana, The Girls of the Golden West, and Lily May Ledford, as well as a host of male stars. Once *Stand By!* proved its worth in not only promoting specific performers, but in shaping audience expectations of those performers, other fan journals followed in the 1940s, including *Rural Radio, Mountain Broadcast and Prairie Recorder*, and Minnie Pearl's *Grinder's Switch Gazette*, which she published from 1944–1946 and which focused on *Grand Ole Opry* talent.[7] These latecomers followed the format established by *Stand By!* whereby a performer appeared on the cover of each magazine with a feature article inside. Other columns gossiped about favorite stars and their daily routines and printed schedules that provided opportunities to hear radio performances or see them at personal appearances, typically listed at the rear of the magazine. Ads also appeared alongside articles, selling songbooks published by performers, clothing, and other goods and services, using imagery and verbiage that fit the barn dance genre's hayseed appeal.

Stand By! and other magazines were published in an era when most listeners heard country music on the radio. At the end of World War II, government controls on shellac, a waterproofing agent deemed essential to the war effort and a key component in record making, ceased, and records began to be sold once again. Jukeboxes reinforced the importance of records in the postwar era because they made records, not radios, an alternative and ultimately successful way a customer could hear country music at any time.[8] Nashville, with its pool of talent nurtured by the *Grand Ole Opry*, and other businesses that supported country music's mission, such as music licenser BMI and Acuff-Rose Music, a publishing firm that licensed music by postwar greats such as Hank Williams Sr., began to emerge as the cultural and economic center of the country and western sound.[9] Artist and repertoire agents ("A&R reps") from large recording companies like Decca also came to capitalize on the region's musical depth. Although California—especially Bakersfield and Los Angeles—gave Nashville a run for its money, Nashville by the end of the 1950s was the firm center of country music production.[10]

The barn dance genre tried to reinvent itself in the postwar era and succeeded well into the late 1940s; programs numbered nearly 650 nationwide by 1949. Television, however, halted that progress as it presented a new visual culture for its audience, one rooted first in cities, then in the suburbs. Television shows of the 1950s valued a national culture, rather than a regional one, one that emphasized suburban homes, demure housewives, and male executives who were firmly in charge of their households (think *Ozzie and Harriet*, *Father Knows Best*, and the *Donna Reed Show*). Barn dance programs attempted to make the transition to television—Patsy Cline's turn on Connie B. Gay's *Town and Country* television show being an obvious example—and were, in some cases, successful, at least regionally.[11] But few shows had the success Gay's show did, probably due to his willingness to move beyond radio formats and build a show based on visual cues rather than other shows' tendency to perform a radio show in front of television cameras. The *Opry*'s television version, for example, was certainly not successful, and only when *Hee Haw* (1969–1971 and in syndication) repackaged the show in a format different from the radio show did *Opry* stars succeed on the air. Barn dance radio was clearly on the wane by the mid-1950s as the deejay format, spotlighting the young man spinning "disks" (records), began supplanting the musical variety show format that barn dance shows followed religiously. By the late 1950s, the shows had all but disappeared.

These transitions are apparent in *Country Song Roundup*, which mimicked some of *Stand By!*'s format when it began publishing in July 1949, but the shift from radio to television and records required a focus on songs and lyrics, rather than an exclusive focus on performers and performance schedules. Nor would Southern Appalachian mothers dominate a fan magazine's pages as they had in barn dance days; now it was the intrepid songwriter or performer who was able to turn a love story into a three-minute hit that became the magazine's focus. Magazine covers changed, too, with a male performer almost exclusively featured, which benefited stars such as Ernest Tubb, Hank Snow, and later, Elvis and other teen idols. The obligatory article still appeared inside. Yet similarities with older fan magazines remained. Articles touted a wide variety of musicians in hopes that the magazine might have found the next big star. Photos dominated all pages in order to give a face to those who sang on records. Gossip columns continued to track favorite stars' antics. The evolution of country music was thus apparent on *Country Song Roundup*'s pages, but it remained true to some of its recent past, an indication that the industry itself was doing the same as it used the past as an anchor to its future.

Embedded in this format was a mixture of old and new roles for women, providing a wholesome image of femininity that hid behind-the-scenes machinations and power-hungry executives. Performer was by far the most popular image as hundreds of women were featured throughout the era. At first, barn dance stars like Lulu Belle Wiseman, the WLS *National Barn Dance* star, were prominent, indicating that the barn dance star was still important.[12] But the recording star also began to appear as more women were signed to recording contracts. New stars and music icons such as Rose Maddox, Dale Evans, and Mother Maybelle and the Carter Sisters all were featured alongside hundreds of now obscure up-and-comers such as Liddie Murphy, Ann Jones, and Lindy Rose.[13] Top-selling performers still caught the audience's attention, most notably Kitty Wells, Martha Carson, and Jean Shepherd. Kitty Wells, with her million-selling hit, "It Wasn't God Who Made Honky Tonk Angels" (1952), caused *Country Song Roundup* to note that "A Star Is Born." In Kitty's case, "Though she may have come into this world with the same opportunities that every other child is afforded, Kitty Wells now holds the distinction of being one of the few women folk singers to ever rise to fame and fortune," the unnamed journalist wrote.[14]

Though the most common role, the solo star was not the only musical option open to women. The family group was a leftover from barn dance and early recording days when the family's performances implied that standing around a microphone and singing was no different from singing near the fireplace. That continued in the 1950s. Siblings, cousins, married couples, and in some cases, entire families (think Carter Family) used their music making to support themselves, but did so in a way that seemed to obviate crass commercialism. This was music making, not money making. Sibling groups such as Maxine, Jim Ed, and Bonnie Brown, members of the Brown Trio, may have found fame and fortune, but features in issues still emphasized the familial intentions behind their music through pictures documenting off-stage domestic bliss. Married duos did likewise as Wilma Lee and Stoney Cooper or the "Mr. and Mrs. Team," Lone Pine and Betty Cody, were also popular in the era.[15]

Although the family effort remained important, individuals affiliated with the industry's new focus on records became more prominent on *Country Song Roundup's* pages as the decade evolved. That new focus had the added benefit of shifting the audience's focus away from rural cabins to more modern suburban venues and away from groups like the Brown Trio to individual artists. Instrumentalists such as Del Woods, who was known in *Country Song Roundup's* pages as the "Queen of the Ragtime Piano," were obvious beneficiaries.[16] But it was the songwriter who became the musical innovator on these pages. She (or he) could write music that captured the ethos of the era, namely an emphasis on the relationships between men and women living in tidy suburban cottages and dancing their woes away in a honky-tonk bar. In the later years, the ability to capture young love, bittersweet and passionate between teenagers, was a good songwriter's focus. Two of the best known were Cindy Walker, a prolific writer best known for Eddy Arnold's "You Don't Know Me," and Felice Bryant, best known for cowriting (with her husband) early Everly Brothers hits such as "Bye Bye Love." Both were named in "Folk Music's Top Songwriters" in *Country Song Roundup*.[17]

Country Song Roundup touted the talented musician on its pages, whether a songwriter or pianist, but it also featured nonmusical roles. It was an industry standard that every show had a male singer, a female singer, and a comedian. That comedic influence was apparent from the magazine's inception with its monthly column, featuring radio star and lovable Ozark rube Judy Canova's "best gags," as it called her jokes. Other female rubes were featured, for example, the *Renfro Valley Barn Dance*'s six-foot, four-inch Little Eller. But the star of the decade, at least comedically, was Minnie Pearl, whose popularity eclipsed almost all other comedians, male and female, country or otherwise. Minnie was featured regularly throughout the 1950s, in articles about her and about the *Grand Ole Opry*, each noting her evolving international stardom.[18] She was also a featured writer—perhaps a nod to her own journalist days writing the *Grinder's Switch Gazette*—and published her first article, entitled "Up in the Air with Minnie Pearl," in 1950.[19]

One legacy from barn dance radio that continued to dominate *Country Song Roundup*'s pages was the rare appearance of women in managerial or technical roles, a continuation from barn dance days that placed men in engineering and managerial roles and, subsequently, in the middle class, and women in secretarial positions and, subsequently, in the working class. On *Country Song Roundup*'s pages, it seemed at first that women would not be excluded from the newest and most visible radio job: deejay. *Country Music Roundup* loved Rosalie Allen, a country music deejay in New York City and promoted her over and over again in the magazine until 1951, when she virtually disappeared from its pages. From there, the female deejay was rare enough for journalists to note her gender when she was featured. In the case of Randy Boone from Oroville, California's KMOR, she was "a little gal who helps everyone start the day right."[20] Thus, the magazine narratively excluded women from the deejay role and reinforced that exclusion by noting gender only in the case of female deejays, which made them unique, rare, and odd.

Whether comedienne, singer, musician, or lyricist, the successful woman was one who could enact an image of the West on a variety of stages, an image that kept a tight hold on performers until the middle of the decade when teen stars like Elvis Presley began to usurp Western performers' popularity. The content of one's (stage) character determined the successful stage performer. Barn dance radio had already helped popularize the West as a counter to depressed urban areas in the 1930s. But its ideological flexibility, the ability to manipulate it for multiple contexts, meant it could be used to fight other battles as well. Scholar Richard Slotkin, in *Gunfighter Nation*, argues that in the 1950s, the mythology of the West became a way to counter a Communist ideology of a collective society by touting the gun-toting man as the individualistic hero of a romantic American past. This was one significant reason that Westerns were repopularized in the 1950s.[21] Country music stages were clearly a site where these multiple ideological struggles took place, struggles that both men and women engaged in. Marking oneself as Western through costuming was a key first step to enacting that Western image and struggle, and multiple photos in *Country Song Roundup* showed readers that clothing. The female Western star wore a dress with fringe, vest, and/or a yoke reminiscent of the West and a cowboy hat, all accessories favored by Patsy Cline. Western stars also behaved like they still lived in the days of old. "Curvaceous Carolina Cotton" was one star whose Western lifestyle was key to her popularity; as *Country Song Roundup* noted, "In addition to being so talented and easy on the eyes, Carolina is a superb horsewoman."[22]

This heavy emphasis on the West was probably the reason Patsy Cline adhered so religiously to the Western image in costume, musical choices, and performances, even though her stardom was eventually founded upon a new kind of image, the svelte chanteuse at home not in a barn, but in front of an orchestra.[23] It is not clear whether she recognized the image's multifaceted use—to wage war against depressions and Communist countries—but it is no surprise that she adhered to it so religiously. She was, literally, surrounded by it, if *Country Song Roundup*'s pages are any indication, as the magazine showcased the multiple stages that engaged in these ideological struggles, musical and otherwise. In many cases, for example, performers featured in *Country Song Roundup* also starred in Western movies, including Roy Rogers and Dale Evans, Tex Ritter, and the Sons of the Pioneers, all of whom were featured in *Country Song Roundup*.[24] The emphasis on the Western film meant, too, that actresses, even those who did not sing a note, were showcased alongside prominent singing cowboys like Rogers and Ritter.

Since its earliest days, barn dance radio invited fans to be a prominent part of its music making even though radio fans could tune in from thousands of miles away. The star performer then was the one who could "pull" or receive thousands of fan letters from radio friends.[25] Fan mail lost its impact at the end of World War II as fan clubs supplanted mail as the main commercial contribution fans made to the industry—besides buying an album, of course.

It became more and more common to find women in unpaid support roles as the heads of these clubs, albeit with fancy titles like "fan club president," doing unpaid work that ensured the industry's success. Presidents invested money and time in publishing newsletters, sending autographed photos to the membership, and in general, building a dedicated group of consumers who seemed guaranteed to purchase new records.[26] By 1954, *Country Song Roundup* recognized fan clubs and fan club presidents for the important role they played in promoting stars and prompted a new *Country Song Roundup* column: "The Fanning Bee," which featured club presidents with their stars. The name implied that fan president was a domestic duty, not unlike sewing, quilting, or cleaning, not an important business role with real financial consequences for the evolving Nashville music business. The columns themselves provided biographic details for both the star and the fan club president as well as information about how to join the club. In the case of Del Woods, she and her fan club president, Doris Land, were featured in one "Fanning Bee" in 1954.[27] Later, fan club presidents were featured in "The President's Report," which reported on stars such as Rex Allen, Pee Wee King, and Roy Acuff.[28] While *Country Song Roundup* saw the role as noncommercial, club presidents did not see their work in exclusively domestic terms. Some, such as Hawkshaw Hawkins's fan club president, Monna Massey, saw these business relationships as a stepping stone for their own careers. Massey, the magazine noted, "did some radio and stage work while in her teens. She's written several songs and has had a couple published."[29]

Fan club president was not the only nonmusical role for women. Perhaps the oddest role for women was the martyred sister, mother, or wife, a role opened exclusively to women and a critical role because the first country music histories began to use a star's early death to create the industry's historical narrative. It had the added benefit of allowing some women to claim a "respectable" middle-class status when their loved ones were inserted into the narrative. Two deceased musicians provided the impetus on *Country Song Roundup*'s pages: Jimmie Rodgers and Hank Williams. In the case of Rodgers, his wife, Carrie, used their marriage to, first, boost attendance at the new Jimmie Rodgers Memorial Celebrations in Meridian, Mississippi, festivals that reinforced his popularity and made his records commercially successful some twenty years after his death. This, of course, ensured her own economic independence and middle-class status. But she also used her fame as a country music man's wife to promote the careers of other country music men, especially Ernest Tubb and Hank Snow. Wife of a dead superstar served as a sort of "cover," meaning she seemed to be acting as a wife rather than as an entrepreneur, nurturing them in their careers since her own husband was deceased. In a May 1952 letter to *Country Song Roundup*, Rodgers touted that year's Jimmie Rodgers Memorial Celebration but took note of Tubb and Snow and their willingness to keep her firmly in the middle class by buying her expensive consumer items. She wrote,

> Two such artists, ERNEST TUBB and HANK SNOW [*sic*] are especially dear to me. In fact, I consider them my "guardian angels." Because of their affection for Jimmie and for me, they keep in close touch and make it their business to be aware of my circumstances always. I am enjoying a lovely RCA television combination set which was recently presented to me by Hank and a 1952 Cadillac sedan—a gift from Ernest.

She ended the letter with another plug for the Jimmie Rodgers fan club.[30] Her role also allowed her to control the ways the first histories of Jimmie appeared in *Country Song Roundup*, also in 1952, making sure his performances were marked as the "true" beginning of the industry (never mind the Carter Family). She characterized his death from tuberculosis at age thirty-six in May 1933 as a tragedy, not just for his family but for the industry as a whole. The first histories of the industry repeated that narrative without realizing the economic context for its initial incarnation.[31]

In the case of Hank Williams, his mother first filled the role of grief-stricken family member as a way to manage the late icon's evolving mythology and to control the dollars that continued to be spent by fans. She, too, extended her motherly instincts to promote other singers such as RCA Victor artist Jack Turner, called a "protégé of Mama Williams, mother of Hank Williams," according to the magazine.[32] When "Mama" Williams died in the mid-1950s, daughter Irene Williams Smith took over as both the new keeper of Hank's iconography and as a journalist, writing a column for *Country Song Roundup* entitled "Hank's Corner." In her first column, she described Hank's philosophy as, "we really don't have the right to criticize and condemn our fellow man," and in doing so, lent legitimacy to one interpretation of Hank as a live-and-let-live kind of man, an image that did not acknowledge his drug and alcohol use.[33] Irene's journalistic efforts in the meantime mimicked the success other women had as journalists on *Country Song Roundup*'s pages. Industry powerhouse Mae Boren Axton, writer of "Heartbreak Hotel," was another regular contributor to the magazine, writing articles that featured male artists' wives and up-and-coming female artists such as Jo Davis.[34]

The domestic lives of stars were under scrutiny in an era when television shows like *Leave It to Beaver* and *Father Knows Best* touted a suburban domesticity. Certainly, June Cleaver—that suburban icon of taste, respectability, and middle-class status on *Leave It to Beaver*—affected the ways that journalists viewed Kitty Wells and other women. Yet country music's

June Cleaver had her roots in the barn dance radio days. That domestic image was the mountain mother who was the radio barn dance's iconic image: the woman who crooned to her babes as she worked. On the radio, she continued that work, only now she crooned ballads from the mountain South to her audiences. No firm distinction, no absolute dividing line existed between stage and home. Home, at least a fictional one, was also a female performer's stage. This was no more evident than in the case of Lulu Belle Wiseman who was named Radio Queen in a national contest while pregnant with her first child in 1936. Her pregnancy made the mountain mother real and substantial in obvious ways. In the 1950s, however, the mountain mother needed to be transformed for a time and place where suburbs, not war and depression, dominated the imaginations of Americans. *Country Song Roundup* featured female stars like Kitty Wells at home in articles obviously titled, "At Home: Kitty Wells," which featured her cooking and cleaning. "Kitty is a wonderful mother and housekeeper," the magazine gushed, assuring readers that fame had not caused Wells to forget her wifely and motherly duties. Home thus remained a stage for Kitty just as it had done for Lulu Belle.[35]

Other references to domesticity were informal ones that described women who were wives of famous stars or mothers of stars' children: photos pictured Webb Pierce's wife and daughter while Jim Reeves appeared with "wife Mary" in another photo spread.[36] "Meet the Mrs." sketches, which appeared sporadically from April 1952 to January 1954, were more formal examples of defining women as wives and mothers whereby journalists highlighted the women who made country music's men so successful because of their wifely skills. Domesticity did not define these women as performers but instead promoted their husbands' careers. Home seemed, at least at first glance, to be their only stage. Mrs. Ernest Tubb was "a wonderful homemaker and thrills to the responsibility of having to take care of their beautiful home," a home that was "on the outskirts of Nashville in a newly developed section of the city," most likely a new suburb worthy of a country music June Cleaver.[37] At the same time, domestic imagery once again provided cover for women who managed their husbands' careers since domesticity seemed to be more husband management than talent management. Olene Tubb may have made a nice home for Ernest, but she also handled Ernest's career, assisting, as *Country Song Roundup* wrote, "her husband with the necessary details of his trips. She makes constant calls to the airline offices, checking and making reservations for Ernest to fly to his show dates."[38] In 1958 and 1959, similar articles appeared, namely, "The Women Behind the Men" and "Meet Mrs. Faron Young," but without the consistency necessary to make "housewife" the only role open to women.[39] In fact, one anonymous journalist, writing about women's broader duties in the industry, noted that, "It seems that the men in the country field are always getting the glory and headlines," but, "you can be sure, though, there are quite a few women who are doing more than their share in promoting and spreading our favorite type of music."[40]

The Western and suburban images waned by 1955 and 1956 as new country icons surged onto *Country Song Roundup*'s pages: Elvis and his peers singing rock-and-roll music.[41] When these new, younger performers were featured, new audiences were also featured, namely teenagers. *Country Song Roundup* touted the young rock-and-roller like Elvis or Ricky Nelson as well as their female counterparts, especially Brenda Lee and Wanda Jackson. As Elvis, Ricky Nelson, and the Everly Brothers grew in popularity, new articles supplanted the features on fan managers, spotlighting teenagers looking for pen pals—both female and male—who wanted to make friends with those who shared a love of country music in general and for stars such as Nelson or Elvis specifically. Fan club—that group that supported a performer's career—waned in influence, at least on *Country Song Roundup*'s pages, as did its president's influence. Now, individuals reached across pages to other individuals to build relationships with each other rather than societies embracing one performer's commercial success.[42]

As the decline of fan club president suggests, the welcome women received on *Country Song Roundup*'s pages was always within strict limits. First, the big commercial push was and had always been made for men, not women. Star performer, until Kitty Wells proved them wrong in 1952, was a role reserved for Ernest Tubb, Webb Pierce, and other top male stars. The commercially successful man dominated the magazine's covers, and no woman was featured until Jean Shepard appeared with Ferlin Huskey in June 1954. The pairing of the two was not a haphazard choice by any means since, from the industry's inception, men had appeared at public concerts alongside a woman to assure the audience of her morality. This was a ritual *Stand By!* and other magazines ignored when they regularly featured solo women on their covers; journalists considered women essential to the magazine's commercial success because they knew a pretty face sold well.[43] Yet *Country Song Roundup* pictured only a few women on covers after Jean Shepard's appearance, namely Betty Jack Davis after her death from a car accident, Goldie Hill, and Kitty Wells.[44] Second, even though the industry relied on musical sound to sell itself, women's visual appeal was as important as how they sounded. Ugly women, quite frankly, from the earliest days of barn dance radio needed not to apply for stage work, and

Country Song Roundup carried that assumption into the 1950s. Photos and descriptions of women thus were prominent, no matter who wrote the article since the industry standard was so well cemented into place. Singer Jo Davis, Mae Boren Axton wrote, was "a vision of beauty in blonde and blue . . . and as the rays from the stage lights steal gentle caresses of her gold, gold hair and the heavens penetrate the ceiling of the studio to bless her, the audience and televiewers everywhere listen and we know why."[45] The "lovely Jan Crockett is loaded with beauty and plenty of down to earth talent," another photo caption read.[46] The emphasis on beauty was more explicit in 1957 in a series of articles called "Pinning up," which featured attractive female (Wanda Jackson, Jean Shepard) and male (Hank Snow) stars.[47] Moreover, attractiveness was an appeal to men in particular, providing female bodies for men's viewing pleasure. A 1952 article entitled "Eye Appeal," for example, pictured a man gazing literally at the Beaver Valley Sweethearts, Phyllis Brown, Chickie Williams, and other female performers through an optometrist's scope.[48]

That visual appeal was not limited to the articles. Ads that appeared in the margins of articles and on the front and back covers reinforced the assumption that being ugly was bad, but this time aimed their focus on the female readership, linking the purchase of their products to making female readers acceptable to the public. Pimples, dark and oily skin, and overweight women were unsightly; only miracle medicines and crèmes like the Mercolized Wax Cream promised to make those ugly features disappear.[49] Other ads promised women they would increase their chest sizes to the large, angular look favored in the 1950s by using technologically advanced crèmes like "L'Ormone, The Estrogenic Hormone Bust Cream" to manipulate the human body into culturally appropriate standards.[50]

Within these limits, *Country Song Roundup* built Patsy Cline's career during her early days with 4 Star, and Cline was well aware of its influence and its welcome. The magazine first featured her in an article entitled "Hillbilly Queens," in April 1956, and her appearances in the journal became relatively consistent after that, although with little hint that she would become an icon. She appeared in ads for Decca Records, was featured in a December 1957 article alongside the Everly Brothers and Brenda Lee, was named number seven on the list of "Top Ten Females" in the industry in 1956, and was noted as one of the stars who made 1957 a "boom" year for country music.[51] And she was delighted by the attention, knowing that the magazine was helping her achieve her dream of stardom. Letters to her fan club president and newsletters to the fan club members document that excitement. In a May 28, 1956, letter to fan club president, Treva Miller Steinbicker, Patsy wrote, "and in *Country Song Roundup*, [the] Jimmy Rodgers Poll of the 'Top Ten Female Singers,' I was No 7. I'm really happy about that, too."[52]

Patsy Cline's sudden death in an airplane accident in 1963 stopped her career—at least until the 1980s when she was reintroduced to the public, first by the movie *Coal Miner's Daughter* (1980), then by Ellis Nassour's biography (1981), and finally by a rather inept biopic about Cline herself, entitled *Sweet Dreams* (1985). The nearly two decades between her death and resurrection allowed for a "decontextualized" Patsy Cline to emerge, according to scholar Joli Jensen, whereby the 1950s and the grand, though limited, welcome by media such as *Country Song Roundup* was erased. This made it possible for many "posthumous Patsies" to exist, according to whatever context or meaning a given audience preferred.[53] For country music scholars and journalists, their favorite Patsy Cline has tended to be feminist Patsy, no matter the evidence to the contrary. This is no more apparent than in Margaret Jones's biography of Patsy Cline (1994) in which Jones describes a woman with an assertive, bold, and brash personality who was persistent in her pursuit of stardom in a Nashville that was, as Jones calls it, a "boys' club, with boys' games."[54] Ignoring primary source material from the 1950s has, in part, made this interpretation possible, as has using commercial success to identify main characters and actors in country music's narrative. This is another primary source issue because the records recorded in the 1950s are much more accessible than a magazine stuck in a dusty archive. But a 1980s phenomena called "backlash" also helped define Cline as a feminist. As President Ronald Reagan promised Americans a renewed and reinvigorated America, modeled on 1950s domesticity and Cold War politics, he promised to overturn feminist gains from the 1960s and 1970s that had, in his opinion, caused the nation's supposed decline. Calling Patsy a feminist in the 1980s was a political opportunity to reclaim feminism's gains—and reputation—while at the same time, rooting feminism in the 1950s, a time of supposed tranquility, calm, and domestic bliss.[55]

By recontextualizing her—and by this, I mean placing Patsy Cline back into the 1950s industry, as displayed on *Country Song Roundup*'s pages—a different interpretation of her career is possible, especially when reexamining three main assumptions that are wrapped up in the feminist image. The first assumption is that male executives exploited her, her talent, and her sexuality, an implied codicil to the assumption that few women were involved in the country music industry in order to avoid being sexually harassed. The vast number of women *Country Song Roundup* highlighted belies that image as does the wide variety of roles it defined narratively as women's roles. It is also belied by the number of men who mentored Cline in ways that helped, rather than exploited, her. Perhaps a better way to look at industry exploitation would be to look at it from a singer's perspective, rather than from a woman's. The best example is Cline's male counterpart, Roy Clark, who was born a year after Cline and who was someone she worked with in Washington, D.C. Clark also worked with Bill McCall, the notoriously unethical president of 4 Star Records. McCall promised him exclusive use of one song, probably written by McCall, and then promised Cline the same song, again with supposed exclusivity. He did so in order to earn the largest amount of royalties for himself rather than to help the up-and-coming singers. This was devastating for Clark, who believed Mc-Call was investing in Clark's career rather than merely making money for himself; in Patsy's case, she simply refused to record it out of respect to Clark who had already recorded the now-unknown song. Exploitation of singers, unprotected by musicians unions like the American Federation of Musicians, which did protect instrumentalists, was rampant in the industry, and it was only when she contracted with manager Randy Hughes and with producer Owen Bradley that Cline's vulnerability as a *singer* was avoided.[56]

The second hallmark of the feminist Patsy image is the infamous fights with Owen Bradley. Patsy Cline was never a musician, meaning her knowledge of music, scales, and instrumentation was relatively superficial. Her training came on stages in the Moose Lodge circuit in an area circumscribed by Maryland, West Virginia, and Virginia. In short, Patsy was a performer, not a musician, and a confident one at that. Owen Bradley, on the other hand, was a musician, not a performer, who played multiple instruments and was a professional musician (piano) by the time he was fifteen years old.[57] Moreover, his exposure to the big band sound of the 1930s and 1940s caused him to notice Cline's true musical ability: the breadth and range of her voice as well as its tonal quality simply did not fit a music that emphasized a song's narrative over a singer's voice, something typical of 1950s country music.[58] Her voice was more similar to Kay Starr's or Jo Stafford's, other "girl" singers who had sung with bands such as Glenn Miller's, Tommy Dorsey's, or Bob Crosby's. The infamous fights between Cline and Bradley could thus be read as a confident performer, aware of her concert audience's taste, challenging a studio musician whose ear told him something different.

The third hallmark is a version of the performer versus musician argument, but this one focuses on her unwillingness to give up her Western image, particularly her costuming and desire to yodel. Images in *Country Song Roundup* of Roy Rodgers and Dale Evans (etc.) reinforced her commitment to Western clothing styles and musical choices. Moreover, it is not clear whether she bought the Western imagery as part of an ideological struggle with Communist Russia, whereby the frontier man and woman struggled with evil in the form of Native Americans or other evil frontiersmen and won, using American ideals of hard work and ethical behavior. What is clear is that this image charmed her audiences, whether they watched them on the big screen or danced to them at a Moose Lodge event in Hagerstown, Maryland. Cline's reputed unwillingness to shift from Western singer to southern chanteuse was a reaction to her knowledge, gained from standing on stage after stage yodeling her heart out, of her audience's likes and dislikes. What she did not realize was what *Country Song Roundup* did: that the Western image was on the wane because of rock and roll. Bradley was thus offering her a new, innovative singing persona that would survive the collapse of the Western image after rock and roll became popular.[59]

A recontextualized Patsy Cline strips away the veneer of feminism from her career and makes a deeper, more subtle interpretation possible. Primary sources like *Country Song Roundup* are a first step since they display the welcome women received. The range of roles was broad and eclectic; singer, musician, comedienne, journalist, legacy maker, and fan club president all were, narratively at least, roles open to women. Certainly, it was within limits and boundaries of what was considered good womanly behavior: limits, boundaries, and potentials that had been partially inherited from the barn radio genre and by Nashville as the center of country music. But it was in this context that Patsy Cline worked her way up the star ladder, never thinking that successful star singer was *not* an option for her. Perhaps, then, it is time for the country music scholar and journalist alike to look at the industry through Patsy's eyes and see what she saw and experienced.

NOTES

1. Bill C. Malone, *Country Music, U.S.A.,* 2d ed. (Austin: University of Texas Press, 1985), 119. Another example can be found in Charles Wolfe's oral interview with The Girls of the Golden West star Millie Good McCluskey (April 20, 1978, in author's possession) in which he asks her about the pressure to remain home once her children were born. One can almost see the quizzical look on Mrs. McCluskey's face when she responded that she never felt that pressure. See page 8 of transcript, tape 2, side 1.

2. Peter La Chapelle, "Country Music and Domesticity in Cold War Los Angeles," in *A Boy Named Sue: Gender and Country Music,* eds. Kristine M. McCusker and Diane Pecknold, eds. (Jackson: University of Mississippi Press, 2004), 29.

3. Margaret Jones, *Patsy: The Life and Times of Patsy Cline* (New York: Harper-Collins, 1994; New York: De Capo, 1999), 40–41. Quote is on page 34.

4. Barry Lee Pearson and Bill McCulloch, *Robert Johnson: Lost and Found* (Urbana: University of Illinois Press, 2003).

5. Kristine M. McCusker, *Lonesome Cowgirls and Honky-Tonk Angels: The Women of Barn Dance Radio* (Urbana: University of Illinois Press, 2008).

6. For an excellent discussion of how Nashville became the cultural center of country music, see Diane Pecknold, *The Selling Sound: The Rise of the Country Music Industry* (Durham: Duke University Press, 2007).

7. These journals may be found at the Country Music Hall of Fame except for *Stand By!*, which is housed at the Southern Appalachian Archives, Berea College, Berea, Ky. The *Grinder's Switch Gazette* may have been the only fan magazine regularly published for the *Opry*.

8. Jeffrey Lange, *Smile When You Call Me Hillbilly: Country Music's Struggle for Respectability, 1939–1954* (Athens: University of Georgia Press, 2004).

9. Pecknold, *The Selling Sound*, 53–94.

10. Malone, *Country Music, U.S.A.*, 200–13; Pecknold, *The Selling Sound*, 66.

11. Lynn Spigel, *Make Room for TV: Television and the Family Ideal in Postwar America* (Chicago: University of Chicago Press, 1992).

12. See features in *Country Song Roundup* (CSR) 1:1 (July–August 1949): 8–9.

13. See *CSR* issues 1:16 (February 1952): 5, for Lulu Belle Wiseman; 1:7 (July–August 1950): 17, 18, for Rose Maddox, Dale Evans, and Liddie Murphy; 1:10 (February 1951): 12, for the Carter Family; 1:21 (December 1952): 24, for Lindy Rose.

14. No author, "A Star is Born: Kitty Wells," *CSR* 1:21 (December 1952): 9.

15. No author, "Three for the Money," *CSR* 2:45 (August 1956): 6; no author, "WL & SC go WSM," *CSR* 7:51 (August 1947): 10; no author, "Mr. and Mrs. Team," *CSR* 1:39 (January 1955): 62.

16. No author, "Dell Wood: Queen of the Ragtime Piano," *CSR* 10:56 (September 1958): 30.

17. http://www.countrymusichalloffame.com/site/inductees.aspx?cid=196# (accessed August 28, 2009); http://www.countrymusichalloffame.com/site/inductees.aspx?cid=104&search=GO (accessed August 28, 2009); no author, "Folk Music's Top Songwriters," *CSR* 1:26 (October 1953): 6.

18. Judy Canova, "Her Best Gags," *CSR* 1:1 (July–August 1949): 32.

19. No author, "Comedy Capers," *CSR* 1:32 (June 1954): 6, features Lonzo and Oscar, Homer and Jethro, and Stringbean with Minnie Pearl; Minnie Pearl, "Up in the Air with Minnie Pearl," *CSR* 1:7 (1950): 12.

20. No author, "Dee Jay Jamboree," *CSR* 1:42 (February 1956): 23.

21. Richard Slotkin, *Gunfighter Nation: The Myth of the Frontier in Twentieth-Century America* (New York: HarperPerrenial, 1993).

22. No author, "Dale Evans: Western Movie Queen of Song," *CSR* 1:7 (July–August 1951): 18; no author, "That Little Cotton Gal," *CSR* 1:5 (April 1950): 20.

23. Jones, *Patsy*, 166, 187–88.

24. See, for example, no author, "Tex Ritter 'Wandering Minstrel,'" *CSR* 1:3 (December 1949): 13.

25. McCusker, "Dear Radio Friend: Listener Mail and the *National Barn Dance*, 1931–1941," *American Studies* 39 (Summer 1998): 173–95.

26. For a broader discussion of the impact of fan clubs on the country music industry, see Pecknold, *The Selling Sound*, 124–30.

27. No author, "The Fanning Bee: Del Wood," *CSR* 1:34 (September 1954): 17.

28. Willis Glenn, "The President's Report: Report on Roy Acuff," *CSR* 1:36 (January 1955): 14; Delores Klaft, "The President's Report: Report on Pee Wee King," *CSR* 1:37 (March 1955): 21; Wilma Orr, "The President's Report: Report on Rex Allen," *CSR* (March 1955): 20.

29. No author, "The Fanning Bee," *CSR* 1:32 (June 1954): 13.

30. Carrie Rodgers, "My Jimmie," *CSR* 1:20 (October 1952): 10. It was not only country music wives who used their husband's fame to secure their economic independence. Military wives who outlived their husbands, such as La Salle Corbell Pickett (in her case, she outlived husband George Pickett, famed for his disastrous charge at Gettysburg, by nearly sixty years), also used their husbands' fame to control their posthumous image and to maintain their own economic security. See Lesley J. Gordon, *General George E. Pickett in Life and Legend* (Chapel Hill: University of North Carolina, 1998).

31. See, for example, Malone, *Country Music, U.S.A.*

32. "WBAM Deep South Jamboree," *CSR* 1:32 (June 1954): 12.

33. Irene Williams Smith, "Hank's Corner," *CSR* 1:37 (March 1955): 24.

34. Mae Boren Axton, "Jo Davis: Destiny's Darling," *CSR* 10:56 (September 1958): 26; Mae Boren Axton, "The Women Behind the Men," *CSR* 11:60 (May 1959): 24.

35. No author, "At Home: Kitty Wells," *CSR* 2:44 (June 1956): 6.

36. No author, "Spotlight on Webb," *CSR* 1:42 (February 1956): 7; no author, "At Home with the Stars," *CSR* 2:44 (June 1956): 7; La Chapelle, "Country Music and Domesticity."

37. No author, "Meet the Mrs.: Mrs. Ernest Tubb," *CSR* 1:17 (April 1952): 13. See also no author, "Meet the Mrs.: Mrs. Hank Snow," *CSR* 1:18 (June 1952): 9; Wesley Tuttle, "Meet the Mrs.: Marilyn Tuttle," *CSR* 1:20 (October 1952): 13. "Meet the Mrs." articles appeared primarily in 1952 and 1953, although one appeared in 1954.

38. "Mrs. Ernest Tubb," *CSR* 13.

39. No author, "Meet Mrs. Faron Young," *CSR* 10:56 (September 1958): 14; Mae Boren Axton, "The Women behind the Men," *CSR* 11:60 (May 1959): 24.

40. No author, "Women in the News," *CSR* 1:19 (August 1952): 28. See also "Women in the News," *CSR* 1:21 (December 1952): 17.

41. See Michael Bertrand, *Race, Rock and Elvis* (Urbana: University of Illinois Press, 2000), for Elvis's popularity and his representation of his audience.

42. No author, "Elvis Presley 'Win a Date' Contest," *CSR* 3:47 (December 1956): 10.

43. Front Cover, *CSR* 1:32 (June 1954).

44. See *CSR* front covers for 1:34 (September 1954) and 1:38 (May 1955).

45. Mae Boren Axton, "Jo Davis: Destiny's Darling," *CSR* 10:56 (September 1958): 26.

46. Picture with caption, *CSR* 10:54 (February 1958): 9.

47. "Pinning 'Em Up: Jean Shepard," *CSR* 8:52 (October 1957): 16; "Pinning Up Hank Snow," *CSR* 4:48 (February 1957): 18; "Pinning Up Wanda Jackson," *CSR* 4:48 (February 1957): 19.

48. No author, "Eye Appeal," *CSR* 1:6 (February 1952): 14.

49. Ad, "Get Rid of Dark or Oily Skin, Ugly Pimples, Freckles—Fast!" *CSR* 11:58 (January 1959): 25.

50. Ad, "L'Ormone, The Estrogenic Hormone Bust Cream," *CSR* 1:1 (July–August 1949): 26.

51. No author, "Hillbilly Queens: Patsy Cline," *CSR* 1:43 (April 1956): 21; ad, Decca Country and Western Records, *CSR* 10:54 (February 1958): 11; "Country Musics," *CSR* 9:53 (December 1957): 18; "Jimmie Rodgers Poll Winner," *CSR* 2:45 (August 1956): 11; "Country Music's Boom Year," *CSR* 7:51 (August 1957): 19.

52. Cindy Hazen and Mike Freeman, eds. *Love Always, Patsy: Patsy Cline's Letters to a Friend* (New York: Berkley Books, 1999), May 28, 1956 (this book has no page numbers).

53. Joli Jensen, "Patsy Cline's Crossovers: Celebrity, Reputation, and Feminine Identity," in *A Boy Named Sue*, 120, 128.

54. Jones, *Patsy*, 73.

55. Susan Faludi, *Backlash: The Undeclared War against American Women* (New York: Crown Books, 1991).

56. Jones, *Patsy*, 52–54.

57. Robert K. Oermann, "Owen Bradley," *The Encyclopedia of Country Music*, ed. Paul Kingsbury (Oxford: Oxford University Press, 1998), 50.

58. Jones, *Patsy*, 86, 109.

59. Jones, *Patsy*, 97.

THE EARLY YEARS: HARD TIMES AND GOOD TIMES FOR COUNTRY MUSIC IN 1950S WASHINGTON, D.C.

George Hamilton IV

IN JUNE OF 1956 I HAD RECORDED my first nationally released record—a teen ballad, written by John D. Loudermilk, called "A Rose and a Baby Ruth." There was a young law student at Duke University in Durham, North Carolina, who heard it on a local radio station. "Rose" was recorded on the campus of the University of North Carolina in Chapel Hill and was first played in that region. The student was one Jan Gay, who happened to be the son of Connie B. Gay, producer of the *Jimmy Dean Show* on WMAL-TV in Washington, D.C., and also the manager of Jimmy Dean and Patsy Cline. Jan Gay sent a copy of "A Rose and a Baby Ruth" to his dad in D.C., and soon I was invited to come to Washington in the summer of 1956 to be a guest on the Jimmy Dean *Town and Country Jamboree* at the Capitol Arena on Saturday evenings. The *Jamboree* was televised by WMAL-TV on a regional network, and Patsy Cline, who was featured on the show, was already a pretty significant country star in the Washington-Baltimore area, mainly due to her television exposure on Jimmy's show. When I first met Patsy on the *Jamboree*, in the summer of 1956, she was already a "seasoned professional," having played the honky tonks and bars around Washington and the VFW halls, Moose Lodges, and volunteer fire department dances in Northern Virginia and Maryland, all around the D.C. area for several years.

I had just finished my first year at the University of North Carolina and showed up at the *Jamboree* looking every inch the nineteen-year-old college freshman that I was—all decked out in my college blazer with a Roman numeral "IV" on the breast pocket, button-down-collar shirt, tie, and Bass Weejuns (penny loafers). Some folks in my early days even called me the "Ivy League Hillbilly," would you believe?

All the above is to put into "perspective" my first meeting with Patsy Cline. She was singing "Life's Railway to Heaven" on Jimmy Dean's television show, which was my grandfather's favorite song (he was a "railroad man"). I fell in love with her immediately! Before you jump to any conclusions, may I confess that Patsy probably thought I was a bit of a wimp! I was a shy, awkward, "wet behind the ears" nineteen-year-old and, again, she was a seasoned professional in every sense of the word.

She walked up to me and said something like, "I'm Patsy Cline. Who are you?" When I said, "George Hamilton IV," her response (with a hearty laugh) was "the *Fourth*? What kind of country singer are you?" When I assured her I *was* a country singer, she replied, "Where are your cowboy boots?" I said, "I ain't got none—I'm from North Carolina!" Patsy stood there, grinnin' from ear to ear, and said, "Who do you think you are, Hoss?—the Pat Boone of country music?" (She used to call me "Mr. Goody 2 Shoes," as well.) From that moment onward, we were good friends!

Patsy was too young to be a "mother figure" to me, but she certainly was like a "big sister." If she liked you, you knew it. But get ready for some "teasing," 'cause Patsy loved to tease her friends, play practical jokes, and be like "one of the guys." If she *didn't* like you, she wasted very little time pretending to. You always knew where you stood with Patsy! I transferred from UNC to American University in Washington, D.C., in the fall of 1956 and became a "regular" on the Jimmy Dean show along with Patsy, Mary Klick, Dale Turner, and the Texas Wild Cats. Although I was in college in D.C., I appeared on Jimmy Dean's daily local TV show and the Saturday night *Town and Country Jamboree* with Patsy, as well as playing a lot of honky tonks, beer joints, bars, and dance halls on the weekends in the D.C. area for several years, alongside Patsy, Jimmy, and the gang.

D.C. was a "hotbed" of country music in the fifties. Keep in mind there were thousands of young folks—government workers—from the South, who were "homesick" for their hometowns and loved to go to the bars and dances to listen to the music they grew up on and loved. Country was—and still is—*their* music, and Patsy, Jimmy, and the Texas Wild Cats were right in the middle of that, providing the "sound of the South" during what some folks now call "the golden age of country music"!

I was privileged and *blessed* to watch a great artist at work up close during those days, as I traveled with Patsy and Jimmy to all the various places they were performing at in the late fifties.

Connie B. Gay, former manager of Patsy Cline and the founding president of the Country Music Association, once referred to Patsy as "the greatest female *singer* ever to walk the face of the Earth!" (He didn't say "country singer," by the way.) Connie B. Gay was quite possibly right. There are many of us who would certainly not argue the point! Patsy was "a woman ahead of her time"—a "pre-feminist" woman who made a place for female singers—front and center—in what was very much a man's world in her day. She didn't "open the doors" for women in country music; she "kicked them down"! She paved the way and made it much easier for Loretta, Tammy, Dolly, Reba, and all who followed her.

In her day, the girl singers were mostly "window dressing" on shows with the male country stars. Patsy would have none of that. She was determined to play a starring role on the shows she was on, and she *did*! Many of us "guys" had to get used to being an "opening act" for Patsy in those days! And we felt privileged to be so!

I want to make clear, as one who was "there" in the fifties and the early sixties—Patsy and I joined the *Grand Ole Opry* the same year, and I toured with her just before her untimely death. In my memory, Patsy Cline was a *Lady*. She was *strong*—not "tough," but she had a big heart—a *kind* heart—she teased me, but she mentored and encouraged me. She lent her stage costumes and even her wigs to other struggling "Girl Singers" like Dottie West and June Carter. She was never "petty or small" in her relations with her peers and competitors. We all respected Patsy Cline and loved her—and we all now miss her!

CHAPTER 5

PATSY CLINE

A Television Star

Douglas Gomery

Introduction

On December 31, 1955, Patsy Cline first appeared on Connie B. Gay's *Town and Country Jamboree*, a local Washington, D.C., television show. She would perform virtually every Saturday night for a year. This would give her experience so that when she appeared on the national broadcast of CBS's *Arthur Godfrey's Talent Scouts* on January 21, 1957, she was an experienced TV performer. The win on Godfrey provided the needed breakthrough of her career and made her a star. But Cline's earlier work on TV was the key development in her career. It enabled her to move from local clubs, to regional TV popularity, and finally to national television stardom.

Virginia Patterson Hensley had become "Patsy Cline" when in 1952 bandleader Bill Peer named her "Patsy," and in March 1953 she married Gerald Cline. She struggled to make a living by singing in Moose halls, fire stations, carnivals, and roadhouses. She was a professional but on the margins. A Washington, D.C., music entrepreneur, Gay then made stardom possible for Cline. He was a deejay for a radio station in suburban Arlington, Virginia, across the Potomac River from Washington. WARL-AM was one of the first country music radio stations in the United States. Gay had a house band—Jimmy Dean and his Texas Wildcats. Gay then hired Mary Klick to play acoustic bass with Dean and sing "girl songs" to give Dean, the principal vocalist, a rest.

Gay was always on the lookout for a second "girl singer," but first he needed to mount a TV show of more than an hour. He found a hit with the three-hour *Town and Country Jamboree* on Saturday nights on Channel 7, the ABC affiliate in Washington. Many think of Nashville as the home of country music, but more country music on television came out of Washington than Nashville.

Why Washington, D.C.?

First, Patsy Cline lived within the range of over-the-air TV signals from Washington. She probably saw her first TV at G & M Music appliance store in downtown Winchester. Her family was too poor to own a set and too oriented toward the radio. But stores were displaying TVs in their windows throughout the period her family lived in Winchester.

After Patsy set up married life with Cline in March 1953 in Frederick, Maryland, she was even closer to Washington. The Cline family was well-off and owned a TV set that Patsy would have inevitably watched. She later told many interviewers of her early interest in appearing on *Arthur Godfrey's Talent Scouts*. This CBS Monday night program was the number-one show of 1952 and famous for making stars out of struggling professionals.

Yet historians now tell us only of Washington as a site of news events, most notably the infamous televised Army-McCarthy hearings. The networks promoted this image so that broadcasting from the nation's capital counted as part of their "public service." The Federal Communications Commission (FCC) recognized: "Since Washington is the nation's capital there are many important events occurring here which are of great interest to audiences throughout the United States."[1]

But Washington, D.C., functioned as far more. It was important as a growing vital urban place as TV developed, but it was also *the* place where FCC Commissioners, members of Congress, and the president watched what they had wrought—and reacted. On a daily basis, policymakers monitored local Washington television closely, beginning in 1946 when the first experimental TV station in the nation's capital literally began operation from a hotel across the street from the FCC's headquarters. Day after day officials walked over to see how TV worked and then returned to their offices to further ponder the politics of license allocation. Regularly thereafter, members of Congress appeared on early discussion shows. President Dwight Eisenhower even telephoned local news anchors to comment on their coverage of events. By their example and presence, local Washington stations offered feedback and influenced national communications policy far more than any other set of stations in the United States.[2]

The commission looked to Washington TV stations also to live up to their local programming obligations. Since, as historian Howard Gillette has written, Washington "served as a workshop in which to try out new policy initiatives," I argue that historians of mass communication should carefully analyze local television history in the nation's capital because that is where policymakers used and judged the new medium in their daily lives.[3]

Moreover, the formal allocation to D.C. set in motion procedures that established precedents for what the commission expected when it chose among competing applicants for licenses through the late 1940s and early 1950s. In April 1946 the commission used its ruling about D.C. to explain its application of "Blue Book" precepts in general, and "localism" policy in particular. The commission noted in this pioneering decision for TV "maximum opportunity for local expression and development of community activity [should be] afforded."[4]

The Washington metro area, reached throughout by TV signals, represented most of the typical traits of twentieth-century urban development. Carl Abbott reminded us in his *American Historical Review* study of the nation's capital: "Washington as everyday community has remained embedded in its regional environment. Despite frequent comments about its isolation from the American mainstream, [Washington's] residents have maintained many old regional relationships while accommodating and constructing new claims and connections."[5]

It is important to note that during the late 1940s and early 1950s, Washington was richer, more suburbanized, and more racially divided than the average American city. Because its boundaries are fixed by federal law, unlike most other large cities, the District of Columbia never expanded beyond its original borders, following the suburbs. As a consequence, after World War II the percentage of metro area citizens living inside the District constantly fell. At the end of World War II, two of three metro residents lived inside D.C. By 1960, after the region's population doubled, and television was a presence in nearly every household, only one of three metro residents resided inside the District. The well-off and white fled, leaving D.C. a poor black enclave, which by 1960 had become the first major jurisdiction in the United States with a majority African American population. For TV stations, however, the total metro area remained more than three-quarters white.[6]

But in one crucial aspect Washington, D.C., was different. In 1790 Thomas Jefferson and Alexander Hamilton knew they were setting up a southern capital city, and until reapportionment rulings of the 1960s, southern representatives and senators dominated the Congress. Yet at the same time that TV was becoming a force in American society, an influx of northerners transformed Washington. Indeed Abbott finds the constantly changing border status of the nation's capital its defining post–World War II characteristic as a community. By the time that John F. Kennedy arrived as president, Washington was widely known as the southernmost northern city and the northernmost southern city. The local history of the coming of TV to the nation's capital as a community must deal with this ever-growing migration and community transformation.[7]

Here, we ought to look to Ray Allen's "Back Home: Southern Identity and African-American Gospel Quartet Performance," found in Wayne Franklin and Michael Steiner's anthology *Mapping American Culture* to inform a new urban history—as much as the work of Sam Bass Warner. Allen analyzes the role of music in easing the stress of urban accommodation for working-class folks who had come to the big city from the rural South. In the 1950s, as in Allen's study, the majority of Washingtonians had been born elsewhere, principally the South. Since many stayed and located in Washington because it seemed the border South, they continued to identify themselves as southerners. Frequently because of the proximity of Washington to main rail lines south, they would travel back home for family reunions, weddings, and funerals, thus permitting family, social, church, and musical networks to remain intact, despite geographical dislocation. For southerners residing in Washington, on the border of their native South, music played an essential role in constructing and maintaining a mythic vision of the rural South. Songs were often filled with nostalgic images of the old southern home place, the beautiful hills, the devoted family, and the old-time religion. These powerful images comforted southerners confronting the frenzy that was Washington, D.C., fighting wars in Europe, the South Pacific, and later Korea, as well as dealing with a world in which the city itself was under assault from migration to the suburbs and the rebuilding of a new form of city life.[8]

Why Channel 7—the ABC Affiliate in Washington, D.C.?

Four VHF television stations in the nation's capital were all on the air before 1950. Two were in the hands of electronics manufacturers with designs on cornering TV set sales. The DuMont network's WTTG came on line in 1946; Radio Corporation of America and its subsidiary NBC followed a year later with WNBW. Local newspapers owned the other two stations. WMAL began broadcasting in 1947, licensed to the then-dominant after-noon daily, the *Washington Evening Star*, while in 1949 WOIC went on the air, originally licensed to Bamberger Broadcasting but soon sold and in the hands of the *Washington Post*.[9]

Notable for media historians, the *Washington Evening Star* and the *Washington Post* covered the local TV scene with a great deal of space and care because both papers owned TV stations. In response, their rivals, the *Washington Times-Herald* and the *Washington Daily News*, often investigated the emerging TV scene, knowing that two of the four stations were in the hands of their press rivals. Thus, the newspaper coverage of early TV in Washington is rich. As indicated by ratings data and oral histories, metro residents quickly and lovingly embraced television.[10]

By 1954 nearly two hundred thousand homes contained TV sets, representing more than three-quarters of the area's households. The number of TV households rose steadily each year as Washingtonians of all income classes embraced the medium with four channels on the air by the close of the 1940s. By 1958 there were television sets in 90 percent of Washington's living rooms. Television had assumed its central position in the cultural landscapes of the United States and its capital city.[11]

Through the early 1950s station owners set the agenda for the four stations in D.C. NBC used the station it owned and operated as a means to build prestige in front of policymakers. In 1946 John Royal, an NBC vice president, testified that his company wanted to "carry the sight and sound of Washington events into every American home that can be reached by a television network. . . . As a source of television program material, Washington is a city which has no parallel in the United States." The record indicates WNBW carried many special events such as telecasting the opening of Congress each January and the presidential inaugural ceremonies every fourth January. WNBW did not ignore programming for local viewers but aired little more than local college football and basketball games and a few talking-heads discussion shows in off-peak hours.[12]

The *Washington Post*'s WTOP affiliated with CBS and during the early 1950s played corporate catch-up to the long-dominant newspaper in the D.C. market, the *Washington Evening Star*. Thus management chose to draw profits from TV rather than spend money televising either special events or live local programming. WTOP did even less than WNBW for local programming. During these early years the *Washington Post* shamelessly used newspaper space to promote CBS network fare in order to build up profits. The *Post* splashed daily advertisements for CBS shows across its entertainment page while listing—in small type—what the competition had to offer.

Owned and operated by the DuMont Television Network, WTTG was the progeny of neither a rich manufacturer nor an expanding media empire. Without much network programming to fill its day and with no support from newspaper promotion, WTTG management did present a great deal of varied, live local programming. In 1947 WTTG began offering regular telecasts of Washington Senators baseball games. For the opening game of the 1947 season, the station remained on the air for thirty hours, giving thousands of D.C. residents their first true taste of TV. But DuMont presented little in the way of major network programming. Thus sports filled the evenings and weekends, and at other time slots viewers saw old movies and local productions like *Georgetown University Forum*. The latter offered no classroom instruction but rather a weekly discussion by government officials berating Communist threats. But local, inexpensive programming garnered sympathy for DuMont officials while seeking valuable government contracts.[13]

In sum, an analysis of the applications for license renewal by these three stations reveals that through the early years WTTG always carried the most live, local programming. In 1954, for example, local shows constituted a third of total programming. WNBW and WTOP, relying on NBC and CBS, respectively, counted half that.

The Grand Local Experiment

But local programming did thrive in the nation's capital at WMAL-TV, the ABC affiliate of the *Washington Evening Star*. Because of a limited network schedule, WMAL had a large programming hole to fill during its early history, and so its local programming totals ran closer to WTTG-TV than to either WTOP-TV or WNBW-TV. Moreover, the *Washington Evening Star* was rich enough to afford to wait for ABC to grow. During the years immediately after World War II, the *Washington Evening Star* represented as successfully profitable a daily as existed in the United States at the time. As a consequence, the *Star*'s local owners saw TV fulfilling the same supplementary role radio long had: a means of promoting the newspaper and protecting its circulation leadership. Prestige took the place of profits as the *Washington Evening Star* boasted about WMAL's news accomplishments, heralding in 1949, at the end of its second year on the air, the prestige of being the first TV station in the land to broadcast a documentary on the Nuremberg trials, the first to televise a hearing from Capitol Hill, and the first to televise from inside the White House.[14]

Through its first decade on the air, WMAL experimented with many forms of local programming, from the talking heads of *Meet Your Congress* to the highly targeted *Modern Woman*. Ratings were regularly anemic; no genre seemed to work save one—country music. During the 1955–1956 and 1956–1957 TV seasons, WMAL's live, locally produced *Town and Country Time* and *Town and Country Jamboree* ranked as the favorites of Washingtonians. Beyond the marble museums and halls of government deliberations, in the mid-1950s Washington, D.C., ranked with Nashville as a country music capital. Examining this case of an unexpected but successful example of what the FCC had called for in programs of "local interests, activities, and talent" can tell us much about how TV worked on a local level during its emerging years as the dominant mass medium of the late twentieth century.

Ray Allen's "Back Home: Southern Identity and African-American Gospel Quartet Performance" clearly shows that a complete understanding of the role of African American gospel quartets in New York City requires an examination of black migration and the music of new urbanites drawing on ties to the culture of the rural South. Allen shows us how geography informed both social history (migration and settlement) and music history (musical forms reminding one of "back home"). An analogous point comes from studying country music and television in a community on the edge of both North and South: Washington, D.C. WMAL's average of an hour of country music local programming per day in 1956 fulfilled important functions for anxious middle-class white citizens of the national capital metro region, many of whom had come to D.C. from the South looking for work, many of whom were fleeing to the suburbs to escape African American neighbors.[15]

Poor whites were part of a labor-intensive economy. Rather than imagining working-class whites thronging Capitol Hill, think of them fetching books at the Library of Congress or helping print government documents at the Government Printing Office. Indeed southerners of all classes labored all over the District of Columbia. No city lured more southerners off their farms than nearby Washington, D.C. Overwhelmed by the city, new immigrants often felt a sense of loss, and their longing for the familiar rural life led them to embrace cultural forms they had left behind. White southerners, moving to Washington yearned to see and hear country music of the South.[16]

Televising eight hours a week of locally produced, live country music was certainly not what the *Washington Evening Star* had envisioned for WMAL. But by the close of the 1953–1954 TV season, the paper had grown frustrated watching rival stations make more money and so hired Booz, Allen, Hamilton to suggest ways of increasing profits. Consultant Fred Houwink delivered his report during the summer of 1954. The *Star*'s management liked what he had to say and hired Houwink as the new general manager of WMAL. Houwink followed his own advice and promptly boosted WMAL's signal reach. This meant higher ratings, greater revenues, and an instant increase in profits. Policymakers noticed the change; FCC commissioner John Doerfer appeared on air to help dedicate the new "Super Power Channel 7."[17]

Houwink next looked for new programming. He had already noticed Connie B. Gay, a local radio personality who pioneered the country format in the D.C. area and had successfully tapped into the desires of transplanted white southerners for music from back home. Gay had moved his radio stars into DAR Constitution Hall and filled the place. His Club Hillbilly in suburban Prince Georges County, Maryland, regularly turned away customers. "Hillbilly Cruises" down the Potomac River helped make Jimmy Dean a star. Area fans also flocked to hear other local discoveries: guitarist Roy Clark and "girl singer" Patsy Cline.[18]

Houwink knew that throughout cities on the "border South," where rural southerners had moved, advertisers long supported barn dances on radio. Moving them over to TV made sense: costs of production were low and advertisers available. Case after case suggested that local beer distributors and auto dealers would pay top dollar to purchase time. After only weeks on the job as WMAL-TV's general manager, Houwink contacted Gay, and on an otherwise quiet Monday night in January 1955, *Town and Country Time*, starring Jimmy Dean, premiered at 5:00 P.M. Five nights a week, Dean and company faced off against "Pinky Lee" on WRC, and a B-western movie on WTOP. Not surprisingly, the *Washington Post* did not even mention the debut of *Town and Country Time*, while the *Washington Evening Star* gave nearly a full page to herald the top "western and Country Music program on television. Local! Live!"[19]

Town and Country Time moved into second place in its time slot. Local advertisers loved the Arbitron surveys, which indicated three or four persons crowding around their TV sets (more women than men) to see and hear Dean, his band the Texas Wildcats, and local and national guest stars.

No one was surprised that ten months later WMAL-TV launched a three-hour live Saturday night *Town and Country Jamboree*. The *Washington Evening Star* regularly proffered huge advertisements on its television page, heralding the appearance of big name guests, from country music legends Roy Acuff and Kitty Wells to newcomers such as Johnny Cash and Elvis Presley. Overnight the *Jamboree* moved WMAL into second place in the late Saturday night hours.[20]

Town and Country programming helped Houwink reap the rewards of a local economic boom taking place in the D.C. suburbs. At this point the migration to suburban Maryland and Virginia made Washington the second fastest growing metro area in the nation. During one stretch of the early 1950s, enough buildings had gone up in the D.C. suburbs to house all the families in Jacksonville, Florida, or Sacramento, California. The well-off whites in a booming Bethesda, Maryland, and a flourishing Fairfax County, Virginia, had made Washington a metro area with the second highest family income and highest retail sales per family in the nation. And these new suburbanites loved watching Jimmy Dean and company on TV.[21]

As the 1956–1957 TV season commenced in September 1956, ratings were so good that Gay, with Houwink's consent, mounted a third show, *Town and Country Matinee*, starring George Hamilton IV, which aired each weekday afternoon. A college sophomore, Hamilton was Gay's discovery, a good-looking "boy" from back home in North Carolina who was to be the *Town and Country* empire's answer to that unprecedented musical phenomenon, another white southern teen heart throb, Elvis Presley. *TV Guide*'s annual preview edition celebrated *Town and Country* as a true local success story, describing how crowds of supposedly sophisticated Washingtonians lined up each Saturday night to get a chance to be a part of the *Town and Country Jamboree*.[22]

Gay aspired to expand his empire and wealth. During the first three months of 1957, he convinced CBS to let him produce a live morning show to go up against NBC's long-running morning hit, *Today*. Jimmy Dean, George Hamilton IV, and the gang premiered *Country Style* at 7:00 A.M. on Monday, April 8, 1957, live from a Washington, D.C., studio. They repeated the telecast at 8:00 A.M. for the West Coast. *Variety* noted that there was "nothing Hayseed About Connie Gay" and heralded the possibility that like Lawrence Welk emerging from Los Angeles eighteen months earlier, a "local [TV] show breaking into network TV" might become a hit. Meanwhile at WMAL-TV, Houwink replaced *Town and Country Jamboree* with a late movie, and *Town and Country Time* with the syndicated TV show *Three Musketeers*. Houwink saw this decision as a low-cost alternative aimed at children.[23]

The Arthur Godfrey Television Colossus

As the 1954–1955 TV season commenced, *TV Guide* called Godfrey "television's No. 1 male entertainer." Godfrey achieved this distinction with a variety show each morning, Monday through Friday. He also had a variety show on Wednesday nights, but his most popular show was *Talent Scouts*. In 1957, it was the lead-in to the number-one TV show in the United States, *I Love Lucy*. With these two programs CBS dominated TV ratings.

Because CBS owned the Columbia record label, CBS owner William S. Paley pushed Godfrey to discover and feature pop talent. CBS did not want just to attract country music fans but to feature singers who appealed to the nation at large. To discover crossover singers, Godfrey tried everything, even a handful of singers who were sold and publicized as country acts.[24]

Most significantly, in the middle of May 1956, Jack Carney, Godfrey's producer and chief aide for *Talent Scouts*, took a medical leave, with Janette Davis "temporarily" taking his duties. By the end of 1956 Carney was dead, and Godfrey's new *Talent Scouts* crew was thus wholly new—from top to bottom. As a pop singer from the South, Davis was on the lookout for female singers like Patsy Cline.[25]

It was well known that Davis was past her prime as a singer, but she was loyal, and Godfrey promoted her. Davis—a husky-voiced, brown-eyed, auburn-haired Dinah Shore–like singer—had started with Godfrey in 1946. Growing up in Pine Bluff, Arkansas, she won amateur contests and a radio contract, and she supported her family. After several local shows and a family move to Illinois, she got her first break with CBS-owned and -operated WBBM-AM in Chicago. After the end of the World War II, she struck out on her own and moved to New York just, as luck would have it, when CBS and Godfrey were auditioning "girl singers" for his CBS show. She had married at age nineteen, quickly divorced, and settled in as a well-paid divorcee making at one point a reported $10,000 week from CBS.[26]

Davis made Godfrey feel like nothing had changed. The one group to whom he remained loyal as they to him were his core band members: guitarist Reno Palmier, organist Lee Erwin, clarinetist Johnny Mince, trombonist Sy Shaffer, and bassist Gene Traxler. More a small ensemble than a band, this combo played any form of popular music. Davis kept the well-oiled machine chugging along. Godfrey, for the record, indirectly praised her matter-of-factly: "The *Talent Scouts* show on Monday nights requires absolutely no effort [for me] other than the 30 minutes on the air." He still arrived at 8:25 P.M., and left at 9:05 P.M. Godfrey was comfortable battling the press, as Davis and the musicians kept the express train rolling.[27]

Commentator Andy Rooney best summarized Godfrey's place in TV history: "The most thoroughly forgotten man in the history of television is Arthur Godfrey. CBS has bought the Broadway studio from which Godfrey's two nighttime shows emanated and they've named it the Ed Sullivan Theater. Ed Sullivan's show, 'Toast of the Town,' was done at that theater, too, but someone has forgotten that both Arthur Godfrey's 'Talent Scouts' on Monday nights and 'Arthur Godfrey and His Friends' on Wednesday nights were more popular and got better ratings than Sullivan's 'Toast of the Town.'" Rooney confessed he never liked Godfrey personally, but for the five years Rooney wrote for Godfrey there was no bigger star on television in the United States.[28]

From the beginning Arthur Godfrey and his assistants were regularly inundated by agents and talent impresarios seeking to gain a spot on *Talent Scouts*. Pop singers did anything they could to get on the show. Male crooners such as Tony Bennett and African American female singers such as Diahann Carroll took their breaks by way of *Talent Scouts*. Patsy Cline knew as she became a professional singer that the way to a national break could really be accomplished only by way of *Talent Scouts*.

Godfrey embraced the female side of pop singing. In the early 1950s, there was no singer more popular than Rosemary Clooney. Born in Maysville, Kentucky, she first took to regional fame on WLW in Cincinnati. With a victory on *Talent Scouts*, she also then began to record for the CBS-owned Columbia record label and covered country hits like "Half As Much" (by Hank Williams). Clooney was so hot that on February 23, 1953, she made the cover of *Time* magazine.[29]

But Godfrey himself preferred female quartets, not soloists. We know this because he had helped take *Talent Scouts* winners, the Chordettes, to the pop charts in the early 1950s. Their records were familiar to Patsy Cline. These four Sheboygan, Wisconsin, women sounded like a barbershop quartet. Carol Busman, baritone vocals; her sister-in-law Janet Ertel, bass vocals; Jinny Osborn, tenor vocals; and Dorothy Schwartz, lead vocals, were Godfrey regulars through the early 1950s appearing on his morning and evening variety shows. They left only in October 1953 when Janet Ertel and Arthur Godfrey bandleader Archie Bleyer announced their marriage. Godfrey fired Bleyer and replaced the Chordettes with the sound-alike McGuire Sisters.

On Bleyer's Cadence record company, the Chordettes went on to score hits with "Mr. Sandman," "Lollipop," and "Born to Be with You." Indeed the Chordettes gave Cadence its first number-one record in 1954 with "Mr. Sandman," a song that, more than any of the group's other hits, reflected the influence of barbershop quartet singing on their sound. On December 6, 1954, it became number one on *Billboard*'s pop charts. The song, in fact, uses the bell chord—one of barbershop singing's favorite embellishments—as its central motif. Interestingly, the male voice representing Mr. Sandman heard on the record was none other than Bleyer. The next big hit for the Chordettes came in 1956 with their recording of "Eddie My Love," which made it into the top twenty. In the wake of the sensation they had created with "Mr. Sandman," the Chordettes found themselves in demand throughout the show business world. They made innumerable appearances on television variety shows, including those hosted by Ed Sullivan. Later in 1956, the Chordettes enjoyed a major hit with "Born to Be with You," which made it into the top ten. Patsy Cline wanted the same national exposure from *Arthur Godfrey's Talent Scouts* as achieved by the Chordettes.[30]

Godfrey would push even nontraditional music into the mainstream. For example, on November 12, 1951, polka legend Frankie Yankovic won. He and his polka band "The Yanks" beat out a Hispanic opera baritone and an African American soprano. Mrs. June Yankovic as their scout "brought" her husband (an accordionist) and the small five-member band to do music popular only in Great Lakes–area cities. Yankovic had begun his career playing socials in Cleveland's ethnic neighborhoods. He grew up in the Slovene-Italian section and in time became the best-known practitioner of Slovenian-style polka, which is heavy on the accordion, clarinet and saxophone. (Polish-style polka features accordions and trumpets and has a faster beat.) "The beat that I gave it was different. It was acceptable to teen-agers as well as the older folks," Yankovic said. "I took the real old-time polkas and modernized them." This is exactly what Patsy Cline would do with country music.[31]

Tony Bennett was a hit-maker through the 1950s. His *Talent Scouts* exposure launched a remarkable half-century career. Anthony Dominick Benedetto was born in August 1926 in Queens, New York, the son of a tailor. In 1951 he won *Cash Box*'s award for Best Male Vocalist for his crossover version of country singer-composer Hank Williams's "Cold, Cold Heart." Bennett took a country hit and made it a pop hit. Patsy Cline would do the same thing with her appearance on *Talent Scouts*.

As seen in Tony Bennett's autobiography, here was a classic rags-to-riches tale that would have been well known to Patsy Cline. Like Virginia Hensley, Anthony Benedetto changed his name, first to Joe Bari and then Tony Bennett. He started out as a jazz singer in Greenwich Village in New York City with the likes of Billie Holiday and caught the eye of a *Talent Scouts* producer.

With a distinctively husky baritone voice, Bennett crooned his way into the hearts of listeners with such 1950s hits as "Boulevard of Broken Dreams" and "Blue Velvet." Yet despite the rise of a new form of pop music—led by Elvis Presley, who started as a country singer but transformed country into rock and roll—Bennett crossed over on multiple *Billboard* charts with his 1962 song "I Left My Heart in San Francisco."[32]

Significantly, in March 1955, Godfrey's staff turned down Elvis Presley. One of Presley's staffers, Elliott Kozak, recalled that Tom Parker, Elvis's longtime manager, spent a great deal of time trying to get Elvis on *Talent Scouts*. As Kozak witnessed, Parker and company "took [Presley] down the freight elevator to the CBS office, where Elvis auditioned for [Janette Davis], a girl singer and Godfrey's girl Friday. Elvis sang one bar and was told, 'Don't call us, we'll call you.'" Elvis was crushed. But Colonel Parker brushed the rejection aside and told Elvis he would get him on national TV somehow, and he did. (Ironically in 2002, rock acts would play atop the marquee and inside the former Godfrey *Talent Scouts* theater—as part of David Letterman's late night show.)[33]

Yet Janette Davis was smart enough to realize *Talent Scouts* would need a new musical formula, and as a native of Arkansas, she deemed it would come from country music. A break had commenced, and the later Godfrey *Talent Scouts* era would focus on discovering those who would—as we look back now—become the cornerstones of the "crossover Nashville Sound." This strategy peaked in both music and ratings with Patsy Cline's win on January 21, 1957.

Janette Davis first found talent on Washington, D.C., television with her booking of Patsy Cline's local costar George Hamilton IV. During the summer of 1956, Hamilton recorded "A Rose and a Baby Ruth" at the University of North Carolina, and by the fall of 1956 it was a hit. In early October 1956, Janette Davis called and George did an audition, a folksy self-composition "I've Got a Secret." Here seemed the ultimate crossover act, like Pat Boone with a touch of Elvis. On October 15, 1956, on *Talent Scouts* Hamilton's girl friend and later his wife, Tinky, appeared as his scout. He won and for a time was a substitute Pat Boone. But in time Hamilton made the natural move to Nashville, had a single hit, "Abilene," appeared on the *Grand Ole Opry*, and made a career for himself on the margins of country music. It would be his fellow Washington, D.C., performer—Patsy Cline who would become the legend.[34]

An Internet search for *Arthur Godfrey's Talent Scouts* produces more hits for Patsy Cline than for Godfrey himself. Where are singers Margo McKinnon and Jerry Antes? Both had the misfortune to appear on January 21, 1957, with Cline on the program. Neither became famous, while Patsy Cline has become an international icon. Simply put, Patsy Cline proved one of Arthur Godfrey's greatest discoveries.

December 1956 turned out to be her lucky month. Godfrey conducted her "audition" himself. With a home in nearby Leesburg, Virginia, he is reported to have watched one of Cline's Washington country music TV performances. Probably on December 27, 1956—that Monday morning—at her mother's home in Winchester, the phone rang, and it was Janette Davis calling. Patsy Cline was booked for Monday, January 21, 1957, but needed a "scout." In a tradition that went back a decade to the origins of the show, Patsy convinced Davis this should be "Hilda Hensley" of Winchester, neglecting to tell Davis that Hilda was her mother.

January 21, 1957

On Monday, January 21, 1957, at precisely 8:30 P.M., CBS began *Talent Scouts* with a prerecorded advertisement for Toni hair products. Then announcer Tony Marvin intoned, with the Godfrey theme song behind him,

trombones leading, "*Arthur Godfrey's Talent Scouts*, brought to you by"—
Deep Magic Cream and long-lasting Toni home permanent. Godfrey did a
little patter and reminded the studio audience: "You are going to predict
the winner, and then we can see doors we can open." The first scout, Mrs.
Ronald Smith, from Toronto, introduced light opera singer Margo McKinnon from Windsor, Ontario, and she sang "The Italian Street Song." (All
three scouts receive a box of Toni products.) Margo McKinnon's presentation lasted two minutes, and then Godfrey did a Toni advertisement in
which he mocked Elvis Presley's hit "Hound Dog" as not fair to singers as
good as Margo McKinnon. The pitch for Toni Deep Magic Cream lasted an
astonishing three minutes—as a live advertisement, with Godfrey speaking
directly to the TV audience.

The second scout was Mrs. James Sonnenberg—whose husband was a
ticket broker for Broadway shows. Her "talent" was Jerry Antes, a singer from
Los Angeles. He had sung all over the United States and at twenty-five was
precisely as old as Patsy Cline. Antes in a manner of Tony Bennett sang "You
Make Me Feel So Young." He was well rehearsed with the band, as there was
an instrumental break in the middle, and he had worked out the arrangement
with Bert Farber, the leader of the Arthur Godfrey house orchestra.

Next, Arthur Godfrey did another advertisement for Toni and then introduced Hilda Hensley, Patsy Cline's mother, as her scout. They spoke for a
minute or two, and Hilda stated: "I have brought a young girl from Virginia
to do her next release on the Decca label, Patsy Cline." Then Godfrey announced: "And now in the Toni spotlight, Patsy Cline."

Then Patsy Cline started singing "Walkin' After Midnight" in a version
that seems odd today as she is backed by a classic big band with woodwinds
and brass. Godfrey commented: "cute song." Then Godfrey did another
Toni Deep Magic Cream live advertisement promoting that this product
"softens as it deep cleans." "Now, bring them out in order they appeared,"
and McKinnon, Antes, and Cline each reprised a few bars of their song.
Patsy Cline gained the loudest applause measured by a VU (volume units)
meter, and Godfrey proclaimed her the winner. CBS faded to its famous
"eye logo" with Patsy saying "Oh thank you."[35]

She was heard and seen by millions. *Sponsor*, an advertising trade publica-
tion of the day, reported that the audience was about half of all homes with
television sets in the United States. According to advertising measures, Patsy
Cline had appeared on the fifth most popular show of the week. "Walkin'
After Midnight" zoomed to number two on the *Billboard* country charts.
She had effectively used television to become a national star.[36]

Conclusion

Those interested in the career of Patsy Cline have stressed the importance of her win on Arthur Godfrey's TV show, and its importance cannot be overstated. Patsy Cline had worked as a regional star since 1952, and her first-place finish vaulted her onto the national stage. Because she died in 1963, her national career proved short and would have never happened if not for her appearance on *Arthur Godfrey's Talent Scouts*.

Patsy Cline's timing could not have been better. By January 1957 television had become ubiquitous in the United States, and network TV exposure made national stars overnight. Cline knew this, and the fortuity of Arthur Godfrey watching her was no accident. Cline had tried out for *Arthur Godfrey's Talent Scouts* twice before and failed to gain a spot on this proven means to national stardom. She knew Godfrey had used singers from all genres, so her work in country music or love of pop music could prove no barrier.

That the national careers of famous singers like Tony Bennett, Rosemary Clooney, and the Chordettes started on or advanced by winning Godfrey's *Talent Scouts* was well known to Cline. By the twenty-first century, Arthur Godfrey's star-making power has been lost to television's history. But a rising professional like Patsy Cline saw it as one of the few ways to jump to instant stardom. She could not have had such a career-changing moment through any other means.

Victory on *Talent Scouts* meant exposure for her latest record, "Walkin After Midnight." As Decca promoted Cline as a country star based on the charting of her first hit, she gained needed gigs (and instant cash) from constant appearances around the United States. But "Walkin' After Midnight" also charted as a pop hit in an era when musical genres were being redefined. Patsy Cline proved to be, with her appearance on *Talent Scouts*, exactly what the Decca label wanted—a star like Elvis who had started as country and then crossed over to pop music.

Patsy Cline, Arthur Godfrey, and *Talent Scouts* produced new stars. That was the goal the CBS television network had in mind. CBS did not want traditional country stars like Hank Williams, but ones who were embraced as stars by everyone interested in the new music called rock and roll. When Cline first appeared on television, national networks were being transformed into producers of national celebrities. That she recorded in Nashville—as did Elvis Presley and the Everly Brothers—did not matter. As Patsy Cline rose to stardom, Nashville produced as many pop music hits as longtime pop music centers Los Angeles and New York.

NOTES

DEDICATION: To Marilyn Moon, who inspired *Patsy Cline: The Making of an Icon* (Bloomington, Ind.: Trafford Press, 2011).

1. There has been prior work on television in Washington, D.C., such as F. B. Marbut, *News from the Capital: The Story of Washington Reporting* (Carbondale: Southern Illinois University Press, 1971), but all ask a different question: How has news been reported in Washington, D.C.? The community is simply a site, not an important place. I seek to reverse that line of inquiry. Quotation from Federal Communications Commission, "Proposed Decision," March 7, 1946, Box 79, Records of the Allen B. DuMont Laboratories, Manuscript Division, Library of Congress, Washington, D.C.

2. Thomas T. Goldsmith, letter to Allen B. DuMont, May 10, 1945, and letter, Thomas T. Goldsmith to Alan Hartnick, April 20,1960, both found in the Goldsmith Papers, Records of the Allen B. DuMont Laboratories, Manuscript Division, Library of Congress. See also oral history 1466, Les Arries Jr., December 20, 1995, and oral history 1467, Larry Richardson, October 31, 1995, Library of American Broadcasting, University of Maryland. On Don Richards, see Folders 165 and 217, NBC Collection, Library of Congress, Recorded Sound Division.

3. Thomas T. Goldsmith, letter to Allen B. DuMont, May 10, 1945, and letter, Thomas T. Goldsmith to Alan Hartnick, April 20, 1960, both found in the Goldsmith Papers, Records of the Allen B. DuMont Laboratories, Manuscript Division, Library of Congress. There are any number of examples of local Washington, D.C., media experiments within the Washington, D.C., market. For example, during the late 1940s and early 1950s, CBS used WTOP-TV, channel 9 in Washington, D.C., to "test" its color system as indicated throughout WTOP-TV logbooks on deposit at the Library of American Broadcasting. Since there are no CBS-type color sets in homes in the nation's capital area, these broadcasts are simply aimed at FCC engineers who had CBS apparatus delivered to them. Public policy experts and historians offer countless examples in any number of areas as seen in Sar A. Levitan, *The Federal Social Dollar in Its Own Back Yard* (Washington, D.C.: Bureau of National Affairs, 1973); Howard Gillette, "A National Workshop for Urban Policy: The Metropolitization of Washington, 1946–1968," *Public Historian* 7 (Winter 1975): 7–27.

4. Bamberger Broadcasting Service et al., 211 FCC Reports 211 (1946), quotation at 222. See also *Broadcasting*, March 11, 1946, 17.

5. Carl Abbott, "Dimensions of Regional Change in Washington, D.C.," *American Historical Review* 95 (December 1990): 1368.

6. "Television's Magic Carpet Beckons Eager Washingtonians," *Washington Evening Star*, March 18, 1946, C3; "The Washington Radio Market," *Broadcasting*, March 29, 1948, 33–34. See also Russell Baker, *An American in Washington* (New York: Knopf, 1961); Howard Gillette, *Between Justice and Beauty* (Baltimore: Johns Hopkins University Press, 1995); Eunice Grier, *People and Government: Changing Need in the District of Columbia, 1950–1970* (Washington, D.C.: Washington

Center for Metropolitan Studies, 1970); Francine Curro Cary, ed. *Urban Odyssey: A Multicultural History of Washington, D.C.* (Washington: Smithsonian Institution Press, 1996).

7. Here, the key article is Abbott, "Dimensions of Regional Change," 1367–1394.

8. Ray Allen, "Back Home: Southern Identity and African-American Gospel Quartet Performance," in *Mapping American Culture*, eds. Wayne Franklin and Michael Steiner (Iowa City: University of Iowa Press, 1992), 112–35. On Washington, D.C., as a southern music town, see Mark Opsasnick, *Capitol Rock* (Riverdale, Md.: Fort Center Books, 1996), 10–12, 18–22. See also Robert Fishman, *Bourgeois Utopias: The Rise and Fall of Suburbia* (New York: Basic Books, 1987); Kenneth T. Jackson, *Crabgrass Frontier: The Suburbanization of the United States* (New York: Oxford University Press, 1985); and Gwendolyn Wright, *Building the Dream: A Social History of Housing in America* (New York: Pantheon, 1981).

9. Thomas T. Goldsmith, letter to William Sayer, November 20, 1945, Records of the Allen B. DuMont Laboratories, Manuscript Division, Library of Congress; Howard Fields, "'Temporary' W3XWT Blossomed into Indie Poorhouse, WTTG," *Television/Radio Age*, May 1985, A3-A4; "CBS Sells Interest in WTOP," *Broadcasting*, October 11, 1954, 64; "The Rich Rewards of Pioneering," *Television*, March, 1968, 27–51; Jeff Kisseloff, *The Box: An Oral History of Television* (New York: Viking, 1995): 61–68; *12th Annual FCC Report, Fiscal Year Ended 1946* (Washington, D.C.: USGPO, 1946), 9–17.

10. "Washington Is Source of Nationwide TV Interest," *Washington Times-Herald*, July 16, 1950, 12. Surprisingly only one of the score of histories of the *Washington Post* notes its utter dependence on WTOP-TV. Chalmers M. Roberts writes that prior to the purchase of the *Times-Herald* in 1954, "more than one reporter remembered asking [Phil] Graham for a raise and, as Sam Zagoria [a fellow reporter] recalled it, hearing [Graham] reply, 'Sam, did you get a check the last week from *The Post*? The funds for that [check] came from WTOP. We lost money here [at the newspaper].'" *The Washington Post: The First 100 Years* (Boston: Houghton Mifflin, 1977), 262.

11. For figures on TV sets in use in the Washington, D.C., area, see C. L. Kelly, memo to Julian Armstrong, November 6, 1946, Du Mont Laboratories Collection, Box 79, Library of Congress, Washington, D.C.; "District of Columbia Market Indicators," *Broadcasting-Telecasting, 1954–55 Telecasting Yearbook-Marketbook*, 82; "The Dimensions of Radio and Television," *1958 Broadcasting Yearbook*, September 22, 1958, A-15, A-26.

12. Testimony of John Royal, Box 105, folder WRC 1946, National Broadcasting Company Records, State Historical Society of Wisconsin, Madison, Wisconsin; "WNBW," *Television*, July 1947, 10, 39; WRC—Television and Radio, Folder 313, NBC Collection, Recorded Sound Division Library of Congress; David Sarnoff, *Looking Ahead* (New York: McGraw-Hill, 1968), 125–45.

13. Oral history 1143, Neal Edwards, April 17, 1978, Library of American Broadcasting; William McAndrew, memo to Carlton Smith, January 26, 1948, Box 596, Folder 23, NBC Collection, State Historical Society of Wisconsin; Kisseloff, *The*

Box, 206–9, 222–24; memo (1953), from Carl McCardle, assistant secretary of state, February 9, Department of State, Record Group 59, Series 911.44, National Archives, Washington, D.C.; "DuMont Turns Its Corporate Back on TV Network," *Broadcasting*, August 29, 1955, 80; Nancy E. Bernhard, "Ready, Willing, and Able: Network Television News and the Federal Government, 1948–1953," in *Ruthless Criticism: New Perspectives in U.S. Communications History*, eds. William S. Solomon and Robert W. McChesney (Minneapolis: University of Minnesota Press, 1993), 291–312.

14. License renewal forms from this period are found in the records of the Federal Communications Commission, Record Group 173, National Archives; oral history, Fred S. Houwink, April 11, 1979, and oral history, John William Thompson Jr., March 27, 1978, Library of American Broadcasting, University of Maryland; "WMAL Launches TV Service," *Washington Evening Star*, October 4, 1947, 12A; "WMAL-TV, 2 Years Old," *Washington Evening Star*, October 2, 1949, A6; "WMAL-TV," *Broadcasting*, special issue July, 1951, 56, 84–85; Joseph C. Goulden, "The Evening Star," *Washingtonian*, January 1970, 28–33, 64–69; John Morton, "Saving the Star," *Washingtonian*, November 1975, 108–11, 165–74; "ABC Fights for Survival," *Business Week*, July 10, 1954, 52–56; Leonard Goldenson, *Beating the Odds* (New York: Scribner's, 1991).

15. Allen, "Back Home," 112–35.

16. E. Barbara Phillips, *City Lights: Urban-Suburban Life in the Global Society*, 2d ed. (New York: Oxford University Press, 1996), 201–3; Wladislava S. Frost, "Cities and Towns Mobilize for War," *American Sociological Review* 9 (February 1944): 85–89; Samuel Lubell, "So You're Going to Washington," *Saturday Evening Post*, February 7, 1942, 18–19, 62, 64; Lewis M. Killian, *White Southerners*, rev. ed. (Amherst: University of Massachusetts Press, 1985).

17. Oral history, Fred S. Houwink, April 11, 1979, and oral history 1138, John William Thompson Jr., March 27, 1978, Library of American Broadcasting. See also "WMAL Makes Switch," *Washington Evening Star*, September 21, 1955, A14.

18. Oral history, Fred S. Houwink, April 11, 1979, and oral history Connie B. Gay, April 1, 1976, Library of American Broadcasting. On southerners migrating to D.C., see Laurie M. Sharp, *Social Organization and Life Patterns in the District of Columbia* (Washington, D.C.: Bureau of Social Science Research, 1965); Joseph T. Holl, *Hard Living on Clay Street* (New York: Anchor, 1973); Frederick Gutheim, *Worthy of a Nation* (Washington: Smithsonian Institution Press, 1977); James N. Gregory, "The Southern Diaspora and the Urban Dispossessed: Demonstrating the Census Public Use Microdata Samples," *Journal of American History* 82 (June 1995): 111–34. On Connie B. Gay's early activities, see "Washington's Hillbilly Impresario Goes Far in 5 Years," *Washington Evening Star*, September 13, 1951, B1, and "Our Respects to Connie Barriot Gay," *Broadcasting*, February 2, 1959, 81.

19. Oral history, Fred S. Houwink, April 11, 1979, and oral history, Connie B. Gay, April 1, 1976, Library of American Broadcasting; the advertisement is found in *Washington Evening Star*, January 16, 1955, E6. A key article is "Why Sponsors

Hate to Leave the Barn Dance," *Sponsor*, May 3, 1954, 42–43. See also *Sponsor*, July 11, 1955, 30; *Sponsor*, October 17, 1955, 33; *Business Week*, March 10, 1956, 30–31; *Sponsor*, May 14, 1956, 29; *Radio-Television Daily*, July 16, 1956, 7.

20. Oral history, Connie B. Gay, April 1, 1976, Library of American Broadcasting; Roy Clark's autobiography colorfully describes his experiences working for Connie B. Gay and with Jimmy Dean in *My Life* (New York: Simon and Schuster, 1994), 29–70. The ratings information is from Hargrett Library, Rare Book and Manuscript Library, University of Georgia, Arbitron TV Collection, ARB Television Audience Reports, Washington, D.C., Television Audience for April 1–7, 1954, March 10-April 5, 1955, October 8–14, 1955, December 1–7, 1955, February 1–7, 1956, April 7–13, 1956, October 8–14, 1956, December 1–7, 1956, February 1–7, 1957, May 6–12, 1957, June 1–7, 1957, and October 8–14, 1957.

21. Oral history, Connie B. Gay, April 1, 1976, Library of American Broadcasting. The ratings information is from Arbitron TV Collection, ARB Television Audience Reports, Washington, D.C. Television Audience for April 1–7, 1954, March 10-April 5, 1955, October 8–14, 1955, December 1–7, 1955, February 1–7, 1956, April 7–13, 1956, October 8–14, 1956, December 1–7, 1956, February 1–7, 1957, May 6–12, 1957, June 1–7, 1957, and October 8–14, 1957, Hargrett Library, Rare Book and Manuscript Library, University of Georgia. See also *Radio Daily-Television Daily*, May 23, 1956, 3; *Broadcasting*, April 23, 1956, 30; *Broadcasting* March 11, 1957, 71; *Television, Data Book for 1955*, 178; *Broadcasting-Telecasting, 1955–56 Yearbook*, 83. *Broadcasting Yearbook of 1958*, A-15, A-26, A-51, and A-93 asserts that in the D.C. area by March 1958, 9 in 10 area households had TV sets, with the greatest concentration in the suburbs.

22. "The Town and Country Story," *TV Guide* (Washington, D.C.–Baltimore edition), September 15, 1955, A7-A8; oral history, Connie B. Gay, April 1, 1976, Library of American Broadcasting. Dale Vinicur, *George Hamilton IV* (Hamergen, Germany: Bear Family Records, 1995), 25–32, describes Hamilton's Washington, D.C., experiences. From a far different perspective Richard Revere noticed the rural side of the nation's capital in his "'Hick Town or World Capital?'" *New York Times Magazine*, April 17, 1955, 13, 56, 58, 60.

23. Oral history, Fred S. Houwink, April 11, 1979, oral history, John William Thompson Jr., March 27,1978, and oral history, Connie B. Gay, April 1, 1976, Library of American Broadcasting; *TV Guide*, April 8, 1957 (Washington, D.C.–Baltimore edition), A-28; "Nothing Hayseed about Connie Gay," *Variety*, March 20, 1957, 35, 43; "Country Stylist," *New York Times*, September 8, 1957, X17. Gay's efforts as a network producer failed, and he turned to other ventures, as did Jimmy Dean and Patsy Cline. See "Our Respects to Connie Barriot Gay," *Broadcasting*, February 2, 1959, 81; "Pappy's Advice and Country Music Launched Gay's Radio-TV Empire," *Washington Evening Star*, August 18, 1960, 37.

24. Bob Stahl, "Godfrey Snaps Back at 'Untruths,'" *TV Guide*, August 7, 1954, 13–14; Martin Cohen, "The Greatest Talent Scout of All," *TV Radio Mirror*, May, 1955, 38–39, 106–7.

25. "Lost Sense of Team Play, Godfrey Says of Fired 9," *Washington Evening Star*, April 19, 1955, C14. "People Going Places," *Ross Reports*, May 16, 1956, 3, clippings, Box 5, Library of American Broadcasting.

26. "He Never Asked Them Back," *TV Guide*, July 30, 1955, 14; Martin Cohen, "Jan Davis: Talent Scout," *TV Radio Mirror*, August 1955, 64–66; Janette Davis entry, *Almanac of Famous People* (Detroit: Gale, 1993); "Arthur Godfrey and His Gang," Box 5b, 26–28, Library of American Broadcasting.

27. "Nielsen Ratings," *Radio-Television Daily*, February 7, 1956, 8; "Trendex Ratings," *Radio-Television Daily*, March 19, 1956, 7; "Pulse Ratings," *Radio-Television Daily*, April 2, 1956, 8; "Nielsen Ratings," *Radio-Television Daily*, April 4, 1956, 12; "Nielsen Ratings," *Radio-Television Daily*, July 11, 1956, 8; "Nielsen Ratings," *Radio-Television Daily*, July 24, 1956, 5; "ARB Ratings," *Radio-Television Daily*, August 6, 1956, 6; "Trendex Ratings," *Radio-Television Daily*, September 20, 1956, 7. Thereafter on a weekly basis, *Radio-Television Daily* offers ratings top tens, absent *Talent Scouts*.

28. Rooney's various remarks on Godfrey were originally printed in his syndicated newspaper column but can be most easily found in Andy Rooney, *Sincerely, Andy Rooney* (New York: Public Affairs Press, 1999).

29. Rosemary Clooney wrote two autobiographies: *This for Remembrance* (Chicago: Playboy Press, 1977) and *Girl Singer: An Autobiography* (New York: Doubleday, 1999), which details her appearance.

30. The Chordettes entry, *Contemporary Musicians* (Detroit: Gale, 2001).

31. See Yankovic's autobiography *Polka King* (Cleveland: Dillion/Liederback, 1977).

32. Tony Bennett, *Tony Bennett, The Good Life* (New York: Pocket Books, 1998), 91–92 tells of losing to Rosemary Clooney. The rest offers details of his life.

33. Patricia Jobe Pierce, *The Ultimate Elvis* (New York: Simon and Schuster, 1994), 85; Peter Guranick, *Last Train to Memphis: The Rise of Elvis Presley* (Boston: Little Brown, 1994), 181, 510; Tom Powell, "Kozak's Career: An Odyssey in the Entertainment Business; Elliott Kozak," *Amusement Business*, March 21, 1994, 3.

34. *TV Guide* (Washington, D.C.–Baltimore edition), November 3, 1956, A3; Dale Vinicur, *George Hamilton*, Bear Family Album BCD 15773 FK, 1995. George Hamilton fully cooperated with this project and it reads like an autobiography.

35. Library of American Broadcasting, Box 12.

36. "Research," *Sponsor*, February 16, 1957, 40–41; "Nielsen TV," *Broadcasting*, February 25, 1957, 35; "Tops in Talent," *Winchester Evening Star*, January 22, 1957, 1.

CHAPTER 6

"Nothing but a Little Ole Pop Song"

Patsy Cline's Music Style and the Evolution of Genre in the 1950s

Jocelyn R. Neal

On September 13, 2009, Taylor Swift stood on the stage at MTV's Video Music Awards (VMAs), stunning in an elegant, floor-length, silver, bespangled gown. Microphone in hand, she began her acceptance speech for "Best Female Video." Although barely nineteen years old, the blonde singer-songwriter had enjoyed a banner year that would culminate soon thereafter with her crowned as the Country Music Association's Entertainer of the Year. She had secured the fierce loyalty of a huge population of young fans and had racked up a stack of radio hits and impressive sales records in just three short years. "Thank you so much!" Swift began. "I always dreamed about what it would be like to maybe win one of these someday, but I never actually thought it would have happened. I sing country music," she reflected, "so thank you so much for giving me a chance to win a VMA award!"

Moments later, Swift was interrupted when a hip-hop star snatched the microphone from her and cut off her acceptance speech, generating a scandal that overshadowed everything else in the world of entertainment that month. But it was Swift's speech before the commotion that was the most controversial of all. "I sing country music," she declared, a reference meant to acknowledge that no country singer had ever before been honored with a VMA. But her assertion of genre identity, namely that she is a country singer, was a claim that has been widely challenged by country music traditionalists. Her detractors have not just been hardcore fans outside of the mainstream, listening to scratchy, old 78s of the original Carter Family. A few months before the VMA debacle, journalist Steve Tuttle penned a scathing critique of contemporary country music in *Newsweek*, citing Taylor Swift in the article's subtitle as poster girl for inauthentic country. "How did we get to this strange, alien land where there's a country-awards show that honors pop-music teenyboppers and a lot of the songs aren't really country by even the stretchiest definition?" complained Tuttle.[1] Web readers posted comments that were far less eloquent in their condemnation of Swift's claims on country music. In an accompanying photo essay, Sarah Ball presented *Newsweek*'s "scale of fifteen [country] artists who span the continuum, from traditional to trite," or "from diamonds to zircons."[2] Holding the top position on the "trite" end was Taylor Swift. Squarely on the "traditional" side of the scale was Patsy Cline.

Fifty years earlier, however, Patsy Cline was not widely regarded as a traditional country singer. Instead, she, too, stood in the center of a heated debate over what was (traditional) country and what was (trite) pop. The style in which she performed was dubbed the Nashville Sound, characterized by musical accompaniments with smooth strings; background vocal quartets adding velvety "oohs" and "aahs"; subtle drums; slip-note piano; and catchy, lilting rhythmic grooves. All of these backed lead vocals that were resonant, shimmering with vibrato, and devoid of the nasal harshness that had characterized honky-tonk singers just a few years earlier. The style was commercially a wild success, but it drew the ire of fans who were self-styled traditionalists and who decried its perceived inauthenticity. During her lifetime, Cline's musical style was viewed by many as the antithesis of traditional and the worst example of selling out one's musical roots. Yet in the decades following her death, Cline's music underwent a retrospective transformation from pop to traditional country—a move that reflects more than a mere change in vocabulary.

As has been widely recounted by scholars and journalists, Cline purportedly wanted to model her career on traditional country music as she understood it: she preferred a wardrobe of fringed western wear; she sought songs that referenced down-home, rural lifestyles; she loved to cover numbers by Hank Williams and Bob Wills; and she resisted mightily the musical innovations foisted on her by her studio producer. Most famous of all is her encounter with the song "Walkin' After Midnight." When the song was pitched to her, recalled its writer Don Hecht, Cline dismissed it as "nothing but a little ole pop song" with a lyric that "didn't have any 'balls.'"[3] Of course, that song became her breakthrough hit and ticket to stardom; it has also been a catalyst prompting writers to attempt to categorize her recordings as either pop or country within an endless debate: was Cline a pop singer trapped in a country career? Was Cline a country singer forced to adopt an unnatural guise as a pop singer?

That long-standing debate, let me suggest, is principally a rhetorical strategy employed by generations of fans and writers seeking to explain one perplexing question: why did it take so long for Patsy Cline to become a commercial success? Many of us regard her as a brilliant, gifted, and talented performer who stands out even among the pantheon of yesteryear's country stars. There must be some explanation, we tell ourselves, why Cline faced such a rocky start to her commercial career that it took several years to score her first hit, and several more before she managed another. One framework through which fans and writers have attempted to answer that question is the tension between pop music, associated in that context with cultural values of artifice, selling out, and role-playing, and country music, associated with cultural values of authenticity, integrity, and identity. But in attempting these explanations, writers inevitably run into the task of attempting to codify country and pop, and then categorizing various songs, performances, and gestures as falling in one camp or the other. Those efforts are severely hampered by common confusions between musical genre and musical style, and by the historical lens through which we view the music of the 1950s and 1960s.

In this essay, I hope to reposition our understanding of Cline's recordings in the context of late 1950s popular music, examine Cline's own conception of country music as a genre, explore the recordings that have been used as evidence in the debate, and suggest why a half-century of country fans have invested so much in the pop/country dichotomy of Cline's legacy. Finally, that dichotomy, along with the distinctions between style and genre, provides an interpretive means through which fans later recast Cline as a "traditional" part of country music's past, even though her recordings challenged the same stylistic boundaries of country music that Taylor Swift's do today.

Setting the Scene: Pop Music in Patsy's Time

The early 1960s were dark days in the history of popular music in America. Just a decade earlier, rock and roll had not yet been conceived. Then came Elvis and a fusion of honky tonk and rhythm and blues (R&B) that gave rise to a new musical era. Accounts of the 1950s often convey a sense of radical newness and excitement as old boundaries were shattered and a reckless, teen music invaded the public imagination. Country music was swept up in the excitement, too, as new recording technologies, new musical styles, and—perhaps most significant—new recognition of segmented audiences emerged.[4] One of the most striking changes was the adoption of single-format programming by radio stations, with formats chosen to reach particular segments of the audience via particular musical genres. Those genres, however, were defined more by their audiences than by the sound of the music that they purported to label, and consequently, the sounds of the music within any particular genre ranged considerably.

In their most basic taxonomy, musical genres are generally defined as categories sanctioned by social convention, yet the means by which those conventions are sanctioned, and the voices of authority within those processes, vary greatly. Prior to the 1950s, genres of popular music (by which I mean the broad swath of music defined by a commercial industry and marketed as entertainment to a general and diverse audience of interested consumers, or in other words, not "art music," "classical music," or "folk music") were largely distinguished by factors such as the geographic origins and racial identity of the performers, the particular catalog in which record labels listed a particular recording, and the demographics of the audience to whom the recording was principally marketed. Trade publications such as *Billboard* reinforced notions of distinct musical genres through their charting systems, which were essentially designed to segment the audience, not the recordings themselves. Songs that ranked high on the country charts were those that the country audience—a demographic defined by the music industry, and determined in part by race and class—were listening to; songs that ranked high on the R&B charts were those that a specific African American demographic was listening to; songs that ranked high on the various "pop charts" were songs that an unspecified mainstream audience—basically a code for white, urban, and middle- to upper-middle class—was listening to. When songs and artists "crossed over," it meant that they simply found a welcome reception in a segment of the audience to whom they had not been originally pitched. What is crucial in this context is that audience demographics and marketing strategies were the strongest delineators of musical genre, not musical style.

Musical style is deeply entangled with ideas of musical genre, yet it is useful to consider the two concepts as distinct.[5] As a term, *musical style* represents the audible characteristics of a particular performance or, in other words, a way of categorizing the sounds themselves. Features such as instrumentation, vocal timbre, techniques with which an instrument is played, particular rhythmic grooves set up in the performance, and even the audible vestiges of the studio techniques used in the recording process contribute to the musical style of a recording. Over the years, through a variety of complex cultural processes, certain musical styles have become representative of musical genres, and value judgments have been imposed on the relations between various styles and genres with which they are most associated.

Throughout country music's history, successive generations of fans have frequently viewed new styles with some degree of skepticism while asserting the cultural superiority of an older style. For instance, partisans of old-time string bands and the nasal vocal styles of 1920s country music were resistant to the smoother, sweeter vocal styles and polished sounds of the 1930s performers, a musical development that was facilitated in part by advances in microphone, recording, and broadcast technology.[6] Another creation of the 1930s and 1940s, the Western Swing bands of Bob Wills and Tex Williams with their drums, horns, and jazz-infused harmonies were initially eschewed by the cultural gatekeepers of the country genre such as the management of the *Grand Ole Opry*. Retrospectively, however, Western Swing has been embraced as a core part of the tradition, and George Strait's allegiance to the style helped him claim a traditional country identity in the 1980s. In yet another example, the arrival of honky tonk in the late 1940s, with its rough-hewn vocals and raucous dance rhythms performed by Hank Williams and others, was off-putting to listeners who loved the more traditional 1940s barn dance repertory. Decades later, in the mid-1990s, Garth Brooks was dubbed the "anti-Hank" for purportedly displacing all sense of tradition in country music.[7] In another instance of shifting perceptions, a decade later, journalists instead nostalgically longed for the good old days of Garth Brooks, describing him as "a modern-day Hank Williams."[8] When Taylor Swift won the Female Vocalist of the Year award from the Country Music Association, fans posted comments on message boards longing for the past when singers such as Carrie Underwood, whom they thought of as more "real," were honored, never mind the fact that just a few years earlier, Underwood herself was in the crosshairs under accusations of inauthenticity. In other words, for nearly a century, country fans have been reminiscing about how much better country music "used to be" and bemoaning the trite shortcomings of present styles.

Yet even within this ongoing pattern, honky tonk has earned a unique stylistic identity among many fans as the most authentic representative of the country genre, the measuring stick by which other styles' country relevance is judged. The honky-tonk style, characterized by expressive fiddling, electric lead guitar solos, sock rhythm acoustic guitar, upright bass, "crying" pedal steel interjections, and nasal, raw vocals (all characteristics of the sounds one actually hears on the recordings), had three unique features that have set it apart. First, it crystallized as a style in the late 1940s and early 1950s with artists such as Ernest Tubb, Webb Pierce, and of course, Hank Williams, during a post–World War II boom in country's popularity and—most important—right before the advent of rock and roll. The honky-tonk heyday was still an era of monophonic recording, when the record captured an actual live performance by the whole band, before overdubbing became common studio practice. The instrumentation, although firmly rooted in the electric lead guitar and—by 1953—the pedal steel guitar, still matched the general look of traditional string bands with its fiddle and upright bass. The second significant feature of honky tonk was that one of its major stars, namely Hank Williams, lived a reckless, troubled personal life and died tragically and dramatically, permanently linking his biography to the pathos of his music.[9] As Williams's fame grew after his death, the symbolic importance of honky tonk as a musical style grew, too. The third feature of honky tonk was that the sound of the music was indelibly linked to a space: the honky tonk as venue, a smoky dance hall where beer flowed freely and dramas of both love and heartbreak played out among sympathetic, working-class friends. For subsequent generations of fans, these three elements together helped cast honky tonk as a uniquely important and symbolic stylistic representative of country music. This association was reinforced when—after the musical and cultural changes brought on by rock and roll, new technologies, and the new societal norms for the baby boomers—country fans reminisced about an idealized time before all of those changes. As they looked back through the history of the genre, honky tonk sat just before the seismic shift. And of great relevance to our explorations of Patsy Cline's music within country music, it was the Nashville Sound that had displaced honky tonk most directly in the mid-1950s. Given that honky tonk was symbolically the core style of country music, the Nashville Sound was rejected from any such representation of country music.

Musical genre and musical style clashed in radical ways in the 1950s. For starters, the rate at which musical styles changed accelerated with the advent of new technologies. And at the same time, the relationship between audience demographics and musical styles shifted in ways that threatened the social order, especially along lines of age and race. The conventional story of how rock and roll came into being—admittedly a vast oversimplification, but one that is oft repeated nonetheless—is one of just such an unexpected intersection. Middle-class, white youth—a "pop" demographic and one that prior to the 1950s had little market recognition because teens before World War II had less purchasing power and leisure time—began listening to and dancing to R&B records—which contained musical styles that had not previously been pitched to that audience. Furthermore, radio stations and independent record labels capitalized on this trend by facilitating new intersections of musical styles and audience segments. Deejays started to host dance parties where they played R&B records; radio stations told listeners where to buy this music; small record labels aggressively promoted their new acts. This new rock and roll was particularly disruptive to the cultural scene. It was wildly popular among teenagers, and on many fronts it challenged the established order of what pop music was supposed to be according to past practice—accessible, pleasant entertainment for the middle- to upper-middle-class (predominantly white) audiences of mostly adults.

But what is most relevant to the cultural context of Patsy Cline is that in the midst of these changes, pop music itself was a moving stylistic target during the 1950s. Even after Elvis hit the scene, there was no consistency in what so-called pop music actually sounded like. At the start of the decade, *Billboard*'s pop charts were full of the Andrews Sisters, Perry Como, Tony Bennett, Rosemary Clooney, and other white, crooning singers backed by polished dance bands and sophisticated orchestras. Although there was some deviation in musical style among those sorts of performers, there was also a tremendous base-level continuity that provided a recognizable pop style. By the middle of the fifties, any such continuity of style had been dislodged. Rock and roll, which sounded nothing at all like earlier pop music, was acting like the new pop style. The pop charts were topped by Elvis Presley's rockabilly (a sound derived from a combination of honky-tonk and hill-billy music on the one hand and R&B and jump blues on the other), small bands featuring raw electric guitar solos, and black R&B groups such as the Coasters. But just a few years later, distinctions between genres that had seemed so clear just a decade earlier were entirely muddied: the pop charts featured number-one hits by everyone from Elvis Presley to Ray Charles, Connie Francis, and Marty Robbins: black artists and white artists, rock and roll and R&B, shimmering crooners backed by an orchestra, gunfighter country songs. In short, there was no musical-stylistic consistency in what constituted the pop genre.

One of trade magazine's charts that is generally referred to as "the pop chart" was *Billboard*'s "Hot 100" chart, which was purportedly not linked to any genre at all. So what appeared on that chart was supposedly what was popular or, in other words, what was widely consumed by the broadest audience surveyed in *Billboard*'s methodologies, and that music included a wide spectrum of styles. Of course, reporting and counting mechanisms in the 1950s and 1960s were even less automated and inclusive than they are today, and so chart positions were subject to the wills, wiles, preju-dices, and corruptions of the industry. But even allowing for those sorts of discrepancies, "crossing over" in Patsy Cline's era simply meant finding a large audience and one that was not bound by decades-old demographic partitions. In the musical upheaval of the late 1950s, many different and distinct musical styles found eager audiences. What the charts really tell us is that the lines of demarcation for audiences and musical genres were being actively renegotiated to accommodate a post–rock-and-roll world and a powerful new youth market.

The biggest question at the end of the 1960s was what musical style would be the next pop music. Between the time Patsy Cline started recording in 1955 and landed her first number-one country hit in 1961, rock and roll was born, shook up the world, and, at least in the minds of many fans, died and left musical chaos in its wake. Of the first generation of rock-and-roll stars, Buddy Holly, Ritchie Valens, and the Big Bopper all perished in a tragic plane crash on February 3, 1959. Elvis Presley was drafted into the army in 1958. Jerry Lee Lewis was embroiled in a scandal over his marriage, and Chuck Berry had been charged with violating the Mann Act. Little Richard had turned to full-time Christian ministry. Most of the other early stars such as Bill Haley and Fats Domino were older and insulated from the teen fever that had flared up. Payola was beginning to taint the disk jockeys' world. Doo-wop was passé, Motown was just starting up, Southern Soul was in its fledgling state, and cookie-cutter girl groups were a dime a dozen. As rock historian John Covach has written, the period from 1959 until the arrival of the Beatles in 1964 was one of vast experimentation, with "everyone in the music business . . . on the lookout for the 'next big thing.'"[10] Pop music was whatever happened to be popular, and the sound of it varied drastically from one hit to the next. In that climate, if the next style to become popular was a country style, so be it.

Country music was not immune from the musical upheaval of the late fifties. Juxtapositions of distinct musical styles within a single genre occurred in country as well. During those years, the country charts were crowded by the sweet, teen-love, crooner sounds of Sonny James and George Hamilton IV; the reckless, electric exuberance of rockabilly; the acoustic, banjo-driven twang of Flatt and Scruggs; and everything in between; the very idea that R&B legend Ray Charles would shortly be in Nashville making a soul-drenched album of country classics illustrates just how ungrounded the relationships between musical style and genre were during this era. All too often, our perception of Patsy Cline conceives of her in motion against a static background: traditional country music and pop music are portrayed as distinct and fixed fields, with Cline's music violating convention to switch from one to the other (against her wishes). But during that era, the genres of country and pop had already lost their traditional demarcations, and any consistent relationship between musical style and musical genre had long since been destroyed.

Role Models and Women

The names Jo Stafford and Kay Starr—both established pop singers—are often bandied about when discussing the role models Patsy Cline adopted. Her producer Owen Bradley suggested those were the women Patsy had listened to, adding yet another point of reference for the idea that Patsy was recording pop music and passing it off for country.[11] Yet one might fairly wonder whom else she could have chosen as the model of a female singer in full command of her performances.

Between 1950 and 1960, only two solo women managed to score number-one hits in country music, and both instances occurred before the arrival of rock and roll. Kitty Wells and Goldie Hill did so in 1952 and 1953, respectively, but in each case, the song was an "answer song," a recording that recast the lyrics to a current (male) hit in a female perspective and then rode the coattails of that male hit to its own success.[12] No other solo female topped the country charts in that entire decade, and certainly not after the arrival of Elvis![13]

Although there had always been women singers in country music, the genre held an unmistakable bias that coded country hits not only as white, rural, and working class, but also as predominantly male. As Kristine McCusker has eloquently described in Chapter 4, the role of "Nashville star"—and most of the other powerful positions within the country music industry—had been cast as male by the country music establishment. This is not to discount the fact that women were often fan favorites on barn dance programs and in concerts, or that a few, such as Patsy Montana, had sold scores of records. Their critical roles in the formation of the genre have been well documented in recent scholarship.[14] But the gendered nature of the country music superstar identity was not a new development in the 1950s. The trade magazines that charted country music in the 1940s reveal the same trends: not a single woman held the number-one spot on *Billboard*'s various country and western charts (initially called "folk") between their advent in 1944 and 1952. That male-dominant trend would continue within country music in many different manifestations: for instance, when the Country Music Hall of Fame was established in 1961, its first three inductees were male (Jimmie Rodgers, Fred Rose, and Hank Williams). Through 1970, an additional thirteen people were inducted, all of them male. In fact, Patsy Cline was the first solo woman to earn that recognition (inducted in 1973), and the only other women in the Hall of Fame at that time were Sara and Maybelle Carter. They were not inducted under their own names but rather in what was an accepted role for women: that of (unnamed) family members. Whatever the country women had been doing, however important it was to the genre's development, and however much they held their fans' affections, they were not becoming commercial stars with any degree of consistency. Their careers were consistently relegated in the public's perception to, as McCusker describes, less powerful and carefully circumscribed roles, almost always tempered and filtered through a male-centric industry, as in the case of those "answer songs" that Kitty Wells and Goldie Hill sang.

The pop charts—especially prior to the arrival of rock and roll—were a much more accepting home for female superstars. Jo Stafford and Kay Starr were joined by everyone from girl groups such as the Chordettes to Rosemary Clooney, Kitty Kallen, and Doris Day in those hit-making ranks. So if Patsy Cline was looking for role models who had enjoyed unbridled and recognized national success, or if Owen Bradley was looking for inspiration for the career of his new singer, female pop stars were not only a logical option: they were the only option.

Along with rock and roll and the shock waves that it sent through the entertainment business, another factor altering the country music industry in the late 1950s was the newfound awareness of just how big the business could become. Patsy Cline's recording career overlapped with the formation of the Country Music Association in 1958, the establishment of a Hall of Fame for country artists in 1961, and the branding of Nashville as "Music City, U.S.A." In the decade following her death, countless artists ranging from Bob Dylan and the Byrds to Connie Francis would make pilgrimages to Nashville in search of the headwaters of their musical inspiration, and both the city and the genre gained new prominence as a gateway to the essence of real and rootsy American popular music. Country singers soon thereafter realized just what power they could wield in negotiating business deals, and in 1974, even the *Grand Ole Opry* abandoned the wooden pews of its old-fashioned "Mother Church," the Ryman Auditorium, and headed to suburbia to glitzy, larger, state-of-the-art facilities. In short, Cline's career overlapped with the awakenings of bold, commercial ambition in country music and the simultaneous branding of Nashville as a musical mecca.

Cline found herself in Owen Bradley's recording studio at the start of that seismic shift. It is all too easy to look back half a century and forget both how few women had achieved lasting, recognized success in commercial country music at that point and how much the socioeconomic forces of the time had already launched drastic changes in the music industry. Just as the genre of pop music from earlier in the decade offered role models of successful female superstars, it also offered business models to support bolder ambitions. And country music producers, record executives, and stars alike were taking notice.

I Know It When I Hear It: Examining the Pop/Country Evidence

In explaining the pop/country dichotomy in Cline's music, many fans and writers are quick to resort to the old adage, "I know it when I hear it," to distinguish between the two. What exactly one might mean by pop versus country, however, and by what criteria critics are making their distinctions, remains murky at best. On November 8, 1956, Cline walked into a recording studio in Nashville, and three hours later walked out with her first hit record. "Walkin' After Midnight" would peak at number two, with its B-side, "A Poor Man's Roses (Or a Rich Man's Gold)" topping out at number fourteen on the *Billboard* country chart. Foreshadowing her future crossover success, the record also reached number twelve on *Billboard*'s pop chart (or, more specifically, the "Top 100" chart). But where the contents of this record fall on the pop/country continuum is a matter of differing opinions for many writers, and these examples underscore the tensions between genre, style, and cultural values that fuel the debate.

Cline was coerced by manager Bill McCall to do "Walkin' After Midnight," a song she felt was not right for her and that she had no interest in recording. According to the extant accounts, Cline agreed to do it only if she got to choose the B-side, for which she picked "A Poor Man's Roses." Cultural historian Joli Jensen described that choice as a "more traditional country song."[15] On the other hand, the author of a biography of Cline, Margaret Jones, pigeonholed the song as a Tin Pan Alley pop number that Cline picked up from a song plugger working for the song's publisher.[16] So, one might be led to wonder, is the song more traditional country or more Tin Pan Alley pop?

The answer is either, neither, or both, depending on one's criteria, all of which renders any binary distinction between pop and country relatively unhelpful, particularly when authors leave unstated the criteria by which they make their distinctions. Those criteria often include the song's text, its writers' biographies, its provenance, its instrumentation, its rhythmic groove, and its marketing, along with the vocal performance style of the soloist. In the case of "A Poor Man's Roses," the lyrics focus on the protagonist's dilemma: choosing between a loveless relationship with a wealthy but callous man and a sweet, passion-filled life with a poor man. In an instance where art imitates life, when she recorded this song, Cline was caught between her estranged husband and businessman, Gerald Cline, and new boyfriend, future husband, and linotype operator, Charlie Dick. Historians have pointed to that biographical resonance when explaining why Cline found the song so appealing, and why her performance of it was so compelling that it became a commercial success.[17] The parallels between the song's protagonist and Cline's personal life has been viewed as markers of the song's so-called country authenticity by many fans.[18]

More important, perhaps, is the theme of love triumphing over money, a theme that emerged in the decade following World War II as a significant trope in country music. The story line appeared commonly in two heavily gendered versions: the first, as heard in Hank Williams's "The Mansion on the Hill," is a poor, male protagonist suggesting to a woman that he knows she will be miserable in her wealthy life compared to what he would have offered her. The second, as heard in Cline's recording, is a female protagonist affirming that she would rather have true love from a poor man than wealth and material goods in the absence of love. Although a few prewar instances of the theme can be found (such as Rex Griffin's "The Last Letter"), the storyline became firmly entrenched in country music in the 1950s, the same time that the American working class was enjoying newfound economic opportunities and increased standards of living. In that context, the songs provided cultural grounding and working-class nostalgia as a counterbalance to the potentially destabilizing prosperity and upward mobility of the country audience. Those themes have persisted as a core part of country music (Jeanne Pruett, "Satin Sheets"; Reba McEntire, "Little Rock"; Buck Owens, "Above and Beyond"; and Travis Tritt, "Country Club," to name only a few of countless examples). In fact, it was Cline's generation of performers who made this theme synonymous with the genre in the first place, but the effect has been that any country fan (or writer) looking back through the years at Patsy Cline's "A Poor Man's Roses" hears the theme as traditionally country.[19]

The songwriters' biographies are another piece of evidence authors draw on when discussing the pop/country reception of "A Poor Man's Roses." These criteria may seem odd at first, particularly since few Cline fans could even name the songwriters (Bob Hilliard and Milton DeLugg) off the top of their heads. Yet it is the songwriters' biographies by which Margaret Jones categorized the genre of "A Poor Man's Roses." Tin Pan Alley refers to the neighborhood in New York that was home to the major songwriting and publishing operations in the early part of the twentieth century, and the phrase has been shorthand for professionally composed, formulaic pop songs ever since. It was unusual that Cline recorded a tune by Hilliard and DeLugg in the first place, given that the pair did not have a publishing contract with McCall and McCall contractually insisted that Cline sing songs for which he held publishing rights. In this case, McCall would have been cut out of any royalties, except McCall agreed to let Cline record the song only in exchange for a "promotional incentive," a fact that cast the song once again as a crass commodity in the commercialized world of pop.[20]

The songwriters' biographies also bring to light the relationship between the singer, the songwriter, and the song, which is of great importance in vernacular musical genres. Within the pop genre, fans hold little expectation that singers write their own songs. In other genres and subgenres, including several alternative scenes and much of rock, fans generally expect singers to have written their own songs as part of their projected authenticity. Country music stands in a conflicted middle ground. Fans expect singers to tell stories from personal experience, and much of the value system that is subsumed under the label of authenticity relies on the idea that country songs project the singer's first-person, honest point of view. Yet even from the earliest days of the commercial genre, many respected country singers have not written their own songs. Even Hank Williams, who is often held up as the paragon of country authenticity, frequently had his compositions doctored by his manager, Fred Rose, a professional songwriter.

By the late 1950s, Nashville had become home to a robust professional songwriting industry. It was a core part of the country music business machine, yet at the same time it was oddly insulated from fans' perceptions of the music. Songs were readily associated with the singer who made them famous, not the writers who conceived them, and fans treasured connections between singers and their songs that made the lyrics believably "theirs." Patsy Cline stood in the middle of this culture: her songs have been inextricably linked with her voice and identity, becoming in that sense "hers," but Cline tried her hand at songwriting only twice in her entire recording career. Both of those instances were an experimental New York session in 1957. "A Stranger in My Arms" was Cline's setting of a poem by Mary Lu Jeans and Charlotte White. Unfortunately for Cline, the melody she composed borrowed too liberally from the musical *South Pacific*'s "Some Enchanted Evening," causing complications with the song's copyright, publication, and royalties. "Don't Ever Leave Me Again" was an R&B number that had been published with McCall, so Cline took the opportunity to arrange it, thereby claiming a third of the writer's credit. In neither case were her efforts very successful.

Other than those two instances, Cline never tried to write her own material. As a result, fans have pushed much of the blame for her early commercial failures on the songs that she was recording, arguing that the material was no good, that she was denied access to quality country songs, or at the very least, that the songs were not right for her. With very few exceptions, McCall insisted that she record songs under publishing contract with his company, and as he was located on the West Coast, his writers were, for the most part, not part of the Nashville songwriting establishment. Similarly, the writers for "A Poor Man's Roses" were not part of the country scene. In either case, the writers' biographies offered no redemption for the song's nontraditional provenance.

Writers' biographies aside, there is essentially nothing in a song itself—by which I mean the combination of lyrics, melody, and chord progression in a particular musical form—that is specific to one genre or another. In the case of "A Poor Man's Roses," the song's melody and chord progressions are not specific to any genre or musical style. The song's form is the conventional thirty-two-bar form known as AABA or Standard Song Form (see fig. 6.1), consisting of four sections. The first, second, and fourth share the same rhyme scheme, chord progression, and melody; the third (beginning "then the poor . . .") uses a contrasting chord progression and melody that is open-ended, concluding on a half cadence (at the lyrics " . . . never miss") and requires the song musically to continue into the fourth section. In practice, most AABA songs were arranged so that at the conclusion of the complete AABA form, an instrumental solo occurred, followed by the singer reprising the last two sections, BA, as is the case in this instance.

A more detailed examination of the AABA form, both as an analytic model and in this particular song, is beyond the scope of this essay. But it is of relevance here because in the early twentieth century, this song's form became the standard in music composed for the popular stage, specifically out of Tin Pan Alley.[21] From that perspective, one might assume that the musical form carried with it associations with the pop genre. By the mid-1950s, however, that form had been thoroughly co-opted by country music and referred as strongly to early country and hillbilly recordings as to anything from the Broadway stage tradition, thereby negating any pop associations with the musical form.

Part of the reason that this musical form conveyed no particular suggestion of genre was that the songs recorded by earlier generations of country singers had been drawn from a wide range of musical sources with no real consideration as to creating or preserving any pristine repertories or firm genre boundaries. Jimmie Rodgers and the Carter Family both recorded songs in

time	form	lyrics
[0:00]	Introduction	
[0:12]	Section A:	I must make up . . .
[0:33]	Section A:	One's as wealthy . . .
[0:55]	Section B:	Then the poor man's . . .
[1:16]	Section A:	And yet the hand . . .
[1:37]	Instrumental solo	
[1:58]	Section B:	Then the poor man's . . .
[2:20]	Section A:	And yet the hand . . .

Figure 6.1: Musical form in "A Poor Man's Roses (Or a Rich Man's Gold)."

the 1920s that they borrowed from the vaudeville stage; Bob Wills covered numerous jazz and pop standards with his Western Swing band; Hank Williams's songwriting frequently invoked the AABA form, both because by the 1940s it was ubiquitous in country music from all those earlier borrowings and because Fred Rose was thoroughly steeped in a popular-song musical (and theatrical) tradition.[22] Thus, for Cline in 1956, the use of AABA forms was no more or less an indicator of any genre association than the use of verse/chorus forms or blues forms would have been, for that matter.

The question of whether blues form conveys some sense of genre is relevant to Patsy Cline's career because songwriter Don Hecht used that term in his description of "Walkin' After Midnight." Hecht explained that the song was "pure B-flat blues," listing both the key of the song and the complicated label "blues" as its musical characteristics.[23] Both bits of information have been cited as evidence that the song was the turning point that pushed Cline's sound into pop and away from country. Hecht's mention of "B-flat blues" evokes a tradition of jazz improvisation, where that key is common. But for listeners, certainly, the key of the song was irrelevant to its genre associations (and as a matter of trivia, Patsy sang it in the key of C, not B-flat). As for Hecht's descriptor "blues," the term could refer to the song's sentiment, the song's use of melodic fragments and scales with "blue notes," most frequently lowered scale-degrees 3 and 7, or to a particular chord progression and form strongly associated with blues. In this instance, the song's lyrics bemoaned lost love, which is a textual invocation of the blues, and the song used lowered scale-degree 3 to great effect. As for the chord progression and form, however, the song did not adopt any conventional blues progressions or patterns. Instead, the song was crafted in the same form as "A Poor Man's Roses," the AABA, and more specifically, in the same arrangement of AABA followed by a short instrumental solo and a reprise of the final two sections, BA. In other words, the song's form in what Cline dismissed as a pop song was identical to that used on the B-side recording of "A Poor Man's Roses," which was either a traditional country song or a pop song, depending on one's perspective.

Although any song's musical construction fails to determine genre, its provenance certainly carries sway. Historically, songs have become marked as country when they were sung convincingly by an artist whom country fans embraced as authentic. That was the case when singers such as Jimmie Rodgers or Bob Wills borrowed songs from pop and jazz performance traditions but turned them into country classics, "In the Jailhouse Now" and "Right or Wrong" being two prime examples. From that time onward, those songs carried a stamp of country approval, and later artists could sing them as a way of claiming country identity, too. One way for her recordings to be unequivocally considered country by the country fan base was for Cline to tap into the tradition of covering songs made famous by iconic country stars. She did this later in her career, partly because she loved that music. But those covers also afforded her some measure of balance for all the new compositions and changing musical styles that, at least according to the letters to the editor received by various fan magazines, were pushing the sound of the music too far from its roots. Among the traditional country music Cline chose to cover were well-known hits by Western Swing star Bob Wills, honky-tonk legend Floyd Tillman, bluegrass father Bill Monroe, Hank Williams, and Buck Owens, to name just a few.

These covers were Cline's chance to finally sing the types of country songs that bespoke traditional country music in her view, but her choices also highlight how male-dominated the singers and role models of canonic country music were in Cline's era. Furthermore, covers are a businessman's conundrum: they have instant audience appeal because they are well known and liked, but on the other hand, fans tend to be protective of original versions that they view as belonging to the original artist and consequently often resist new performances of old favorites. Covers also reduce the number of ways a singer and his or her producer can cash in—literally—on writers' and publishers' royalties, because those royalties flow back to the original songwriter. This fact was of paramount importance to Bill McCall and one reason why Cline was not allowed to record those sorts of songs while under his contract. Finally, cover songs reduce the opportunity for a new singer to establish an independent brand name, something more easily accomplished with new songs that lack any association with another star and that carry that cachet of first-person, autobiographical believability (even if written by professional songwriters). But even with all these obstacles that come with cover songs, they remain one of the most powerful ways a singer can establish musical lineage and pedigree and thereby construct genre associations in the minds of fans and claim a space in country music. Patsy Cline's later insistence on covering those iconic country songs provided fans and writers with evidence of Cline's devotion to country tradition, especially since she had to thwart conventional business practice to record them. And yet early on, that avenue to establishing country roots was closed to her.

For Patsy Cline's recordings, the pop/country dichotomy was grounded neither in the musical substance of the songs (her comments about "Walkin' After Midnight" notwithstanding) nor in her songs' provenance, given that covers were essentially off limits to her for business reasons in the first several years of her career. Instead, the pop versus country rhetoric offered a strategy to wrestle with her musical style. That style, particularly with regard to the instrumentation, was the most audible break from established country traditions and—by extension—from some fans' conceptions of the genre.

Even in 1956 before the full-blown, lush orchestration of the Nashville Sound had coalesced, Cline's producer Owen Bradley steered her away from the solo fiddle and crying steel guitar that had characterized honky-tonk music for the previous half decade. The session at which she recorded both "Walkin' After Midnight" and "A Poor Man's Roses" utilized the standard midfifties honky-tonk lineup of electric lead guitar, acoustic guitar, fiddle, steel guitar, piano, bass, and drums, but what is heard on the recording is very different from the way that same lineup had been used just a few years earlier or on contemporaneous records by other artists. On "A Poor Man's Roses," the fiddle is missing entirely from the final mix, and there is no prominent cry of the steel guitar. The piano pounds out repetitive, triplet-rhythm chords that define a shuffle groove and evoke R&B. The drums and lilting bass further distance the groove from the traditions of hillbilly and honky-tonk music and instead adopt a medium shuffle reminiscent of Fats Domino's "Blueberry Hill" (a connection that the piano playing amplifies further). Finally, Cline's vocals not only deliver the story but also serve as an expressive sonic instrument. Her rich resonance, silky vibrato, and extensive use of breaks, catches, and cries all stretch the sonic palette well beyond what was typically heard in country singles of that era. Cline starts out with a more perfunctory delivery, but as the song unfolds, she begins to back-phrase more extensively, singing behind the beat and stretching out the duration of each phrase to allow for greater expressive nuance. After the instrumental solo, when her vocals reenter two-thirds of the way through the recording, she milks each syllable—extending each one far longer than the rhythmic patterns of the song's melody indicate—and adds a catch to her voice. The performance demonstrates her remarkable skill as a stylist along with her refusal to adhere to established stylistic norms of country music, even before the mature Nashville Sound had fully come into existence.

From the wider view of social context, a change in sound and style was inevitable in the late fifties. Since its inception as a recorded genre in the 1920s, country music had always conveyed a sense of nostalgia, but that sentiment had been injected into the music by producers and record label executives who were certain that reflective, homespun recordings with an affect of retrospection were what the mostly rural, largely southern, working-class audience wanted to hear.[24] Performers in those first few decades, by contrast, often saw themselves as contemporary, forward-looking entertainers. In the years immediately after World War II, the idea of country music as a sonic space to preserve something old, idealized, and unfettered by modernity gained momentum, as seen in the rise of nostalgic, old-time images and song lyrics within country. But as the entire entertainment industry boomed in the 1950s, country musicians—meaning those who self-identified with the genre and who were received warmly by the fan base—also figured out how to capture their share of that newly expanding market. The changes heard in the music were the very fruits of ambition that earlier generations of country singers had planted, and now the country industry had the clout, recording technologies, and source pool of experienced session musicians to make that happen.

As for the sound of Cline's recordings, they were no more derived from some fixed pop genre than anything else, primarily because there was no clearly defined, single sound or style known as pop music in the late 1950s. They were indeed different from the honky-tonk sounds Kitty Wells had offered fans in the early fifties, and they shared commonalities with both rhythm and blues and the newly birthed rock and roll. They also pulled stylistic influence from female pop stars, but that was mainly because so few female singers of any genre were available role models for a major, national-profile career. And Cline's recordings connected with an extensive new audience, one whose tastes and rising purchasing power happened to be catalogued in the pop charts and one that eschewed the hillbilly twang of earlier generations of country singers. Thus, although this new sound was inarguably different from the country styles that preceded it, it did not match any definitive stylistic category of pop.

Repositioning Patsy's Music

Over the span of her short recording career, Cline changed her singing style, a move that some have described as her abandoning any country leanings and fully embracing a pop sound. That transition is often identified as the moment that the Nashville Sound sold out and abandoned its authentic identity in a quest for commercial success. A clear illustration of that stylistic change can be heard by comparing her original recording of "Walkin' After Midnight" to the remake of the song she did in 1961. In the latter version, the tempo is slightly faster, the backup vocalists fill in the sonic texture with tight, close harmonies, and the tic-tac bass lays down a crisp foundation for the song. Cline's voice is drenched in reverb, reflecting new recording technologies in use by 1961. Floyd Cramer's slip-note piano dances around the singers. A modulation in the middle of the song from the key of C Major to the key of D-flat Major (at time 1:37 in the recording) reveals the hand of a more sophisticated musical arranger. Most notable, whereas in 1956 Cline's rhythmic performance of "Walkin' After Midnight" was relatively straightforward, in 1961 Cline adds extensive back-phrasing, at times singing a full beat behind the band.[25]

That prominent back-phrasing untethers the singer from the metric framework of the song and grants her emotional (and rhythmic) freedom in telling the song's story. It pulls the focus off of the song and puts it instead squarely on the singer as stylist. For Patsy, heavy back-phrasing was a manifestation of her maturation as a performer: she had mastered how to own a song, how to command it, and how to make it belong to her alone, even though she had not written it.[26] Even though Patsy Cline was far from the first country singer to make use of the technique (Kitty Wells, for instance, used it albeit to a lesser extent on some of her ballads), it was undeniably a stylistic trait that normally characterized pop stars and pop ballad singers. For skeptics, that symbolized Patsy crossing into the foreign territory of a pop singer. For fans, it merely symbolized Patsy singing her "own" country classic. Once Patsy Cline committed fully to this new singing style (and consequently scored major hits on the pop charts), her music no longer fit within the stylistic boundaries of traditional country music, but it became wildly popular. In the last few years of her career, she enjoyed resounding commercial success. Yet just as Patsy had needed to untether herself from the rhythms of the songs in order to emerge as a masterful stylist and superstar, later generations of fans would have to untether Patsy the star from the actual musical style in which she recorded in order to reposition her as a classic country singer.

Reconciling Patsy Cline and the Nashville Sound

The Nashville Sound's heyday as a musical style remains—to this day—a troublesome era in country music history. A harsh retrospective view of the style emerged in the late 1970s as country music embraced not only the stark twang of outlaw country but also the rebellious sounds of southern rock. From that vantage point, the Nashville Sound was recast as a low point in country's past, when the genre's traditions were abandoned in favor of crossover pop artifice. In 1979, authors Bill Ivey and Douglas B. Greene penned an apologist view of the condemned Nashville Sound, arguing that it was a desperate move on the part of the country music industry to save the genre from the onslaught of rock and roll.[27] Such a charged perspective, which casts rock and roll as the evil attacker and the Nashville Sound as a necessary, albeit drastic, sacrificial and compromising defensive maneuver, has since been thoroughly and critically reevaluated by scholars including Joli Jensen.[28] But the Nashville Sound remains vilified in many historical narratives that seek to establish values of authenticity in country music. And that interpretation complicates efforts to view Patsy Cline as one of the genre's most celebrated stars, since she was also the voice of the Nashville Sound.

How the Nashville Sound could be both country music and, simultaneously, popular posed a conundrum to its fans. As a musical genre, country has always been defined in opposition to various "others," and country fans took pride in their music being distinct from the mainstream pop music. Of all the styles that required careful handling in historical retrospectives, the Nashville Sound was the most problematic because its commercial success had turned it, in effect, into pop(ular) music.

Thus, fans of Patsy Cline faced a dilemma: how could they claim Cline and her crossover recordings as a core part of country music, while still adhering to the idea that country was a distinct musical genre, different from pop music? The first step was to separate Cline the star from judgments about larger stylistic trends. In that frame of mind, fans can characterize the Nashville Sound as an inauthentic, sold-out style that undercut country's traditionalism, while simultaneously adoring its biggest star and leaving her musical reputation untarnished. Yet to her fans, the long-dead Patsy Cline exists primarily in her recordings, and thus the fans must reconcile the musical style of those recordings—irrefutably Nashville Sound—with the historical narrative that describes the Nashville Sound so negatively.

The rhetoric of the pop/country dichotomy provides a remarkable solution: the fans' answer to that question has been to propagate the rhetoric of pop versus country as an intrinsic struggle that persisted throughout Cline's career. We mentally cordon off the parts of her career and musical style that were too successful or sonically accessible by labeling them as pop and then highlight how those elements were apparently forced upon her against her will, and we cling to the traditionally country aspects of her persona and career as evidence of her "real" identity. That allows us to reauthenticate Patsy Cline through the pop/country dichotomy.

Can a Country Singer Be Popular?

There is great danger when a country musician actually becomes popular because the genre's identity is constructed in part on the fierce pride of marginalization. Artists who breach that boundary are inevitably stripped of some degree of country authenticity by a core, tradition-centered fan base. For instance, the Recording Industry Association of America (RIAA) currently lists Garth Brooks as third on its list of top-selling acts of all time, behind the Beatles and Elvis Presley.[29] Yet during his ascent to fame, Brooks became the target of endless diatribes, including that famously scathing accusation that he was the "anti-Hank."[30] Among many fans, no insult is intended to carry as much vituperation as that of losing one's country roots and selling out to commercial or crossover interests, which leads to the unsolvable paradox in country music: success actually implies failure.

Why did it take so long in Patsy's short career for her to become a star? The real answer, if there is such a thing, has much to do with the fickle nature of the music industry. Although fans like to believe that natural talent triumphs, reality dictates that it takes a tiresome amount of work and a healthy dose of luck to manufacture a number-one hit record. There is no single reason why she found commercial success briefly in 1956 and then had a long, four-year wait for the next big hit. But when we look back on our beloved Patsy Cline, we inevitably try to explain what held her back from the spotlight we feel she deserved in the late fifties prior to the triumph of "I Fall to Pieces." The answers to which we turn are usually couched in the struggle to reconcile pop and country in her voice, song selections, interference on the part of her manager or unfair business contracts, musical arrangements, etc., but none of those answers is fully defensible as an explanation. Those responses tell us little about alternate trajectories that Patsy's career might have taken (because the should-have-could-have-would-have options they imply are always untestable speculation), but those responses tell us much about the way country fans construct narratives of authenticity in country music history against a very complicated notion of "pop music," as we have explored throughout this chapter. Pop music, with all its abstractions, becomes the foil to which we turn to explain country music.

The more interesting question is why it took so many years after her death for Patsy to be widely embraced as a legend of country music, even tipping the scales as a "traditional" star, as in the *Newsweek* article that pitted her against Taylor Swift. Although Cline was inducted into the Country Music Hall of Fame in 1973, Patsy Cline's memory lay dormant through most of the 1970s, which is when the harshest assessments of the Nashville Sound emerged. It is no small accident that Cline's reputation rose to new heights of fame in the 1980s and crested with a biography and Hollywood film about her, accompanied by increased attention from fans and country artists alike. During the early to mid-1980s, country music once again favored a number of extreme pop-crossover styles, and in that context, Patsy Cline offered a unique figure of redemption from country music's past.

In the 1970s, the country music genre found new styles in the form of defiant, antiestablishment revivals of twang through the outlaw movement, country rock, and a streak of mainstream Nashville records that returned to a honky-tonk aesthetic. Yet during that time, Cline's music was quietly incubating in a number of places, most notably the careers of female country vocalists. Unsurprisingly, the first of these came from a woman whose career started out more in pop than in country. In 1971, Linda Ronstadt's self-titled third studio album included a live performance of "I Fall to Pieces," along with several other country covers. At the time, Ronstadt's songs were not even appearing on the country charts, although that would change within a few years. But she was widely respected as a vocalist. In 1975, Emmylou Harris offered several country retrospectives on *Elite Hotel*, including a cover of "Sweet Dreams" that became a number-one country hit for Harris. Here again, Harris was weaving Cline's music into the fabric of country standards. Two years later, Loretta Lynn revived the memory of Patsy Cline with a full tribute album, *I Remember Patsy*. The album appeared just a few years after Lynn had reached full star status as the first woman to win the Country Music Association's Entertainer of the Year award (1972) and as the best-known female country singer of the mid-1970s. Owen Bradley produced the tribute album, and the last cut was a lengthy, personal, and nostalgic conversation in which Lynn and Bradley reminisced together about Cline. The album's cover version of "She's Got You" topped the *Billboard* country chart, and another single, "Why Can't He Be You," peaked at an impressive number seven.

Lynn had always claimed Cline as a major influence as well as a dear friend, and when Lynn's autobiography appeared in 1976, it pointed yet more attention to Cline's memory. In that climate, it is unsurprising that Reba McEntire, a young country stylist with a great big voice, included a Patsy Cline cover on each of her first three albums (1977–1980). In 1980, film producer Bernard Schwartz turned Lynn's autobiography into a major Hollywood film, *Coal Miner's Daughter*, and Cline featured prominently in the story line. Thus, at the dawn of the 1980s, Cline was already shifting back into the public's attention as a major figure in country music's past.

The 1980s began with a country fad fueled by cultural politics and Hollywood. Cowboys were once again heroes in the Reagan era (even the president wore boots), and a sense of patriotic pride and a new social conservatism emerged. Country music offered an all-American soundtrack for this new nationalist identity, best signified by hits such as Lee Greenwood's "God Bless the U.S.A." John Travolta and Debra Winger two-stepped their way across the silver screen in *Urban Cowboy* (1980), and fans who had never before listened to country music turned to the genre in droves. The country music styles during those years incorporated aspects of New Wave, electronica, and pop dance music in their sounds. The resulting country records were wildly popular, and not just with a conventionally country audience. Those country singles began crossing over to the pop charts. Dolly Parton's "9 to 5" was a number-one hit on the *Billboard* country chart, but also the number-one hit on the pop chart *and* the adult contemporary chart.[31] That trend continued, with numbers such as Kenny Rogers and Dolly Parton's "Islands in the Stream" (number one on both the country and pop charts) and Alabama's "Love in the First Degree" (number one country and number fifteen pop). Country music was once again popular, to the point that it was undeniably part of pop music.

An enormous audience loved the new trends, which left the 1980s country airwaves full of vapid love ballads, hand-clap rhythmic grooves, and catchy, synthesizer-backed guitar hooks, while the radio blared Janie Frickie, Crystal Gayle, Marie Osmond (as a country star!), and Juice Newton. Dolly Parton was a pop sensation, while Loretta Lynn's hard country twang could scarcely even crack the top twenty on the *Billboard* country chart. Country music faced a crisis of genre identity more severe than at any previous time since its first recordings. Where the Nashville Sound had invoked apologists, the era after *Urban Cowboy* seemed almost beyond salvation. Country music's problem was in part its own commercial success, which once again threatened the genre with obsolescence as it became pop(ular). Even those who loved the country-pop styles saw the challenges that the genre faced in terms of self-preservation: was there any precedent for country music that was commercially successful and lacking twang?

In that context, Patsy Cline's story offered a path to redemption. Within the pop/country rhetoric, she provided a story of struggle and triumph—country roots and passion surviving a career wrapped in pop aesthetics. She was a country star, and yet her music had landed on the pop charts, her vocals were silky smooth and produced with the full arsenal of available technologies. And she sounded, well, "good." Unforgettably and irreproachably good.

Indeed, Cline's fame reached new heights in this era. Ellis Nassour penned a detailed biography of her, which she published in 1981. Country songstress kd lang cast herself as a modern-day Patsy Cline and famously covered her songs on lang's first few albums. And in 1985, Bernard Schwartz drew on his success with *Coal Miner's Daughter* to produce the Cline biopic *Sweet*

Dreams, starring Jessica Lange. For country music of the mid-1980s, embracing the Patsy Cline story was a way of affirming that country authenticity could exist in a pop guise, and thereby a way of rationalizing and reconciling country music of the 1980s with notions of tradition. That story, particularly the pop/country struggle through which Patsy triumphed with raw musical talent and an unwavering passion for "real" country music, recast Patsy as a towering legend in country's history. It also set up the grand irony of Cline's appearance later as a traditional foil for Taylor Swift's accused inauthenticity. Four months after *Newsweek*'s photo essay appeared in 2009, Swift's "You Belong with Me" topped the country charts and crested at number two on the pop charts, calling to mind the country/pop landscape of the early 1980s, and that of the early 1960s as well.

As for Patsy Cline, historians of rock and pop music have conveniently left her out of their narratives, while country's authors have burnished her already polished sound into a new form of traditional country music. Perhaps the best lesson to take from the recordings she left behind is that country music has always thrived on paradox: tradition is at odds with innovation, authenticity with accessibility, and country music will never be comfortable with its own occasional mainstream popularity. With our luxury of writing and rewriting history, generations of fans and scholars have found a place for Patsy Cline: timeless only after the passage of time and as country as the genre of country music itself ever really manages to be.

NOTES

1. Steven Tuttle, "Murder on Music Row: Taylor Swift? Songs about Cute Little Kids? What Has Happened to Country?!" *Newsweek*, April 3, 2009. http://www.newsweek.com/id/192377 (accessed September 2012).

2. Ball's photo essay held the original title "From Diamonds to Zircons," with Taylor Swift equated to the cheap, imitative "Zircon." *Newsweek*'s online archive has indexed the photo essay under that title. http://www.newsweek.com/photo/2009/04/03/photos-country-music-from-diamonds-to-zircons.html (accessed September 2012).

3. Recounted in Joli Jensen, *The Nashville Sound: Authenticity, Commercialization, and Country Music* (Nashville: Vanderbilt University Press, 1998), 100, and in Margaret Jones, *Patsy: The Life and Times of Patsy Cline* (New York: HarperCollins, 1994; New York: De Capo, 1999), 119–20.

4. Diane Pecknold, *The Selling Sound: The Rise of the Country Music Industry* (Durham: Duke University Press, 2007), 143.

5. Allan F. Moore explores how *genre* and *style* have been defined in different analytic disciplines and elaborates on how *genre* in analyses of popular music encompasses audience reception in its meaning; see "Categorical Conventions in Musical Discourse: Style and Genre," *Music and Letters* 82 (August 2001): 432–42.

6. See, for instance, Charles K. Wolfe's accounts of the *Grand Ole Opry*'s hiring practices in the 1930s, as pertains to the Delmore Brothers and Roy Acuff in particular: *A Good-Natured Riot: The Birth of the Grand Ole Opry* (Nashville: Vanderbilt University Press, 1999), 214–15 and 256–57. Richard Peterson offers a detailed account of the tensions between what he calls soft-shell and hardcore country in the *Opry* and the early career of Roy Acuff in *Creating Country Music: Fabricating Authenticity* (Chicago: University of Chicago Press, 1997), 138–48.

7. David Goodman, *Modern Twang: An Alternative Country Music Guide and Directory* (Nashville: Dowling Press, 1999), vii.

8. Tuttle, "Murder on Music Row."

9. Curtis Ellison has described the "tragic troubadour" aspects of his career in *Country Music Culture: From Hard Times to Heaven* (Jackson: University Press of Mississippi, 1995).

10. Covach, *What's That Sound?* (New York: W. W. Norton, 2006), 106; countless other accounts of rock's history during this period echo the same idea.

11. Jones, *Patsy*, 109.

12. Wells scored a top hit with "It Wasn't God Who Made Honky Tonk Angels," and Hill with "I Let the Stars Get in My Eyes."

13. Both Kitty Wells and Jean Shepard had number-one records that were duets with male singers, the Browns (including Maxine) had scored one top hit, and the Davis Sisters had a single number one.

14. See, for instance, Mary A. Bufwack and Robert K. Oermann, *Finding Her Voice: Women in Country Music, 1800–2000* (Nashville: Vanderbilt University Press, 2003); Bufwack and Oermann's pathbreaking 1993 edition of the same book; Kristine M. McCusker, *Lonesome Cowgirls and Honky-Tonk Angels* (Urbana: University of Illinois Press, 2008); and Stephanie Vander Wel, "'I'm a Honky-Tonk Girl: Country Music, Gender, and Migration," PhD diss, University of California Los Angeles, 2008, to name just a few such sources.

15. Jensen, *Nashville Sound*, 100.

16. Jones, *Patsy*, 123.

17. See, for instance, Paul Kingsbury, *The Patsy Cline Collection*, liner notes (MCA Records MCAD4-10421, 1991) 18.

18. Country fans have often granted cultural superiority to songs in which the singer appears to be singing from first-person, lived experience, even when that song was written by another songwriter. These connections are often traced to the impact of Hank Williams; see, for instance, Peterson, *Creating Country Music*, esp. 178–79.

19. Ronnie Pugh provided me with an invaluable list of songs to help in tracing this theme through country music's past.

20. Jones, *Patsy*, 123.

21. In those instances, the AABA pattern was used for the song's refrain (sometimes called the chorus in that era), and an introductory verse preceded it that was usually loosely used to advance the plot of the show in which the song appeared. A famous example of an AABA form is George Gershwin's "I Got Rhythm."

22. See, for instance, Jimmie Rodgers, "In the Jailhouse Now" (and discussion in Jocelyn R. Neal, *The Songs of Jimmie Rodgers* [Bloomington: Indiana University Press, 2009], esp. chapter three); The Carter Family, "A Hot Time in the Old Town Tonight" (sung as part of the duets with Jimmie Rodgers, recorded in 1931; see Mark Zwonitzer, *Will You Miss Me When I'm Gone?* [New York: Simon and Schuster, 2002], esp. 141–42); Bob Wills, "Right or Wrong." Hank Williams's songs in AABA form included "Hey, Good Lookin.'" Fred Rose's pop songwriting credentials are well documented by John W. Rumble in "Fred Rose and the Development of the Nashville Music Industry, 1942–1954," PhD diss, Vanderbilt University, 1980.

23. Jensen, *Nashville Sound*, 100.

24. See, for instance, Nolan Porterfield's account of producer Ralph Peer searching for songs that sounded "old" in the 1920s and 1930s (*Jimmie Rodgers: The Life and Times of America's Blue Yodeler*, rev. ed. [Urbana: University of Illinois Press, 1992], especially 99).

25. *Back-phrasing* is a vocal technique in which the singer performs the melody behind the beat, or in other words, sings the notes substantially later than the basic rhythmic structure of the song would indicate. This is especially noticeable at the end of phrases, where the band arrives at the final chord before the singer does.

26. Joli Jensen discusses how Cline's rhythmic phrasing changes over the span of her career in *Nashville Sound*, 102–5.

27. "The Nashville Sound," *The Illustrated History of Country Music*, ed. Patrick Carr (Garden City, N.Y.: Doubleday, 1979), chapter 10.

28. For a thorough critique of the Ivey and Greene perspective, see Jensen, *Nashville Sound*, 58–66.

29. According to statistics identified as "Top Selling Artists" on RIAA's Web site, Garth Brooks ranked third as of spring 2011, with certified sales of 128 million units; the next highest ranking country singer was George Strait, twelfth at 68.5 million units. http://www.riaa.com/goldandplatinumdata.php?table=tblTopArt (accessed September 2012).

30. This accusation is printed in the introduction of David Goodman's *Modern Twang: An Alternative Country Music Guide and Directory* (Nashville: Dowling Press, 1999) and has been requoted in countless sources since.

31. The film for which this was the theme song, and which starred Parton, eventually grossed well over one hundred million dollars.

CHAPTER 7

"Becoming a Postage Stamp"

Patsy Cline, Visual Image, and the Celebrity Process

Joli Jensen

This essay is about what Patsy Cline has been made to look like. In the 1950s and early 1960s she was a real person and performer who shaped and was shaped by her visual image, in and through the changing country music industry. Since her 1963 death, her visual image has been shaped by other people. By exploring how Patsy Cline has become a visual icon, we can investigate aspects of how country music and celebrity are culturally processed.

Searching for Patsy

In the summer of 1978 I had no idea what Patsy Cline looked like—she was just a stunning voice on the coverless vinyl record I had checked out from the public library. No one I knew in graduate school had heard of her. My country music disk jockey boyfriend suggested I give her a listen, because she had inspired Linda Ronstadt and Emmylou Harris. In search of a picture, I consulted an illustrated encyclopedia of country music.[1] It had one brief paragraph (and no picture) and implied that she was a pop, not a country, performer.

It is easy to forget that, during her lifetime, Patsy Cline's fame was mostly limited to her fans. After her death in 1963 until the early 1980s, she did not have anything like the wide name recognition she has now. I originally wanted to write her biography and spent the summers of 1979 and 1980 doing interviews and archival research in Nashville; Winchester, Virginia; and Washington, D.C.[2] In the end I wrote a dissertation, not a biography. It was about authenticity and commercialization in the country music industry 1950–1963, and it centered on Patsy Cline's recording career. It was eventually published as a book, and since then I have written several other scholarly articles drawing on the primary research I did in 1979–1983.[3]

It was during this time that Patsy became a posthumous celebrity. So I was part of an early 1980s cultural shift that rediscovered—and remade—Patsy Cline. This process is ongoing, as demonstrated by this book.[4] Thirty years after I failed to find a picture of Patsy Cline in the library, and almost fifty years after her death, she is a "country music icon" who even gets taken seriously as an object of scholarship.

But in 1978 the only way to find out what Patsy Cline looked like was to order her albums. As they arrived one by one, through a local record store, I discovered not only the odd variety of her songs (from twangy to bluesy to novelty tunes to the "classics"), but also the disappointing and confusing assortment of her "looks."

On the *Greatest Hits* album[5] she wears a yellow shirtwaist dress, along with what appears to be a dickie—a turtleneck insert. She has on white pumps and looks like a stereotypical 1950s TV housewife. The next album shows her draped across a stack of pillows wearing a blue lace dress, looking like a pop chanteuse.[6] On each of her album covers she looked different—and none of her images looked "country" to me. On one, she wore a striped top, looking like a college girl;[7] in another she wore sassy gold booties, a white shirt, tight red Capri pants, and a red gauze scarf ascot—a modish twenty-something.[8] In another she looked matronly, with sequined evening gown, permed hair, and long rhinestone earrings.[9]

The visual images of Patsy Cline available in the late 1970s did not add up and certainly did not make her look like I wanted her to look—like a 1950s Emmylou Harris. This was my first indication that I needed to stop projecting onto her what I needed her to be and instead stay open to discovering who she actually might have been.

In the summer of 1979 I was able to track down more pictures from fan magazines and fellow performers, thanks to the archives and helpful staff at the Country Music Hall of Fame Library and Media Center in Nashville.[10] These pictures did not add up either—the Patsy Cline they depicted ranged from sophisticated pop singer in a cocktail dress to pert barn dance girl in a gingham shirtwaist.

It took elaborate procedures to watch a kinescope of Patsy Cline—and so to get my first glimpse of Patsy in performance.[11] She was wearing a checked apron, singing "Walkin' After Midnight" while winding lace trim on a nostalgic general store set with china, fabric, and a grandfather clock set to midnight. This was definitely not the visual Patsy I wanted to find—dutifully pretending to be a clerk, while wearing a pinafore.

Today the Internet has made every one of these once scarce images—including the kinescope—accessible to everyone who wants to find them.[12] A few minutes on Google or Yahoo images or YouTube yields an impressive mix of Patsy album covers, kinescopes, personal photographs, and publicity stills.

Patsy Cline fan sites have lovingly arranged, cataloged, and re-presented these images. Deeply informed fans have uncovered and posted personal photos, obscure biographical details, and a wealth of previously unavailable information, displayed so that any newcomer can quickly and easily become an expert in Patsy arcana. And there is often a playful quality to their fan scholarship—my favorite example of this is the "golden bootie" award on Bill Cox's superb site "Patsy Cline: The Lady, the Legend."[13]

But in spite of this visual proliferation, one image of Patsy Cline has come to dominate the popular imagination. The contradictory images that I pains-takingly gathered in 1979 and 1980 (and that are now easily accessible on the Internet) have been distilled into a specific and iconic Patsy Cline—the one on the postage stamp.

This iconic Patsy Cline is relatively young, with dark wavy hair, big red lips, a gauze kerchief knotted on the side, and a fringed shirt. On the stamp she is singing into a big microphone. In related versions, she may or may not be wearing a white cowboy hat.

This iconic Patsy has also become the "community theater" Patsy—the one that actors adopt in order to portray her on stage in the two most popular theatrical productions, Ted Swindley's *Always . . . Patsy Cline*[14] and Dean Regan's *A Closer Walk with Patsy Cline*[15] For these plays the actors and the posters use approximations of the postage stamp look—dark wig, big red lips, gauze neckerchief, fringed shirt, maybe a microphone and hat.

The poster promoting *Always* has a stylized version of Patsy that may eventually supersede the postage stamp Patsy it resembles. This is the image used to promote the show, and it is available for purchase on coffee cups, pens, and a baseball cap. A graphically stylized Patsy is simply dark-haired, red-lipped, with a red (or blue) neckerchief. There is no fringe or microphone or cowboy hat, and she has been visually distilled to hair/eyes/lips/scarf.

Iconicity and Celebrity

A celebrity's image involves three interacting elements—the actual person, the performing self, and the iconographic image. The person is biological, the performer is more sociological, and the iconic image is more cultural. In other words, a celebrity is simultaneously a biological, sociological, and cultural object. When celebrities die, they become purely cultural objects. Patsy Cline's posthumous visual images show us how a celebrity's biography and performance record become symbolic resources that are selectively used to create and sustain a posthumous visual image.

An iconic visual image is something that the actual and performing selves inform, but can never fully control. Obviously, a celebrity is or was an actual human being, but a celebrity image is always a mediated, cultural process that only partially connects to the "real self" who creates and offers a "performing self" for audiences.[16]

Fans as well as scholars seek the "real" inside the performed and iconic. Meanwhile, various media professionals try to control the iconic image because the biographical and performing selves can disrupt what can be called "the iconization process." Rock Hudson is an example of someone whose biographical self (homosexual) so contradicted his performance self (heterosexual) that he became much more complex as an icon of masculinity.

The country music industry, like all culture industries, relies on real people who perform selves that sometimes become "iconic" so that they can effectively represent (especially posthumously) whatever we want them to mean. Hank Williams remains the most iconic country music performer, but Patsy Cline has now become a parallel female country music icon. Like Marilyn Monroe, Elvis Presley, Pablo Picasso, and others, her stylized image is recognizable by people who know very little about her biographical or performing selves.

Iconic imagery is never directly controlled by the performer or the publicity process. It is instead purely cultural—a symbolic reality we create, collectively. Iconization is a mediated process that creates celebrity images designed to meet audience needs. This obviously means that iconic images have less to do with real people or their actual performances and more to do with what we, culturally, need someone to represent.[17]

An iconic image uses the actual and performing selves to create a short-hand celebrity self—an image that is instantly recognizable as the star. Fame does not just bestow, but requires, this visual shorthand. With iconic dead celebrities—Michael Jackson is a recent example—thousands of visual possibilities are distilled into a signature look (glove, hat, ankle-length pants) that is easily recognized, reproduced, and parodied. Full iconization has been achieved, I argue here, when the icon's "look" can be reliably impersonated.

Patsy Cline offers us a case study of this process, and in the following pages I trace the ways that biographical and performing images of Patsy became distilled into an iconic "Patsy Cline." What happened with Patsy's visual imagery reflects an interaction between what she offered (as a biographical and performing self) and what she has been turned into. Interestingly, she now looks a lot like I wanted her to look back in 1978, when I first began researching her life and recording career and had only the sound of her voice to draw on.

Patsy and Iconicity

The biographical Patsy became a performer in a world that offered a particular set of class and gender markers. Fully understanding her options for her self-created "looks" would require knowing her personally and understanding exactly how social class and femininity were encoded in hair, shoes, clothes, and makeup in the period from the 1940s to the 1960s; in Winchester, Washington, D.C., and Nashville; in live performance and televised performances; in country music in particular and the music business in general.

Since this is impossible, we must instead piece together a story from the archival evidence. We know that Patsy Cline, the person, made her own choices about what she would look like, in everyday life and on stage. The pictures we have of her "real life" show a woman who sometimes chose clothes that showed off her figure making her look "fast" or even "trashy" in the language of the times.

There is one particular snapshot of her leaning against a tree, probably at a picnic or outdoor performance, looking like she is fifteen or sixteen. She is wearing short-shorts—a controversial signifier of female sexual confidence in the late 1940s. Today she just looks impossibly young and sweet and shapely. But I know from my interviews that, at least in Winchester, her short-shorts (and other clothing choices) along with her family background and connection to bandleader Bill Peer were evidence that she was "easy," i.e., sexually promiscuous.[18] She lacked many of the signifiers of 1950s middle-class feminine respectability—a point Beth Bailey makes in her essay in this volume.

But there are other pictures of Patsy from her private life where she is more modestly dressed in jeans and cotton shirt, with a bandanna over her hair—looking like a typical rural housewife and mother from the 1940s or 1950s.

A revealing biographical Patsy "look" involves a recording session where she showed up with her hair still in curlers. In the 1950s and 1960s, before blow dryers, women had two main choices for hair care. They either went to beauticians where their hair was washed, set, and dried under stationary dryer hoods, or they ran errands or did housework with their freshly washed hair rolled onto large metal tubes, usually covered by a scarf, and left to dry by itself.

This "hair in curlers covered by a scarf" look signified casualness and a lower-class look. The implication is that you might dress up later, but for now you are taking care of business. You are doing errands before some later time when you will dress up and style your own hair. Only rich, uptown women spend all day sitting around at beauty shops getting their hair done.

According to Jordanaire Ray Walker, Patsy came to one of her last 4 Star recording sessions with her hair in curlers.[19] He told me he was dismayed by this—it was not typical of Patsy. It was unprofessional and disrespectful of what everyone at the session—herself, her producer Owen Bradley, and the musicians—was working to accomplish. But, he implied, it was understandable. She was discouraged at the time, frustrated by the limits of her 4 Star contract and the lack of any hits since "Walkin' After Midnight." It was her way, he thought, of expressing hostility toward her situation and everyone in it—she just was not going to try anymore. The visual message was that her recording session was an errand she really did not care about. But she really did, he said, "She cared too much."

There are apparently no pictures of this particular session, so Walker's interpretation can be used to frame its meaning.[20] It is an example of how a "real self" uses a "look" to express biographical reality. Understanding it requires being aware of now-anachronistic gender and class signifiers such as curlers. But it is a rare example of how Patsy Cline, the person, controlled her own look for her own purposes. And it is not on the Internet.

Patsy also sought to shape her performing look, although it is hard to know how much power she actually had over her portrayal in publicity photos and on album covers. Many of her album and publicity photos used clothes she owned. Some of this clothing reappears in candid backstage shots, like the lace dress on *Sentimentally Yours*. If those are her personal earrings and evening gowns and Capri pants and gold booties, it is still unclear whether they were bought for photo shoots and then taken home, or selected from her own personal or professional wardrobe. And what were these clothes "trying to say" when she bought and wore them?

Early in her career Patsy worked with her seamstress mother to design the fringed cowgirl outfits that she used for many of her early stage and television performances. When Patsy began focusing on making a living as a singer, she created an interestingly gendered persona that drew from the dominant country and western look that was based largely on movie cowboys—fringed shirts with curlicues and cowboy boots.

The other main clothing option was what can be called the barn dance look—appropriate to a stage set of hay bales, wagon wheels, and wooden siding in a fantasy setting for music, talking, and dancing. This is the look that was used for the live shows broadcast as radio barn dances and for the touring package shows that were connected with them. It draws on the bib-overall and string-tie hillbilly look of the 1920s and 1930s, along with a square dance dress style (fitted bodice and petticoated skirt) worn by female dancers.

By the 1950s, a woman performing country music could choose either the cowgirl or the barn dance look if she wanted to stay within generic boundaries. Her choice said she was either "country western" or "hillbilly," the two terms used for what became in the 1960s officially "country music" on the *Billboard* charts. Patsy's 1950s performance pictures offer examples of both styles, along with the more sedate shirtwaists, before she settled on the pop-identified formfitting cocktail dresses of her 1961–1963 period.

The cowgirl look, made by her mother, was the less demure choice—more gender-bending, actually. It was suited to live performances in roadhouses in the Winchester area, but it was not necessarily the right look for television shows. Interviews with those who worked with her during this period imply that Patsy did not easily give up her cowgirl look in favor of the more sedate gingham pinafores and shirtwaists that she was expected to wear on television. Just as Patsy fought against the "pop sound" that ultimately made her famous, she resisted being visually tamed by wearing demure dresses in her early television appearances.

Pictures and publicity stills from various industry functions in the middle to late 1950s show that she chose to wear tight-fitting "glamour girl" dresses for these appearances—not the down-home, country fringe of her early stage costumes, or the domesticated shirtwaists of her television performances. When she was publically performing the role of 4 Star recording artist, she chose a look that may have seemed uptown or—to her, at least—starlike.

After the early 1960s success of "I Fall To Pieces," "Crazy," and "Sweet Dreams," she went even more "uptown" in her stage look. She wore a mink coat she loved and much dressier gowns for live performances. Her performance persona was still down-home and even raucous (as evidenced in the 1961 performance "Live at the Cimarron"[21]), but her performing look was much more sedate.

The key visual depiction of this would be the picture of her taken in 1962, when she and the Glaser brothers were booked in Las Vegas at the Mint Lounge. This was a well-paying engagement, but the lounge was small and off the beaten path. But visually Patsy went for movie star glamour. In the pictures we see a curvaceous Patsy in a form-fitting, sequin, floor-length evening gown—uptown personified.

Patsy Cline embodied the tension between down-home and uptown country music, particularly during this period.[22] That tension was obvious visually as well as aurally, where hillbilly, cowboy, and pop visual markers all mix together. Pictures of the *Grand Ole Opry* stage include performers in business attire (men) and dressy little suits (women) standing in front of wagon wheels, hay bales, and other barn dance signifiers, with cloggers in petticoats and banjo pickers in dungarees. This disjointed visual quality mirrors the contradictory effort, during the period, to find a commercially successful sound that could stay country but still cross over and appeal to a wider audience.

At the time, a steel-guitar, honky-tonk sound or a fiddle-based hillbilly sound were defined as "traditional." These were being replaced by a more orchestrated, and commercially viable, Nashville Sound that could and did cross over onto the pop charts which, increasingly, were shaping radio airplay and thereby determining record sales. Each of these three styles of country music have their visual components—cowboy look for honky tonk; overalls and gingham for hillbilly; and business suits and evening gowns for the Nashville Sound. As a performer, Patsy both sang and looked all three different styles.

Patsy Cline recorded over one hundred songs in a variety of styles, but her greatest commercial success came with the bluesy "Walkin' After Midnight," eventually followed by pop-sounding orchestrated songs such as "I Fall To Pieces," "Crazy," and "Sweet Dreams." These non-twangy songs were able to cross over onto the pop charts and thereby garner a wider, more lucrative audience in the more radio-driven industry. It is only in comparison with today's Nashville products that those four hit songs can be said to sound "country."

This helps explain why, in the 1970s, the illustrated encyclopedia I found in the public library refused to describe Patsy Cline as a "real" country music performer. As I documented in my dissertation and subsequent book, Patsy Cline and the Nashville Sound she exemplified was criticized as having "sold out." I was told over and over that Nashville Sound producers had commercialized the authentic country music of the 1940s and early 1950s. Giving up the rural sound (twang) and the rural look (cowboy or hillbilly) implied a disloyalty to tradition and to fans. It implied you were choosing to shed your down-home roots and instead join the upper class. Going pop was selling out. In spite of Patsy Cline's clearly country biography, her post-1961 performance style and look made her seem (until her posthumous 1980s revival) not-really-country.

But what was once dismissed as pop-crossover—Patsy and her music—has now retrospectively become "classic" country music. The Nashville Sound of the 1950s and 1960s, once defined as commercialized, now represents an era of lost authenticity.

Which means that Patsy Cline can now represent country music's lost authenticity, too. Few know or care that there was a time when she was perceived as "not really country." Her recent mobilization as a signifier of "real" country music is secure and embodied in the same way that her multiple, contradictory down-home/uptown images have been narrowed to the iconic scarf, fringe, and red lips.

So for today's audiences, Patsy Cline has come to signify some combination of female energy and independence. How? Partly through newly created images in two movies and two plays. Part of the explanation is that new media portrayals were being made available. People who may never have heard a Patsy Cline song in the 1970s were able, in the 1980s, to see a dynamic, engaging Beverly D'Angelo portrayal of Patsy in the 1980 movie *Coal Miner's Daughter*. And then they had Jessica Lange's version of a strong, fiery, mistreated wife in the 1985 biopic *Sweet Dreams*.

In the 1990s two plays brought that same figure to local theater audiences. In both *Always . . . Patsy Cline* and *A Closer Walk with Patsy Cline* she is brash, down home, and delightful—her "countryness" symbolized by her being so authentic, unpretentious, and down-to-earth.

The cinematic and staged Patsy tells an inspiring story of a brave, generous woman who grew up on the wrong side of the tracks, was in a difficult marriage, and lived the heartache she sang about. She was "natural" and "unaffected," a strong woman ahead of her time, who died tragically at the height of her powers.

This combination of obstacles, strength, individuality, and tragedy apparently helped ensure that Patsy would also become popular with gay and lesbian audience members. Jim White, writing in 1993 about the "gay craze" for Patsy Cline,[23] quotes Sussex University researcher Andy Medhurst, who studies gay icons. Medhurst argues that the story of Patsy overcoming her husband's abuse "adds to the tone of disappointment and despair in her songs . . . she is the nearest thing to a diva country music has."

White quotes Caz Gorham, who says that Patsy's music has the heartache that "is meaningful to those who are unable . . . to express feelings openly." But, Gorham adds, "there is a tongue-in-cheek element. Those clothes, that style. I don't think you can buy into it without a sense of irony." And Mandy Merck, producer of a BBC film called *Gay Rodeo*, says of Patsy's look: "It's feminine without being at all hesitant or little-girlish. And she looked big. She was a forcefully featured woman."

And, of course, the public embrace of Patsy by Canadian lesbian chanteuse k. d. lang in the 1980s cemented the identification of Patsy as lesbian-friendly. Lang named her band the Re-Clines, used producer Owen Bradley for several albums, and claimed to be in spiritual contact with Patsy who gave her advice from beyond the grave.

In 1996, Roseanne Cash wrote about Patsy in a *New York Times Magazine* special issue on "Women as Icons." She describes Patsy as someone who "is rooted in her body like a redwood in the earth, who is in command of a startling sexuality that infuses everything and who is the vehicle for a preternaturally affecting voice that both reveals and obscures her essence." Cash admires Patsy's "confidence and lack of self-consciousness" and says that she "lived a life utterly her own, messy and self-defined, and it all fed and merged with that voice."[24]

The Patsy that all these people admire is not a Patsy they have ever met personally or seen perform live. She is a symbolically constructed figure who meets the interpretive needs of the viewer. Cash is not really describing the person her stepmother (June Carter Cash) actually knew. Instead, she is describing the posthumous Patsy Cline portrayed in the movies and the plays. It is a culturally constructed Patsy, created from selected, repackaged elements of Patsy Cline's biographical and performing selves. When Patsy Cline was being rediscovered in the 1980s, she could be made to mean almost anything. The "country music icon" she has become washes away most of her biographical and performing contradictions—and offers instead a recognizable idealized inspiration.

Explaining Visual Transformation

Four different perspectives—production, consumption, aesthetics, and se-miotics—can be used to explain how Patsy was "rediscovered" in the 1980s and remains famous until the present day.[25] These same four perspectives can be used to explore, at least briefly, why her signature look may have developed in the ways that it has.

From a production perspective, the media seek to "brand" celebrities, and so the media distill a proliferation of images into a single, easy to recognize and reproduce, iconic image. It is always in the interest of media producers to define an image that is recognizable and widely appealing—not confusing or ridiculous. In Patsy's case, the movies and plays offered simplified options that became even more simplified and distilled into the posters and postage stamp.

From a consumption perspective, audience members need branding—they prefer a coherent and simple version of a contradictory and complicated visual record. Consumers do not want to have to sift through a bunch of complicated, anachronistic images—they need visual images that make quick and clear sense. In Patsy's case, fans barely born when she died desired a strong and independent but still tragic and poignant figure to represent the authentic experience that musical performance—especially country music performance—supposedly once offered.

And from an aesthetic point of view iconic images are streamlined and timeless—a way to abstract visual elements so that they can reliably appeal to a wider audience across time. Patsy's iconic image—lips/scarf/hair—is more desirable than the puzzling, various, dated images that the actual photographic record offers. From an aesthetic perspective, iconicity is a process that captures someone's visual traits in a fulfilling way—it winnows distracting details and finds the essential core.

But the semiotic perspective is probably the most productive perspective from which to analyze what has happened to Patsy's image, because it visually represents what happened, overall, with Patsy Cline's posthumous reputation. Semiotics explores how particular visual elements make meaning. Patsy's full cowgirl outfit was too country, just as her full chanteuse look was too pop, and her shirtwaist too 1950s housewife, and her Capris and golden booties too dated, unless interpreted ironically. But the semiotic meaning of the scarf, and the dark hair, and the lips that became her signature look are a little country, a touch pop, a bit of 1950s housewife, and a little dated. Just enough to be aesthetically valid, appealing to an audience, and useful to the media. A coherent visual image that allows Patsy to be recognizably "past" in the present, "country" in the world of popular music, "authentic" in a commercial context, strong and female and admirable.

Iconization Reconsidered

What does it mean when someone gets "iconized"—becomes an easily recognized, coherent image? What is gained and lost, in general, and with Patsy Cline in particular?

Obviously, an iconic image offers wider access to a celebrity. A single, simple image allows someone to become truly famous, rather than recognizable only to those "in the know." A unified and coherent look allows audience members who are not deeply interested in the biographical or performing selves to identify, and identify with, what that celebrity has been "made to mean."

In Patsy's case, when nonfans look at the Patsy poster or stamp, they see a woman who is presumed to be "real" and "ahead of her time" and "timeless." The inspiring posthumous Patsy Cline persona (brash, confident, comfortable in her own skin) is a construction. It is based in selected fragments of her story. Her "look" is only part of how she has been "made to mean," but it is a crucial part.

What is gained by iconization, then, is that we get another cultural figure onto whom we can inscribe our own desires. Once Patsy Cline becomes a postage stamp, she can mean whatever we want her to mean. She can stand in for whatever we want to believe in. Iconic Patsy can be made to represent the qualities we want a legendary country music star to have.

So what has been lost? The complexities of Patsy Cline's biography and performing career are mostly absent from the iconic image. She is country for sure, thanks to the fringe and neck scarf, and safely midcentury with the wavy black hair and large microphone. Her full red lips and direct gaze say she was confidently female, but not dangerously seductive. This particular iconic image gives us a Patsy Cline just country enough to be authentic, just retro enough to be cool, and just seductive enough to be desirable.

It does not give us the tensions between rural and urban, down-home and uptown that so deeply shaped her career. It also does not reveal the ambivalence about her social class. It does not give us the scarred forehead from her 1961 car accident, or her tumultuous marriages, or her motherhood, or her hair in curlers. Why should it? It gives us a Patsy that can tell us the story we want to be told about a strong, caring woman whose talent and temperament were ahead of her time and made her a star.

Is this a bad thing? Not necessarily. We never understand the world fully and in all its contradictory detail. An iconic image does not destroy our ability to read or understand other "selves." But an iconic image does inflect and organize all the other images. Once it has been created, it changes how we see every other depiction.

An iconic image comes to seem the essential one, and so it retroactively affects the understanding of the biographical and performing selves. Once someone becomes iconized, other visual images of the celebrity seem like deviations, or rough drafts, or bad copies.

With Patsy Cline, this is true with sound as well as look. Once iconic Patsy Cline songs are heard, her other recordings sound "not quite there" or "not really Patsy songs." But obviously all her recordings, however different in sound, are Patsy Cline songs. And all those different, seemingly contradictory looks are all "real" Patsy Cline images. They just do not sound or look like what we have led ourselves to expect.

So iconization is a process that locates, defines, and visualizes what people want a celebrity to be. It allows a general audience to "make the celebrity mean." And what celebrities have been made to mean is selectively and partially informed by their actual biographical and performing selves.

Patsy Cline's iconic image (like the Nashville Sound she helped to popularize) is designed to be just country enough to be widely appealing. It is also just dated enough to feel nostalgic, and just sexual enough to be "ahead of her time." That was, it seems, the Patsy Cline that people wanted in the 1980s and 1990s and that continues to entertain audiences in community theaters all over the world.

Scholars and fans share a dilemma—the more we find out about someone, the farther we are from connecting with them. In 1978, when all I knew about Patsy Cline was what I heard in her voice, I may have been as close as I will ever be to directly experiencing Patsy Cline. As I absorbed more and more images and facts and interpretations, I became less and less able to listen to her songs with pleasure, rather than analysis.

In a wonderful essay, novelist Walker Percy details how difficult it is to wrest direct experience from its symbolic packaging.[26] People are forever trying to achieve direct, intense, unmediated experience, using strategies to try to get to "it"—the really real. What Percy implies is that "culture" is the inescapable symbolic packaging in which all human experience is wrapped.

The consequences of iconization, therefore, are the same as the consequences of symbolic packaging. The question is—in an age of visual, auditory, and narrative proliferation—are we getting closer or farther from Percy's "it"? In other words, does iconization help or hurt our ability to directly experience reality?

Percy's notion of symbolic packaging supports both helping and hurting. A visual icon could represent a distillation, a way to break through the proliferating packaging to the essence of a celebrity. In an era of visual "too muchness" an iconic image could offer sanctuary. Because it is so simple and open ended, an iconic image might give us easier access to a celebrity's symbolically distilled essence. Iconicity, in this explanation, helps us "see through" the packaging. Or it could be the opposite—an iconic image offers even more impermeable packaging, keeping us even further away from apprehending contradictory, messy reality. It stands in the way, preventing acknowledgment of how confusing, even incoherent, people, including celebrities, really are.

My sense is that iconization makes it harder to know and appreciate contradictions in lived experience. Obviously not everyone wants to know every detail of Patsy's biographical and performing selves. But Patsy Cline's image has been shaped and selected to tell us mostly what we want to find. There were lots of things she was trying to say, using her looks. Do we really want to sift through all the contradictory images and decipher what she might be trying to show? No. It is easier to settle for iconic images, and find only what we always, already, wanted to see.

NOTES

1. This was probably Fred Dellar, Roy Thompson, and Douglas B. Green, *The Illustrated Encyclopedia of Country Music*, with an introduction by Roy Acuff (New York: Harmony Books, 1977).

2. My primary research included recorded interviews with Mae Boren Axton, Owen Bradley, Charlie Dick, Ralph Emery, Connie B. Gay, Harlan Howard, Kathy

Copas Hughes, Joe Johnson, Brenda Lee, Jim McCoy, Redd O'Donnell, Gordon Stoker, Ray Walker, and Faron Young, as well as review of coverage of country music and Patsy Cline 1953–1965 in *Billboard Music Week*, *Country Song Roundup*, *Country and Western Jamboree*, *Trail Magazine*, and other archival material of the period housed in the Country Music Hall of Fame Library and Media Center.

3. Joli Jensen, *The Nashville Sound: Authenticity, Commercialization, and Country Music* (Nashville: Country Music Foundation Press and Vanderbilt University Press, 1998); Jensen, "Patsy Cline's Recording Career: The Search for a Sound," *Journal of Country Music* 9 (1982): 34–46; "'Walkin' After Midnight': Patsy Cline, Musical Negotiation, and the Nashville Sound," in *All That Glitters: Country Music in America*, ed. George H. Lewis (Bowling Green: Popular Press, 1992); "Patsy Cline's Crossovers: Celebrity, Reputation, and Feminine Identity," in *A Boy Named Sue: Gender and Country Music*, eds. Kris McCusker and Diane Pecknold (Jackson: University of Mississippi Press, 2004), 107–31.

4. Thanks to colleague Douglas Gomery for suggesting to me and Warren Hofstra that I participate in "Sweet Dreams: The Life and Times of Patsy Cline," the conference held on April 4, 2008, in Richmond, Virginia, sponsored by the Virginia Historical Society. It was a delightful and humbling experience to discuss Patsy Cline's visual image with such knowledgeable panelists and audience members.

5. *Patsy Cline's Greatest Hits*, Decca Records, DL 74854, March 13, 1967, cover photo by Hal Buksbaum.

6. *Sentimentally Yours: Patsy Cline*, Decca Records, DL 74202, August 7, 1962.

7. Her first album, *Patsy Cline*, Decca Records, DL 8611D, August 5, 1957.

8. This image is on the rereleased MCA cover of *Patsy Cline Showcase*, MCA 87, photo by Hal Bucksbaum. The original *Patsy Cline Showcase* album cover (Decca Records, DL 74202) has three small identical headshots of Cline wearing an off-shoulder evening dress.

9. *The Legend: Patsy Cline*, 4 Star Records #1/2/3, 1985.

10. I remain grateful for the knowledge and support I received from those who worked there at the time—including Ronnie Pugh, Robert K. Oermann, John Lomax III, Don Roy, and then editor of the *Journal of Country Music*, Kyle Young.

11. Available on YouTube at http://www.youtube.com/watch?v=96SNCWuCWNM (accessed September 2012).

12. Permission could not be obtained to reproduce images of Patsy Cline in this chapter. Interested readers are encouraged to use the Internet to find the images referenced throughout.

13. The URL for this impressive site is www.patsified.com (accessed September 2012). Other fan sites demonstrating the tremendous dedication and acumen of particular fans are A Tribute to Patsy Cline: Her Life and Career, www.patsy.nu; Patsy Cline: A Fan's Tribute, www.patsyclinetribute.com; and The Incomparable Patsy Cline: Sean's Award Winning On-line Museum, www.reclinerclub.com (accessed September 2012). On YouTube, a French teenager, Arnaud (crazy4patsycline), has been posting rare television and radio appearances. All this goes to prove that fans can outstrip scholars in their zeal for accuracy and understanding—for my take

on fan/scholar similarities, see my "Fandom as Pathology: The Consequences of Characterization," in *Reader in Mass Communication Theory*, ed. Denis McQuail (London and Thousand Oaks, Calif.: Sage Publications, 2002), 342–54.

14. *Always . . . Patsy Cline* opened in June 1997, and was one of the most produced plays in 1998. It continues to be performed by community theaters, telling a story about Patsy Cline's inspiring personal relationship with a female fan. The Ted Swindley production Web site (www.tedswindley.com (accessed September 2012) sells Patsy Cline merchandise, including several versions of a fringed cowgirl shirt.

15. This production traces her life and career, using twenty of her songs, and has the approval of Patsy Cline's estate. Marquis Entertainment offers marketing and production assistance, and, by request, will arrange an appearance by Patsy's husband Charlie Dick.

16. Joli Jensen, "On Fandom, Celebrity, and Mediation: Posthumous Possibilities," introduction to *Afterlife as AfterImage: Understanding Posthumous Fame*, eds. Steve Jones and Joli Jensen (New York: Peter Lang, 2005), xv–xxiii.

17. The controversy over whether the 1993 Elvis postage stamp should show the "young" or the "old" Elvis suggests that there were two very different groups commemorating Elvis—those who had aged along with Elvis and accepted his later, larger Vegas incarnation, and those who wanted to think of him as the young, slim rock-and-roller. Few remember he was once billed as "the hillbilly cat."

18. See Margaret Jones, *Patsy Cline: The Life and Times of Patsy Cline* (New York: HarperCollins, 1994; New York: De Capo, 1999), 47–48 on what she calls the "Nudie's-of-Hollywood-meets-Frederick's-of-Hollywood" midriff bearing, fringed short-shorts, western ensemble. "The Outfit" caused quite a stir in the Winchester area and fit in with the notion that Patsy's performing self was too risqué. The image of Patsy Cline in short-shorts can be viewed in Stuart E. Brown Jr. and Lorraine F. Myers, *Patsy Cline: Singing Girl from the Shenandoah Valley* (Berryville, Va.: Chesapeake Book Company, 1996), 41.

19. Ray Walker interview, June 25, 1979. Tapes of these and other interviews I conducted in 1979 and 1980 have been donated to the Library of American Broadcasting at the University of Maryland.

20. In Margaret Jones's interview with Johnny Anderson, May 24, 1991 (quoted in Jones, *Patsy*, 48), there is also a mention of Patsy driving around Winchester in her red-and-white convertible with her hair in rollers.

21. *Patsy Cline: Live at the Cimarron Ballroom*, live performance in Tulsa, Oklahoma, recorded July 19, 1961, but not released until July 29, 1997, by MCA Records, MCAD 11579.

22. See, for example, Richard Peterson "The Dialectic of Hard-Core and Soft-Shell Country Music," *South Atlantic Quarterly* 94 (Winter 1995): 273–300; Peterson, *Creating Country Music: Fabricating Authenticity* (Chicago: University of Chicago Press, 1997).

23. This and following quotes from Jim White, "Is Charlie Making Patsies of Lesbians?" *Independent*, April 16, 1993, 18.

24. Roseanne Cash, "Patsy Cline: Honky Tonk Angel," *New York Times Magazine*, November 24, 1996, 66–67.

25. Joli Jensen, "Posthumous Patsy Clines: Construction of Identities in Hillbilly Heaven," in Jones and Jensen, *Afterlife as AfterImage*, 121–42.

26. Walker Percy, "The Loss of the Creature," in *The Message in a Bottle: How Queer Man Is, How Queer Language Is, and What One Has To Do with the Other* (New York: Farrar, Strauss and Giroux, 1975), 46–63.

The Historical Significance of Patsy Cline

Warren R. Hofstra

Without the resurgence of Cline's posthumous popularity in the 1980s and her subsequent elevation to iconic status—witness the 1993 postage stamp—her story would be very different. Her early death notwithstanding, she has received little of the scholarly attention given to Jimmy Rogers or Hank Williams, each of whose stardom was equally fleeting but whose celebrity today is arguably far less than Cline's. Is then this book more about Cline's enduring legacy than the cultural significance of her life and career? Is it about images of Cline or about the real Cline?

These juxtapositions, however, beg the larger question of Cline's importance in American cultural history since her rise as a country music performer in the early 1950s to the present. Cline would never have achieved stardom or iconization had her character and her career not resonated with some of the deepest chords of history within her community, her region, and the nation. Cline's significance and the significance of writing about her are therefore measured in the depth of her time and the heights touched upon by her story. By these measures, hers is a life well worth examining.

As Bill Malone put it: "the contours of her life, and her evolution as a singer, paralleled the major transformations that were reshaping the cultural moorings of her class and region." These transformations placed Cline at the "most important intersections" of various cultural and economic movements at play in her day. All emanated in some way from the American experience in World War II. What rendered Cline's life and career significant in postwar America was her central position at three of these crossroads: rural tradition and urban modernism, local status and national authority, and finally, industrial production and domestic consumption. Each entailed a transition: from rural to urban, from local to national, and from the economics of production to the economies of consumption—all taking place in the 1950s. Convergences among these trends in the postwar period, however, are traceable in historical currents reaching much deeper into the American past.

The proportion of Americans living in cities had been increasing steadily since the founding of the America republic, but only by the 1920s had a majority of Americans come to live in urban areas.[1] The upheavals and dislocations of the Great Depression and the world war that followed deferred America's true embrace of the city and the culture of modernity until the 1950s. The architecture of New York's Lever House (1952) and then the Seagram Building (1958) proclaimed the demise of classicism and historicism as sources for contemporary design in favor of volumetric massing, geometric irregularity, and the rhythmic repetition of surface features so powerfully characteristic of urban modernism. Similarly, bebop in New York City broke the historical continuity of jazz by projecting a bold new sound largely stripped of reference to the southern music traditions converging in New Orleans at the origin a half-century earlier of this uniquely American music. And in the formless experience of painting as aesthetic process, Jackson Pollock came to symbolize the rejection of traditional meaning at the core of modern art. That country music survived and thrived in such an age and that Patsy Cline rode its wave to stardom in the crossover world of pop music during it underscores the depth of the cultural crosscurrents moving through her era.

Paralleling this rural-urban transition was an equally profound shift in cultural authority away from local, class-bound communities toward national networks of information and celebrity loosely woven together by varied new media—but most notably through television. Since the creation of the U.S. Post Office in 1775, the history of communication in America has been marked by various improvements and inventions that vastly increased the speed and enlarged the content of information flowing throughout the country and the world. From the inception of the modern newspaper and the proliferation of the telegraph in the years before the American Civil War to the discovery of radio and the transmission of moving images in film and on television during the ensuing century, Americans have seen how the influences over their lives, behaviors, beliefs, and ideals have shifted from the face-to-face dynamics of community relations to the faceless power of public relations. Corporations and advertising firms have gained control over the media's marketing of news, sports, entertainment, and most recently, reality itself. In this process the public sphere of American life has expanded from the public spaces and public markets of immediate communities to the intellectual and cultural spaces of imagined communities transecting the nation.

Certainly industrial output has depended upon the rates at which people bought manufactured goods since Samuel Slater built the first mechanical spinning mill in America at Pawtucket, Rhode Island, in 1793. And demand drove the greatest expansion of American industrial production in the years between the Civil War and the World War I, during which the United States came to outproduce all the industrial countries of the world combined. But it was not until the 1930s when New Deal economists began blaming the economic catastrophe of the Great Depression on the inability of working people to afford the selfsame goods they made, did politicians and planners begin to devise the public programs necessary to arm Americans with the buying power needed to drive both production and consumption in an upward spiral of economic recovery. World War II then provided not only for the full employment but also for the accumulation of pent-up consumer demand that exploded in postwar markets as war industries converted rapidly to the manufacture of domestic goods, and the G.I. Bill, the baby boom, and defense spending drove consumer expenditures to ever greater heights. The resulting consumer revolution of the 1950s vastly enlarged the American middle class. Desires for new products—many developed during World War II—crossed lines of region, race, ethnicity, and most significantly, social class. Credit cards, expanded consumer loans, and a burgeoning advertising industry fueled acquisitiveness. Television not only consolidated this new national culture and cultural authority but also transformed the life and career of Patsy Cline.

It is tempting—with Bill Malone's encouragement—to see the national transition from rural life to urban living in the move Patsy Cline's family made in 1948 from its itinerancy in the villages and hamlets of the Shenandoah Valley to the factory town of Winchester, where Patsy's mother remained until the end of her life. Working in Winchester meant living close to the bone at the intersection of rural and urban America. In order to make ends meet, Hilda Hensley took in sewing in a pattern of women's domestic work deeply rooted in rural communities.[2] But when her eldest daughter put herself to labor in the chicken factory, the family clearly joined the urban working class in a real and personal way. And despite a large working class in Winchester, a strong antiunion culture—predicated upon the self-interested commitment of the upper, or proprietary, class to the long-standing freedom of contract and subordination of labor characteristic of rural America—was embedded in the town's class structure.[3] Winchester was, after all, the home of both Harry Byrd Sr. and Jr. The former helped engineer the passage of the Taft-Hartley, Labor-Management Relations Act through Congress in 1947 while the latter secured its stepchild in the Virginia Assembly, the Virginia

Right to Work Act. This measure outlawed the closed union shop and affirmed the dependence of the urban working classes upon their social "betters," many of whom had attained wealth in rural pursuits as farmers and orchardists. It was, then, in the cultural shear of this unstable environment with men and women caught in the crosswinds of urban and rural America that Cline's rise to stardom in the 1950s provoked deep disturbances in the class structure and social history of Winchester that enveloped her legacy in conflict and innuendo for decades.

Turbulence at the convergence of urban and rural life manifested itself throughout Cline's career. After she left Winchester and settled in Nashville, she helped pioneer the Nashville Sound and a style of country music tellingly called "countrypolitan." If rural tradition was embodied in the hard sound of high country, then it was the fiddle, the steel guitar, and the nasal intonations of traditional singing by the likes of Hank Snow, Hank Williams, Rose Maddox, Ernest Tubb, Webb Pierce, Kitty Wells, and others that linked country music to its rural roots at the same time it attracted a nostalgic urban working-class audience in the honky-tonk era of the late 1940s and early 1950s. And honky tonk had been the music that so powerfully attracted Patsy Cline at the precise moment she began working in Winchester. Honky tonk dominated jukeboxes in city bars, diners, and beer joints or shows in the roadhouses and small-town dance halls where she launched her singing career. For a city girl, cowgirl dress provided another connection to rural life. Cline had never ventured much beyond the Valley and had seen western attire only in the movies or live at the Palace Theater in Winchester. But western fringe, bandanas, and high boots made for strong signifiers of her attachment to the rural ambience and sonic culture of hard country. So did the yodels and yelps with which she peppered her songs.

According to Kris McCusker, western imagery and cowboy dress provided an antidote to the anonymity and the hard edge of city living. For a 1950s generation the individualism and personal freedom of the great American West were cultural standards to rally around in defense of American nationhood and an idealized rural past. Thus the western contrivances of country music positioned the genre at one of the most prominent intersections of modernism and history in American life. If the new urban architecture rejected the historicism of classical form, gothic ornament, and revivalist decoration, then massing and rhythm played a structural role in Cline's dress as well. For gigs in nightclubs such as the York Inn near Winchester or Front Royal's John Marshall Nightclub, Cline donned a stripped-down, form-fitting, sleek, black cocktail dress—a sartorial accompaniment to the refined glass-walled skyscrapers of her age—to sing pop songs with the Jack Fretwell Orchestra. Something similar could be said about the sonic design of the Nashville Sound. In crafting it, Owen Bradley, Paul Cohen, Chet Atkins, and others expunged the embellishments of honky tonk and stripped it of its country referents by replacing the fiddle with violins, rebuilding rhythm sections with pianos, vibraphones, and drums, all the while moving accompaniments upscale to the smooth sounds of vocal groups like the Anita Kerr Singers or the Jordanaires. And, of course, they relied on Cline's voice at its country bel canto best.[4] Claiming that these architects of the Nashville Sound accomplished for music what the likes of Mies van der Rohe or designers at Skidmore, Owings, and Merrill did for America's greatest cities seems pretentious at face value, but with varied media and meaning all were artists and artisans working in the aesthetics of one of Bill Malone's "most important intersections" of cultural production in American life.

Cline's posturing as a "new woman" as well as a "girl singer" in country music also created turbulence at the intersection of urban and rural strains of life in the 1950s. Some would say that Cline's greatest contribution to the social history of country music came through her role as a feminist who broke gender barriers in a male-dominated world. In this volume, for instance, Joli Jensen asserts that Cline was a "natural" and "strong" woman who was "ahead of her time." George Hamilton IV takes the argument a step further in proclaiming that Cline did not just "open the doors" for women in country music but she "kicked them down."[5] The feminist Cline certainly became a prominent feature of her legacy as it was reconstituted beginning in the 1980s. The Cline that Joli Jensen rediscovered during that decade and who became a cultural icon in the next was a version already appropriated by a feminist movement devoted to equal rights for women in a modern, urban America. The strength of American feminism lay in the nation's cities. It was here that women made original contributions to American politics, intellectual life, and culture while seeking new opportunities in education, employment, and the professions. Feminism in the late twentieth century was modernism—women rejecting the past and with it the male ascendency and sequestered domesticity of traditional rural life in America. It was Malone who wrote in this volume that city life for country migrants challenged the "old social hierarchies" that had promised "stability" and "security" in "masculine dominance, white supremacy, [and] the unquestioned obedience of youth."

But in a detailed examination of gender and women's roles in country music from the period in which the radio barn dance dominated the genre to the 1950s, McCusker parses out evidence of a much more complex and elaborately gendered world in which Cline crafted her career. Although Cline was one of country music's first women to achieve stardom as a solo performer, she did so in a field crowded with women playing various roles, from girl singer in a family band to singing housewife, from fan club president to production assistant, from songwriter to deejay, and from music journalist to successful lyricist. McCusker's point is that in the rural traditions of barn dance radio, Cline's celebrity as a woman was nothing extraordinary. Her argument not only "tears away the image of a feminist Patsy Cline," but with the collapse of the barn dance paradigm in the music media and the rise of a new one based on the transforming medium of television, she positions Cline clearly at one of the most important and contested cultural intersections of her era. That Cline never advocated women's rights publicly, however, fails to gainsay her legacy as a protofeminist who, if only in retrospect, parted the waters for women performers in a sea of male domination.

The question remaining, therefore, concerns the cultural process of appropriation in which Cline as a legacy became something she was not in life. An answer may come in the forceful persona for which Cline is justly famed. She certainly exploited her straight-shooting, hard-hitting qualities of character that many people, mostly men, found equally alluring and off-putting. In the absence of the kind of institutional support the feminist movement later provided ambitious, aggressive women, Cline, relying solely on her own devices, perfected the gruff language, jocular humor, and overt sexuality needed to be always on the offense in relations with men. No one provides a more vivid account of how Cline made her way in a male world of 1950s country music than George Hamilton IV. All the varied roles played by women in this world notwithstanding, it was nonetheless a realm men still governed. When Cline moved to Washington in fall 1954 shortly after having mastered and dismissed two dominant men in her life—her first husband, Gerald Cline, and her lover and bandleader, Bill Peer—she remained under the thumb of men, at least professionally, in the characters of Connie B. Gay and Jimmy Dean, and in the masculine culture of the D.C. dance halls where she performed.[6] But it was on Gay's *Town and Country Jamboree* with Dean that Cline met Hamilton. Hamilton was a disarming young college student from North Carolina on his way up in the music world on the strength of great talent, good looks, and lucky breaks. But by his own account, he "was a shy, awkward, 'wet behind the ears' nineteen-year-old." Cline, by contrast, was a "seasoned professional in every sense of the word." But in her notorious patter of gibes and jokes, she established who unquestionably was the boss. "Who do you think you are, Hoss?—the Pat Boone of country music?" she demanded of him on one occasion when he came across as a little too clean-cut. Hamilton took these quips in good humor and as a sign more of affection than affront, but Cline's blunt directness and coarse earthiness clearly worked to clear a wide path for her in a highly gendered world in which women otherwise were expected to compromise in the presence of men. It would be too great a stretch to impose the grand scheme of rural-urban conflict over Cline's encounter with Hamilton—Hamilton the country rube and Cline the streetwise new woman—but the qualities of Cline's character that emerge therein certainly positioned her for appropriation as either augur or oracle of feminism in one of the great reform movements dominating the latter age of Cline's iconization.[7]

If feminism was an impulse of urban life, then it was also an expression of national culture. Reformers in smaller communities and rural areas throughout America relied on leadership from national organizations. The National Organization for Women (NOW) was founded in 1966 three years after Cline died and Betty Friedan published *The Feminine Mystique*, the book that made the modern women's movement. If local communities in the years before 1963 were bound tight by interconnected lines of gender, race, age, and social class as Bill Malone has indicated, then the emergence of a new national women's rights reform movement was one expression of the larger transformation of local into national sources of cultural authority. This was the deep change traced by Beth Bailey as moral respectability—the glue holding face-to-face communities together—gave way to amoral celebrity in a consumer society in which household spending defined personal identity, and lifestyle increasingly challenged gender, race, age, and class as the structural principle of social order.[8]

Country music had always possessed a national following since it emerged as hillbilly music in 1920s recordings and on radio broadcasts of barn dance programs such as the *Grand Ole Opry* or the *National Barn Dance* at the same time. The outward migration of southerners—including many African Americans—to take jobs in northern industries beginning in World War I was responsible in part for the nationalization of this genre of rural culture, but as already discussed, new media—notably television in the 1950s—completed this important transition from local to national as one of the great intersections of modern life. Patsy Cline's career is itself a study in this monumental movement from local to national culture—a story of her spiraling outward from community to region and then nation in epicycles of performance and recognition.[9]

Cline began singing locally, mostly in the company of her mother, at roadhouses and supper clubs, anywhere a woman under twenty could get gigs. In September 1952, however, she persuaded Bill Peer to take her on as the girl singer with his Melody Boys, a territory band. In Peer's company she appeared before audiences within the band's reach extending from West Virginia to Brunswick, Maryland, and including the Northern Virginia piedmont and occasionally the country music bar scene in Washington, D.C. And it was with Peer that Cline made her first trip to New York City in November 1954. By this time, however, she had already won the National Country Music Championship, in reality a local affair held every summer at the Warrenton, Virginia, fairgrounds but drawing major audiences. In addition to attracting fans, this victory also captured the attention of Connie B. Gay and brought Cline to Washington.[10]

In the nation's capital, Cline's circle of attraction grew dramatically. Gay booked Cline, Dean, and others including Dale Turner, Mary Klick, and the Texas Wildcats at major venues, including Constitution Hall, the National Guard Armory, Griffith Stadium, and on at least one occasion, the Lincoln Memorial. But the full circle of clubs and dance halls where Gay's crew performed stretched for a hundred miles from Washington. It encompassed Winchester, where Cline's mother still lived. And, as Douglas Gomery has written in this volume, it was with Gay that Cline received her first experiences performing regularly on radio and then, more significantly, on television. She learned the body language of visual appeal so necessary to success on this new medium. Thus the ground for Cline's rise to national stardom had been well prepared regionally long before her appearance on *Arthur Godfrey's Talent Scouts* in January 1957. Unlike the large majority of people in her hometown who stayed put for a lifetime, Cline outgrew the confines of Winchester in stages that paralleled an alternative American experience of moving from local to national sources of cultural authority. That she was often out of step with a community she nonetheless called home throughout her own lifetime is hardly surprising.

Just as Cline broke through the geographical barriers enclosing Winchester society in the 1950s, so she also penetrated the cultural boundaries by which respectability shaped middle-class life. It was in this sense that the course of Cline's career fulfilled the local-to-national metamorphosis that in Beth Bailey's formulation gave it national significance. Cline, according to Bailey, lacked respectability not simply due to rumors of affairs but additionally because of her latent sexuality. White women of Washington Street could rightly worry about their husbands in the presence of such a woman. So could their Kent Street counterparts, who might feel betrayed by one of their own. White men suffered the temptation she represented. Cline's innocence aside, she became the object of sexual slander because she trespassed the borderlands of class distinction and its vital function of validating how some in town could live better off the labor of others. Or so say Hofstra and Foreman in an argument that what was contested in Cline's legacy was not some peccadillo festering beneath the social skin of community life but a sign of the way in which middle-class consumption deprived society of the material and affective distinctions upon which the social order had traditionally depended. It was no accident therefore that Cline's celebrity rested upon the sale of a music commodity her producers crafted for a popular audience in which sales defined popularity. Throughout the nation, this formula for celebrity worked brilliantly, but locally it rancored. This contradiction underscores the national significance of our third major intersection that Cline crossed in her career: production and consumption.

By the 1950s many economists felt that Americans had solved the technical problems of industrial production. American industry could deliver goods seemingly in excess of any demand.[11] World War II had demonstrated this. In 1940, President Roosevelt's call for aircraft manufacturers to produce fifty thousand planes a year had been condemned as unrealistic. Four years later the industry turned out almost twice that number. One B-24 rolled out of Henry Ford's Willow Run plant every hour; shipyards in California launched a new merchant ship every other week. In the postwar years this kind of productivity was redirected toward consumer goods. Within a few years of the outbreak of peace, American industry was meeting the huge domestic demand for cars, appliances, and other goods. What Ford, GM, and Chrysler accomplished in automaking, William Levitt achieved for home-building. By mass producing more than seventeen thousand homes in Levittowns in New York and Pennsylvania, he could offer a two-bedroom Cape Cod for less than $8,000. These are only a few examples of the immense productivity of postwar America. By 1960 the output of the American economy measured in the gross national product exceeded consumer expenditures by more than 50 percent.[12]

Developments in the cultural production of music in the 1950s mirrored the productivity gains in consumer industries. Many of the innovations behind the mass marketing of music can be traced to the early twentieth century and Tin Pan Alley's success in streamlining the creation and sale of songs and sheet music. Due to this achievement and the rise of the radio and recording industries, a large number of Americans could listen to music regularly at home by World War II. After the war, however, the LP, the 45, format radio, the Top Ten, and most significantly, television placed the consumption of mass-produced music within the grasp of practically every American. Teenagers emerged as a distinct market segment, and their musical demands fueled the rock-and-roll revolution as well as a national fixation with youth culture and musical taste. Despite a freshet of high school garage bands, the immensity of consumer choice in the 1950s created a culture of music consumption while it initiated a long-term decline in music making at home and within communities.[13]

But the meta-narrative of consumption does not tell the whole story of American music in the age of middle-class consumption, nor does it give credit to the position Patsy Cline assumed at the crossroads of production and consumption during the era of her rising fame. Automakers quickly learned that yearly style changes and a parade of new models each fall timed with the seasonality of television shows piqued the desires of auto buyers to replace their old machines every several years or so. Scheduled innovation and planned obsolescence, moreover, created a constant turn-over of new appliances in the home. Producers, in other words, learned that goods could be engineered in production for maximizing consumption by linking need with novelty and necessity with desire.[14] Bradley, Cohen, and Atkins, of course, did much the same for the Nashville Sound in their own studios. No longer did they simply open their doors and wait for talent to walk through. Nor did they put together a singer's accompaniment out of an assemblage of studio musicians on the ready. They carefully crafted every element of the sound they transferred from the studio to vinyl disk. This may be an oversimplification of the recording process, but the point is that the Nashville Sound emerged from Bradley's Quonset Hut and RCA's Studio B as a conscious creation fine tuned for an explicit market of pop and country listeners. Cline, of course, was Bradley's critical ingredient in this new mix.[15]

In the end, Cline became the icon for a new music aesthetic because she grew up loving the popular sound of big bands, saw a future in country music as a rising star in the honky-tonk era, and lusted after celebrity for the freedom it brought from the steel trap of poverty and respectability. With a house in the Nashville suburbs, a white convertible, and a new husband, she too joined the middle class insofar as that class had come to be defined by consumption. And with his singer's success, Bradley closed the loop of music production and consumption through the intentional creation of a sound crafted for popularity. Self-styling for stardom would in the years to come place country music among the top-grossing musical genres in America. But country also surrounded itself with a culture of disingenuousness in which, as Jocelyn Neal demonstrates, a Taylor Swift could become the Country Music Association's Entertainer of the Year at the same time that media surveys placed Swift squarely at the trite end of a country continuum that began with tradition and sincerity. Patsy Cline as progenitor of the Nashville Sound, however, came across in the same survey as traditional, and by contrast, authentic. What Cline in her legacy became only underscores the significance of the intersection between production and consumption from which that legacy derives.

One cannot help wonder what if Cline had survived? What if she had become a living legend instead of a country music legacy? Her brief existence bracketed the life experience of America's "Greatest Generation" that fought the Great Depression, won World War II, and prospered in the 1950s. But this was also a generation its own children rejected in the 1960s only to be refurbished in American popular culture in the 1980s and 1990s, the era of resurgence for Cline's own reputation.[16] The fall and rise of Cline's legacy may have resonated with the broad cultural movements shaping American history during the half-century after her demise, but causal connections are difficult to establish. Cline's violent death during the same year that John F. Kennedy suffered an assassin's bullet in an incident that unhinged a nation seems rationale enough for the immediate eclipse of her popularity. If Cline rode to stardom on the wave of the Nashville Sound's popularity among white, middle-class suburbanites, then it is doubtful that her talent, no matter how brilliant, would have survived the onslaught of the British rock music invasion, the rise of soul music, and the sonic frenzy of the counterculture revolution against middle-class suburbia. Had she lived, her career may have followed the course taken by Jan Howard or Loretta Lynn, both great performers but neither an icon. The central fact of Cline's life, however, is her death. And it was in her death that she bequeathed a legacy that like the contours of her life paralleled the major transformations of the coming history.[17]

In addition to the counterculture, the transformations of the 1960s rested upon civil rights, feminism, the Vietnam War, and the antiwar movement it spawned. All, in one way or another, constituted rejections of the middle-class culture of respectability that Beth Bailey identified as so vulnerable in the 1950s. But so too did these movements condemn the materialism at the heart of the 1950s consumer culture that supplanted respectability with cupidity and produced lifestyles fashioned largely by consumer goods. If Cline, on her own terms, had already rejected respectability, her career was inextricably entwined with the rise of a consumerist middle class in the 1950s and the culture of popular music at its core. It is no wonder, therefore, that her reputation sank with the reaction of 1960s youth against this culture. Unlike Willie Nelson, the author of her most famous song, "Crazy," she was unable to let her hair grow, don bandanas, and abandon Nashville in search of creative freedom under wide-open Texas skies. As leader of the Outlaws, a loosely construed band of Austin singers that included Waylon Jennings,

Kris Kristofferson, and others, Nelson represented an explicit rejection of the Nashville Sound and the system of production behind it. Clearly the focus of American music had shifted away from Cline and the temper of her times.

Less apparent in the 1960s but equally potent were the seeds of a conservative reaction to the revolutions of that era. These sprouted during the next decade not from the business culture of either Wall Street or Main Street but in the fertile ground of evangelical religion and its notions of immutable moral values, militarism, patriotism, and various social concerns regarding abortion, gun control, and government regulation. As discussed in the introduction to this volume, the election of Ronald Reagan in 1980 signified the arrival of the New Right and a populist conservatism that finally fractured the liberal consensus for which the 1950s was famed. As for country music, it offered, according to Jocelyn Neal, an "all-American soundtrack for this new nationalist identity." With patriotic songs such as "God Bless the U.S.A." and movies like *Urban Cowboy*, country music became "wildly popular."

That the renewed interest in Cline through various books, movies, and plays came in on the tide of this conservative reaction oversimplifies the complexity of identity politics in an era better characterized by liberal-conservative polarization than conservative hegemony. Here, too, was one of the great intersections of this age that can account for Cline's resurgent popularity. Cline's renewed appeal, says Neal, was owing to the hardened authenticity of her struggle for success when the story of the triumph of raw talent came across as so much more genuine than the contrived, made-for-success, manufactured sound of highly politicized versions of country music. The idea that the country girl in Cline resisted these same tendencies toward crass commercialism in the Nashville Sound gained favor at the expense of any narrative of her complicity in compromising country music. Her struggle with Owen Bradley—not her cooperation—rose to the surface of Cline's popular image in the 1980s and 1990s as did the story of her role in nobly sacrificing musical ideals to rescue country music from the onslaught of rock and roll. It was in this way that Neal accounts for how Cline could be tied to the traditional side of the country music continuum.

Joli Jensen provides an alternative account of Cline's restored popularity in the crosscurrents of the age bracketed by Ronald Reagan and Bill Clinton. Cline simply rose above the turbulence of the era's culture wars as an icon—a blank, almost Warholesque representation of herself in primary colors. As an icon, Cline could be transformed by any audience into whatever impulse was most popular with it. That a rapidly growing segment of her fans consisted of gay and lesbian consumers both belied and underscored the partisanship of the era.[18] So did her embrace by the country music establishment in numerous awards and recognitions. The industry, however, would undergo profound change in the next century leaving the future of Cline's legacy uncertain but positioning it once again at the critical intersections of a new, historically significant age of music media and technology.

If Cline's own age witnessed a shift of social authority from the class structures of local communities to celebrity status in the national media, then the most recent phase in the history of her legacy has been profoundly altered by the democratization of media authority with the Internet. Cline struggled mightily to launch her career and achieve stardom amid the mutuality of community life and within the corporate world of the American music business wherein the path to success was marked by numerous, well-established authorities guarding the gates of advancement. Bucking the class and gender conventions of small-town life, she sought attention in expanding circles of appearances from local honky tonks to regional clubs, to popular competitions, to major venues in Washington, and ultimately to recording contracts, television appearances, professional managers, Top Ten hits, awards, and various other recognitions becoming a star. Her music followed a conjoining path across barriers of rights and restrictions from composer to agent, record label, recording, release, airplay, charting, and so forth. Whether by radio or record, consumers heard only the small fraction of the music and its performers that ever set out on these journeys. The process of sifting and sorting did not guarantee the best music to the listener, but what the listener heard was the music best calculated to appeal. And the listener could take that on the good authorities of the music business.[19]

With the arrival of the Internet, however, these authorities folded in on themselves. In an oversimplified version of what the music business has become in the digital age, all a singer-songwriter need do today is to buy accompaniment on-line, hire studio time, mix and produce a recording with readily available software, and post an electronic file for sale on-line at a personal or music Web site. Success—and sometimes profit—comes in the number of downloads. Media attention helps, but it usually follows fame instead of promoting it as it did for Cline in the case of television. File sharing and audio streaming has truly made the free market free, and many musicians charge nothing for their music, hoping instead to cash in on the celebrity it might bring.[20]

Will the iconic Cline survive these changes? Thrive on them? If iconization is image making, then the brave new world of on-line music making and marketing could spell the unmaking of music icons in the twenty-first century. As Beth Bailey asserts, the purpose of television programming was not to inform or entertain the people but to make audiences out of them for advertisements. Celebrities were crucial to this process. But technology has democratized both music production and consumption, allowing artists to manufacture and sell music in a marketplace in which audiences coalesce and disperse with the freedom of individual choice, the speed of a few keystrokes, and the fungibility of friends on Facebook. Downloads determine popularity much more than corporate marketing, public relations, *Billboard* charts, or celebrity appearances. Many music files, in fact, come without the liner notes and images that signify celebrity. The iconic Cline may no longer matter.

All along the road of modern history new media has laid out the great intersections of cultural eras, each falling one after the next. Radio and then television helped drive the transition from rural tradition to urban modernism. In no age was this intersection as busy as in the 1950s when Cline's star was born. It was also new media that facilitated the emergence of a national culture in which fame followed the familiarity so essential to commercial success, and notoriety supplanted respectability as the genius of middle-class consumerism. Cline thrived on this very notoriety that freed her from the burden of poverty and the cross of respectability. And finally, the intersection of radio, recording, and television in the 1950s made possible the creation of the Nashville Sound at the nexus of production and consumption wherein Cline achieved the critical mass of celebrity. If on the one hand the new medium of the Internet has democratized consumption and deprived icons of their power to fascinate and possess, then market atomization and reconstitution through social media might generate more power to connect like-minded consumers than icons ever enjoyed. The answer to the question of Cline's future, then, may just depend upon the friends of Patsy Cline.

NOTES

1. Not until the census year of 1920 did the percentage of the American population living in cities of 2,500 exceed 50 percent for the first time. By the era of Patsy Cline's rise to celebrity during the 1950s, three out of five Americans lived in urban areas of this size, which would, of course, have included Winchester. See U.S. Bureau of the Census, Census of Population, Urban and Rural Classification, Urban and Rural Populations, Table 4: Population: 1790 to 1990 available at http://www.census.gov/population/www/censusdata/files/table-4.pdf (accessed July 2010).

2. The Great Depression had ironically reinvigorated the domestic economy of home production among rural Virginians at the same time it strengthened farm

communities and the spirit of economic reciprocity that bound them together; see Ronald L. Heinemann, *Depression and New Deal in Virginia: The Enduring Dominion* (Charlottesville: University Press of Virginia, 1983), 22–23.

3. On the legal and cultural tradition of "liberty of contract" as the basis of opposition to the collective bargaining so fundamental to the American labor movement, see Eric Foner, *Give Me Liberty: An American History*, 2nd ed. (New York: W. W. Norton, 2009), 668, 767, 776, 793.

4. One of the most thorough and detailed accounts of how Bradley and Cohen crafted the Nashville Sound is found in Douglas Gomery, *Patsy Cline: The Making of an Icon* (Bloomington, Ind.: Trafford Publishing, 2011), 118–27, 202–15; see also Joli Jensen, *Nashville Sound: Authenticity, Commercialization, and Country Music* (Nashville: Country Music Foundation Press and Vanderbilt University Press, 1998), 89–118; Diane Pecknold, *The Selling Sound: The Rise of the Country Music Industry* (Durham: Duke University Press, 2007).

5. According to Loretta Lynn, "Patsy didn't let nobody tell her what to do. She done what she felt, and if a man got in her way she let 'em know they couldn't stand there"; see Lynn, "Foreword," in Margaret Jones, *Patsy: The Life and Times of Patsy Cline* (New York: HarperCollins, 1994; New York: De Capo, 1999), viii. Also quoted by Jones, Brenda Lee observed that Patsy "would talk to me about show business, about women and the kind of tough row they had to hoe. She would tell me things like we had to stay in there and fight for the things we believe in and don't give up, because we can do it"; see Jones, *Patsy Cline*, 155. Ellis Nassour, another of Cline's biographers, however, portrayed Cline more aggressively as a reformer, as a "woman not only twenty years ahead of the pack musically—the female singer responsible for changing the course of country music—but also twenty years ahead as a feminist"; see Nassour, *Honky Tonk Angel: The Intimate Story of Patsy Cline* (New York: St. Martin's, 1993), xiii.

6. Connie B. Gay, in fact, produced and broadcasted the *Town and Country Jamboree* from Turner's Arena, a converted hall built for boxing and wrestling matches in a white, working-class area of Washington, D.C.; see Gomery, *Patsy Cline*, 128.

7. For more on the feminist construction of Cline during the era of her resurgent celebrity beginning in the 1980s, see Douglas R. Anderson, *Philosophy Americana: Making Philosophy at Home in American Culture* (New York: Fordham University Press, 2006), 95–98; James L. Dickerson, *Go, Girl, Go!: The Women's Revolution in Music* (New York: Schirmer Trade Books, 2005), 34–36; Steve Jones and Joli Jensen, eds. *Afterlife as Afterimage: Understanding Posthumous Fame* (New York: P. Lang, 2005); Elayne Rapping, *Media-tions: Forays into the Culture and Gender Wars* (Boston: South End Press, 1994), 30–31; Dana Jennings, *Sing Me Back Home: Love, Death, and Country Music* (New York: Faber and Faber, 2008), 75–77; Joli Jensen, "Patsy Cline's Crossovers: Celebrity, Reputation, and Feminine Identity," in *A Boy Named Sue: Gender and Country Music*, eds. Kristine M. McCusker and Diane Pecknold (Jackson: University Press of Mississippi, 2004), 107–31.

8. As Lizabeth Cohen brilliantly argues, the principles and practices of market segmentation captured the fields of advertising and consumer product marketing

in the 1950s as manufacturers and businesses realized that their goods and services sold better when pitched specifically to the people most likely by reason of lifestyle to use them; see Cohen, *A Consumers' Republic: The Politics of Mass Consumption in Postwar America* (New York: Alfred A. Knopf, 2003); see also David Bell and Joanne Hollows, *Historicizing Lifestyle: Mediating Taste, Consumption and Identity from the 1900s to 1970s* (Aldershot, Eng.: Ashgate, 2006); Dennis J. Cahill, *Lifestyle Market Segmentation* (New York: Haworth Press, 2006); Mark Tomlinson, "Lifestyle and Social Class," *European Sociological Review* 19 (February 2003): 97–111; Glenn D. Walters, *Lifestyle Theory: Past, Present, and Future* (New York: Nova Science, 2006).

9. The American population in Cline's era was, in fact, more mobile geographically than it is today. Whereas one in five Americans moved during a year in 1950s, only about one in eight did so throughout the last decade of the twentieth century. See U.S. Bureau of the Census, Geographical Mobility/Migration, Geographical Mobility Reports and Tables from 1950–1959 and 1990–1999, available at http://www.census.gov/hhes/migration/data/cps/archive.html (accessed July 2010).

10. This account of Cline's expanding career draws on all her biographies; see Mark Bego, *I Fall to Pieces: The Music and the Life of Patsy Cline* (Holbrook, Mass.: Adams, 1995); Gomery, *Patsy Cline*; Cindy Hazen and Mike Freeman, *Love Always, Patsy: Patsy Cline's Letters to a Friend* (New York: Berkley Books, 1999); Jones, *Patsy*; Brian Mansfield, *Remembering Patsy* (Nashville: Rutledge Hill, 2002); Nassour, *Honky Tonk Angel*.

11. Writing in the early 1960s, the economic historian Harold G. Vatter observed that the "remarkable capacity of the United States economy in 1960 represents the crossing of a great divide in the history of humanity. . . . The full significance for all mankind lies in the possibility that poverty can be eliminated within the foreseeable future"; see Vatter, *The U.S. Economy in the 1950's* (New York: W. W. Norton, 1963), 1.

12. William H. Chafe, *The Unfinished Journey: America since World War II*, 5th ed. (New York: Oxford University Press, 2003), 8–9, 112–17; Dan McNichol, *The Roads That Built America: The Incredible Story of the U.S. Interstate System* (New York: Sterling, 2005), 110; Thomas C. Reeves, *Twentieth-Century America: A Brief History* (New York: Oxford University Press, 2000), 127; Vatter, *U.S. Economy in the 1950's*, 1.

13. The evolution of commercial music in the United States is a well-known story, and some of the best accounts can be found in Glenn C. Altschuler, *All Shook Up: How Rock 'n' Roll Changed America* (Oxford: Oxford University Press, 2003); Pecknold, *Selling Sound*; David Suisman, *Selling Sounds: The Commercial Revolution in American Music* (Cambridge: Harvard University Press, 2009); Larry Starr and Christopher Waterman, *American Popular Music: From Minstrelsy to MP3* (New York: Oxford University Press, 2007). On teenagers and teenage culture in the 1950s, see Ronald D. Cohen, "The Delinquents: Censorship and Youth Culture in Recent U.S. History," *History of Education Quarterly* 37 (Autumn 1997): 251–70; James Gilbert, *A Cycle of Outrage: America's Reaction to the Juvenile Delinquent in the*

1950s (New York: Oxford University Press, 1986); John Modell, *Into One's Own: From Youth to Adulthood in the United States, 1920–1975* (Berkeley: University of California Press, 1989); Grace Palladino, *Teenagers: An American History* (New York: Basic Books, 1996); Jon Savage, *Teenage: The Creation of Youth Culture* (London: Viking Penguin, 2007).

14. Regarded as the godfather of contemporary marketing, Theodore Levitt called on each automaker to consider that "what it offers for sale is determined not by the seller but by the buyer. The seller takes his cues from the buyer in such a way that the product becomes a consequence of the marketing effort, not vice versa"; see Levitt, "Marketing Myopia," *Harvard Business Review* (July/August 1960): 3–13; see also John A. Heitmann, *The Automobile and American Life* (Jefferson, N.C.: McFarland, 2009); James M. Rubenstein, *Making and Selling Cars: Innovation and Change in the U.S. Automotive Industry* (Baltimore: Johns Hopkins University Press, 2001); John B. Rae, *The American Automobile: A Brief History* (Chicago: University of Chicago Press, 1969); Giles Slade, *Made to Break: Technology and Obsolescence in America* (Cambridge: Harvard University Press, 2006); Nigel Whiteley, *Design for Society* (London: Reaktion Books, 1993), 19–21.

15. Gomery, *Patsy Cline*, 247–74.

16. In his 1998 book by that name, NBC reporter Tom Brokaw coined the term the "Greatest Generation" for those born in the first decades of the twentieth century, and who came of age during the Great Depression, fought World War II, and created the Affluent Society during the 1950s. Cline was born too late for this generation, but her birth coincided with the depths of the Great Depression, and her death in 1963 came at the time the cultural consensus about courage, idealism, and hard work that defined greatness for this generation began to break up. See Brokaw, *The Greatest Generation* (New York: Random House, 1998).

17. In a 1997 review of the tribute show *Always . . . Patsy Cline*, the *New York Post* critic Clive Barnes commented on possible meanings of Cline's early death: "Ever since the premature but romantic deaths of Shelly and Keats, it has been evident to the cynically inclined that, for an artist, an early demise can prove a shrewd career move. There is little more poignant or tantalizing than the specter of lost promise," as quoted in Gomery, *Patsy Cline*, 381.

18. Patsy Cline's appeal among gay and lesbian audiences may have been best described by filmmaker Caz Gorham: "Her music has a sense of unrequited passion, you know, heartache, which is meaningful to those who are unable, because of outside pressures, to express feelings openly. But there is also a tongue-in-cheek element. Those clothes, that style. I don't think you can buy into it without a sense of irony," as quoted in Jim White, "Is Charlie Making Patsies of Lesbians?" *The Independent*, April 16, 1993, 18.

19. Amid the vast literature on American music in the twentieth century and the contemporary music business, there is little that focuses on the historical development of the music business in America with the notable exception of the multivolume works of Russell Sanjek, most ably summarized in the volume published with his

son; see Russell Sanjek and David Sanjek, *American Popular Music Business in the 20th Century* (New York: Oxford University Press, 1991).

20. In reality the music business is still highly complex and complicated by conflict among the freedoms of the digital age and the restrictive processes that developed throughout the late nineteenth and twentieth centuries to create, produce, reproduce, promote, distribute, and market music as well as profit from it at each stage in its development and consumption. A number of works endeavor to make sense of this new era; see Otto D'Agnolo, *The Music Business Is Burning Down—Thank God!* (Bloomington, Ind.: Trafford Publishing, 2007); Greg Kot, *Ripped: How the Wired Generation Revolutionized Music* (New York: Scribner, 2009); David Kusek and Gerd Leonhard, *The Future of Music: Manifesto for the Digital Music Revolution* (Boston: Berklee Press, 2005); Patrik Wikström, *The Music Industry: Music in the Cloud* (Cambridge, Eng.: Polity, 2009).

CONTRIBUTORS

BETH BAILEY, professor of history at Temple University, is a social and cultural historian of the twentieth-century United States who specializes in the history of gender and sexuality. Her books include *From Front Porch to Back Seat: Courtship in Twentieth-Century America* (Johns Hopkins University Press, 1988); *The First Strange Place: Race and Sex in World War II Hawaii*, with David Farber (Free Press, 1992); *Sex in the Heartland* (Harvard University Press, 1999); and *America's Army: Making the All-Volunteer Force* (Harvard University Press, 2009). She is also coauthor of the American history survey text, *A People and a Nation* (Houghton Mifflin, 2008; Cengage, 2011). Her research has been supported by fellowships from the Woodrow Wilson Center for International Studies and the National Endowment for the Humanities.

MIKE FOREMAN was a native of Winchester and a graduate of the John Handley High School. He received a BA degree from the University of Richmond and his MA with additional graduate work at the University of Virginia. During his career he served as teacher and administrator in the Winchester Public Schools, as an adjunct assistant professor of political science at Shenandoah University, and as a member of the Winchester City Council. For twenty-eight years, he was clerk of the Winchester Circuit Court, retiring on December 31, 2003. He coedited the pictorial history *Images of the Past* (Winchester–Frederick County Historical Society, 1980); authored *A History of the Nurses Training School, Winchester Memorial Hospital, 1903–1964* (1990); and most recently completed *Some Worthy Women* (Winchester–Frederick County Historical Society, 2008), biographical sketches of women leaders from Winchester and Frederick County, Virginia.

DOUGLAS GOMERY is professor emeritus of media studies at the University of Maryland and resident scholar in "Mass Media and Culture," Special

Collections, University of Maryland Library. He is the author of twenty-one books, including *Patsy Cline: The Making of an Icon* (Trafford Press, 2011), and two national award–winning volumes: *Shared Pleasures: A History of Movie Presentation* (University of Wisconsin Press, 1991) and *Who Owns the Media?* (with Benjamin Compaine) (Routledge, 2000). In 2005 Gomery became official historian for the Patsy Cline Historic House in Winchester, Virginia, and authored the historic marker in front of this museum. He is author of more than 500 academic articles and book chapters. He has taught at the University of Wisconsin at Madison and Milwaukee, Northwestern University, the University of Iowa, New York University, and the University of Utrecht in the Netherlands.

GEORGE HAMILTON IV began his career in the late 1950s as a teen-oriented pop star. After his first hit, "A Rose and a Baby Ruth," reached number six on the pop charts in 1956, he toured with Buddy Holly and the Everly Brothers but reached the pop Top Ten only one more time. Hamilton moved to the country charts by 1959, where nine of his hits spent time in the Top Ten, including his only number one, "Abilene." Hamilton joined the *Grand Ole Opry* in 1959 but was increasingly inspired by folk music during the 1960s. He took country music around the world during the 1970s. In addition to more than ten tours of Great Britain and several BBC-TV productions, he hosted the Gospel Celebration and the International Country Festival, both of which were held in England. In 1973, he organized the longest international tour ever by a country artist, doing seventy-three shows over a period of three months. One year later, Hamilton became the first country artist to perform behind the Iron Curtain, where he also lectured about country music. Besides Europe, he has toured Africa, the Orient, New Zealand, Australia, and the Middle East.

WARREN R. HOFSTRA is Stewart Bell Professor of History at Shenandoah University in Winchester, Virginia. In addition to teaching in the fields of American social and cultural history and directing the Community History Project of Shenandoah University, he has written, edited, or coedited books on various aspects of American regional history, including *The Planting of New Virginia: Settlement and Landscape in the Shenandoah Valley* (Johns Hopkins University Press, 2004); *A Separate Place: The Formation of Clarke County, Virginia* (Rowman and Littlefield, 1999); *George Washington and the Virginia Backcountry* (Madison House, 1998); *After the Backcountry: Rural Life in the Great Valley of Virginia, 1800–1900* (University of Tennessee Press, 2000); *Virginia Reconsidered: New Histories of the Old*

Dominion (University of Virginia Press, 2003); *Cultures in Conflict: The Seven Years' War in North America* (Rowman and Littlefield, 2007); *The Great Valley Road of Virginia: Shenandoah Landscapes from Prehistory to the Present* (University of Virginia Press, 2010); and *Ulster to America: The Scots-Irish Migration Experience, 1680–1830* (University of Tennessee Press, 2012). His long-term research program focuses on the regional history of the Shenandoah Valley and its communities from the eighteenth through the twentieth century.

JOLI JENSEN holds the Hazel Rogers Chair in communication at the University of Tulsa. She received her PhD in 1985 from the Institute of Communications Research at the University of Illinois and has taught at the University of Virginia and the University of Texas. She is the author of three books: *Redeeming Modernity: Contradictions in Media Criticism* (Sage, 1990); *The Nashville Sound: Authenticity, Commercialization, and Country Music* (Vanderbilt University Press, 1998); and *Is Art Good for Us? Beliefs about High Culture in American Life* (Rowman and Littlefield, 2002).

BILL C. MALONE is professor emeritus of history at Tulane University. His books include *Country Music, U.S.A* (University of Texas Press, 1968, 1985, 2002, 2010); *Singing Cowboys and Musical Mountaineers: Southern Culture and the Roots of Country Music* (University of Georgia Press, 2003); *Don't Get Above Your Raisin': Country Music and the Southern Working Class* (University of Illinois Press, 2001); *Working Girl Blues: The Life and Music of Hazel Dickens* (University of Illinois Press, 2008); and *Music from the True Vine: Mike Seeger's Life and Musical Journey* (University of North Carolina Press, 2011) .

KRISTINE M. MCCUSKER is professor of history at Middle Tennessee State University, where she teaches American history. She holds a PhD from Indiana University, is coeditor of *A Boy Named Sue: Gender and Country Music* (University Press of Mississippi, 2004), and is the author of *Lonesome Cowgirls and Honky-Tonk Angels: The Women of Barn Dance Radio* (University of Illinois Press, 2008). With major funding from the National Library of Medicine at the National Institutes of Health, she is currently at work on a book project about southern death rituals called "Just Enough to Put Him Away Decent."

JOCELYN R. NEAL is an associate professor of music at the University of North Carolina at Chapel Hill. She holds a PhD in music theory from the Eastman School of Music at the University of Rochester. Her articles have appeared in music theory and musicology journals including *Music Theory Spectrum* and *Musical Quarterly*. She is the author of *The Songs of Jimmie Rodgers: A Legacy in Country Music* (Indiana University Press, 2009), coauthor with Bill C. Malone of the third revised edition of *Country Music, U.S.A.* (University of Texas Press, 2010), and author of the college textbook *Country Music* (Oxford University Press, 2012). She is also coeditor of *Southern Cultures*.

INDEX

Music in American Life

Then Sings My Soul: The Culture of Southern Gospel Music
    Douglas Harrison
The Accordion in the Americas: Klezmer, Polka, Tango, Zydeco,
    and More!   *Edited by Helena Simonett*
Bluegrass Bluesman: A Memoir   *Josh Graves; edited by Fred Bartenstein*
One Woman in a Hundred: Edna Phillips
    and the Philadelphia Orchestra   *Mary Sue Welsh*
The Great Orchestrator: Arthur Judson
    and American Arts Management   *James M. Doering*
Charles Ives in the Mirror: American Histories
    of an Iconic Composer   *David C. Paul*
Southern Soul-Blues   *David Whiteis*
Sweet Air: Modernism, Regionalism,
    and American Popular Song   *Edward P. Comentale*
Pretty Good for a Girl: Women in Bluegrass   *Murphy Henry*
Sweet Dreams: The World of Patsy Cline   *Edited by Warren R. Hofstra*

The University of Illinois Press
is a founding member of the
Association of American University Presses.

Composed in 10/13 Sabon
by Lisa Connery
at the University of Illinois Press
Manufactured by Thomson-Shore, Inc.

University of Illinois Press
1325 South Oak Street
Champaign, IL 61820-6903
www.press.uillinois.edu